The history of the last 120 years without oil would be an alternative so profound it is hard to imagine it. Mechanised tanks, bulldozers, chainsaws, aerial bombers, pharmaceutical drugs, cancer epidemics, plastics, artificial fertilisers, high explosives, and US global dominance would all not have happened without it. This volume is a profound engagment with oil and energy and its intersections with divine energeia and climate change: deeply researched and yet lucid and readable, I highly commend it.

Michael Northcott, University of Edinburgh, UK

In our accounts of the economics of climate change, and even of the theology of dominion that lubricates it, we have missed a crucial part of the story: the affects of a particular white masculine individualism that have energized an extractivist civilization. Terra Rowe's critical petro-theology unearths the US enchantment with autonomy and the aesthetic of the open highway flowing through an oily intersectionality. With "terranean" brilliance, she tracks the affective investments, theological and secularized, that keep Western fossil fuel so world-destructively energized.

Catherine Keller, Drew University, USA

Of Modern Extraction situates contemporary discourse about energy and climate change in the context of religious and theological histories that show how modern energy regimes align with gendered, racist, and colonial forms of power. Rowe develops this account of extractivism with an enviable knack for story-telling and an attention to philosophical detail.

Evan Berry, Arizona State University, USA

In *Of Modern Extraction*, Terra Schwerin Rowe provides us with the first great intellectual history of petroculture. By showing just how deeply Western understandings of energy and extraction are connected to theological notions of fulfilment, redemption, and divinity, Rowe opens us new avenues and insights into how power is written into subjective and social experience. Essential reading.

Imre Szeman, University of Waterloo, Canada

This book explores like no other the many enchantments of extractivism. Through Rowe's deep energo-theological lens we discover new sedimentary layers of our petrocultural attachment, including the figuration of oil as divine gift and animated savior. We also discover the urgent need to imagine alternative energy beyond theological modes of redemption and resurrection. *Of Modern Extraction* is a truly pathbreaking work of energy humanities.

Dominic Boyer, Rice University, USA

Of Modern Extraction offers a fascinating account of the theological aspects of energy, and the petro-theology that animates Western extraction. From inter-Scholastic debates about power to the resurrection logic of fossil fuels, Rowe beautifully weaves together unfamiliar histories that will inspire new directions in energy and climate scholarship.

Cara New Daggett, Virginia Polytechnic Institute and State University, USA

In our fossil-fueled, globalized climate changed world, this book is much needed. Terra Rowe takes us through a critical, detailed analysis of how our addiction to speed is tied with extractive colonial practices, and how these practices are fueled by metaphors of an omni-God. Our theological projection of this omni-God fuels our desire to live at a pace that is "out of this world," and as a result, we are outstripping the carrying capacity of the planet and wreaking havoc on many human and other earth bodies. No environmental or energy humanities analysis is complete without this type of sustained focus on petro-cultures and petro-theology.

Whitney A. Bauman, Florida International University, USA

Energy humanities has emerged as a cutting-edge field, and *Of Modern Extraction* is an extraordinary ground-breaking synthesis. Here Rowe takes her place as a leading scholar whose comprehensive treatment shows how energy, extraction, oil, and capital are interlinked, and how petro-theologies of redemption continue to impact us in dangerous ways.

Clayton Crockett, University of Central Arkansas, USA

With striking analytical precision *and* breadth, Rowe unearths the enchantments of modern energy that have kept western (Christian) societies beholden to its material functions, wealth, and weight. By carefully assessing the sacred workings (and burdens) of petro-culture she forces us to recognize just how essential it will be to pursue a sustainable future by imagining alternative theological as well as technological paths.

Darren Dochuk, University of Notre Dame, USA

OF MODERN EXTRACTION

T&T Clark Explorations in Theology, Gender and Ecology

Series editors
Hilda P. Koster: University of St Michael's College, Toronto, Canada
Arnfríður Guðmundsdóttir: University of Iceland, Reykjavík, Iceland

OF MODERN EXTRACTION

Experiments in Critical Petro-theology

Terra Schwerin Rowe

LONDON • NEW YORK • OXFORD • NEW DELHI • SYDNEY

T&T CLARK

Bloomsbury Publishing Plc

50 Bedford Square, London, WC1B 3DP, UK
1385 Broadway, New York, NY 10018, USA
29 Earlsfort Terrace, Dublin 2, Ireland

BLOOMSBURY, T&T CLARK, and the T&T Clark logo are trademarks of Bloomsbury Publishing Plc

First published in Great Britain 2023
Paperback edition published 2024

Copyright © Terra Schwerin Rowe, 2023

Terra Schwerin Rowe has asserted her right under the Copyright, Designs and Patents Act, 1988, to be identified as Author of this work.

For legal purposes the Acknowledgments on p. x constitute an extension of this copyright page.

Cover image: Mari Dein/500px via Getty

All rights reserved. No part of this publication may be reproduced or transmitted in any form or by any means, electronic or mechanical, including photocopying, recording, or any information storage or retrieval system, without prior permission in writing from the publishers.

Bloomsbury Publishing Plc does not have any control over, or responsibility for, any third-party websites referred to or in this book. All internet addresses given in this book were correct at the time of going to press. The author and publisher regret any inconvenience caused if addresses have changed or sites have ceased to exist, but can accept no responsibility for any such changes.

A catalogue record for this book is available from the British Library.

Library of Congress Cataloging-in-Publication Data

Names: Rowe, Terra Schwerin, author.
Title: Of modern extraction : a critical petro-theology / Terra Schwerin Rowe.
Description: London ; New York : T&TClark, 2022. | Series: T&T Clark explorations in theology, gender and ecology | Includes bibliographical references and index. |
Identifiers: LCCN 2022012241 (print) | LCCN 2022012242 (ebook) | ISBN 9780567708342 (HB) | ISBN 9780567708359 (ePDF) | ISBN 9780567708380 (ePUB)
Subjects: LCSH: Petroleum industry and trade–Social aspects–Middle West. | Energy consumption–Religious aspects–Middle West. | Petroleum–Political aspects–United States. | Environmental justice–Middle West. | United States–Social life and customs. | Environmentalism–United States.
Classification: LCC HD9567.M55 R69 2022 (print) | LCC HD9567.M55 (ebook) | DDC 338.2/72820977–dc23/eng/20220718
LC record available at https://lccn.loc.gov/2022012241
LC ebook record available at https://lccn.loc.gov/2022012242

ISBN: HB: 978-0-5677-0834-2
PB: 978-0-5677-0839-7
ePDF: 978-0-5677-0835-9
ePUB: 978-0-5677-0838-0

Series: T&T Clark Explorations in Theology, Gender and Ecology

Typeset by Deanta Global Publishing Services, Chennai, India

To find out more about our authors and books visit www.bloomsbury.com and sign up for our newsletters.

*To Mica and Bea
and all those cultivating alternate worlds*

CONTENTS

Acknowledgments   x

INTRODUCTION   1

Chapter 1
ENERGY   29

Chapter 2
EXTRACTION   61

Chapter 3
CAPITAL   91

Chapter 4
OIL   123

Chapter 5
ALTERNATE ENERGIES   149

Bibliography   177
Index   192

ACKNOWLEDGMENTS

Debt often embroils one in uncomfortable, if not precarious, situations. Acknowledging one's debts unravels any certain sense of self-sustenance, pride, and isolated selfhood that troubles even a solid or secure understanding of authorship or ownership. Indebtedness also has a way of revealing the impurity of one's grounds. In writing a text on oil, religion, white supremacy, and colonialism, I recognize the impurities of the conceptual and material ground I stand on. This is a text on extractivism written from sites of land extraction, funded in significant ways by historical and current extraction in what is now known as the Bible Belt. The university I am indebted to for employing me and funding my research stands on the occupied and unceded territory of the Wichita and Caddo Affiliated Tribes. These tribes have, for generations, stewarded this land. With the University of North Texas (UNT) Native American Student Association I articulate this land recognition as an "expression of gratitude and appreciation to those whose territory we reside on, and a way of honoring the Indigenous people who have been living and working on the land from time immemorial."[1] I would also like to express my profound gratitude to the Chickasaw Nation. When lines for vaccines were still months long, they generously offered their extra vaccines to educators like myself and their families.

I never intended to write this book during a pandemic and, on the whole, don't recommend it. Finishing this project would not have been possible without our Covid pod—Kim, Steven, Jade, Jordan, Melissa, Day, Kit, and Neve—who shared parenting, meal prep, and made lockdowns (and ice storms!) less isolating.

When conferences and presentation opportunities were lost over the past couple of years, brilliant and generous colleagues and friends stepped in to read chapters and offer critical advice and support. I'm especially grateful to my UNT colleagues, Irene Klaver, Kim De Wolff, Miguel Gualdrón Ramírez, Leah Kalmanson, Ricardo Rozzi, Adam Briggle, and Rachel Moran, who voiced key concerns, made crucial suggestions, and pointed to helpful resources. Former and current department chairs Klaver and David Kaplan, respectively, have been remarkably supportive psychologically as well as materially.

UNT grad and undergrad students are passionate advocates of social and environmental justice. I am a better scholar because of their hopes, challenges, and expectations. In particular, I'm grateful for the conversations and feedback I received when presenting parts of Chapter 5 at a department colloquium over Zoom during the pandemic. Conversations that took place in my Spring 2021 Religion and Science grad class were also key as important themes and organizing threads were coalescing at this time. A special thanks to Maureen Trussell who offered her adept research skills during the summer of 2021, thanks to a UNT Faculty Summer Research Grant.

Early versions of Chapter 1 benefited from a presentation at the Ecofeminisms unit of the AAR and Chapter 4 has been enhanced by feedback from a presentation at the 2021 virtual European Forum for the Study of Religion and the Environment on "Religion, Materialism, and Ecology." Presenting at and participating in the 2019 Rice Cultures of Energy Symposium was inspiring and even transformational as it gave me a strong sense that this project would need a lot of work, but had real potential. The valuable feedback I received at Rice informed another iteration of early research by the summer of 2019 at the International Society for the Study of Religion, Nature, and Culture (ISSRNC) at Cork University, Ireland. This presentation allowed not only for valuable feedback from co-panelists Hilda Koster, Marion Grau, Jacob Erickson, and Jan Pranger but also for a growing sense that my project could contribute to building an intellectual community around the themes of petroculture, energy, extraction, and religion.

Coalescing now as the new Energy, Extraction, and Religion Seminar (EER) at the American Academy of Religion, this group of friends and scholars has inspired and encouraged this work for the past three years. In particular, Evan Berry has been a remarkable co-organizer on a number of different panels and proposals, including the EER and a virtual ISSRNC panel in 2020 with Darren Dochuk on his remarkable history of petroleum and Christianity in the United States. Many thanks also to Berry for his generosity in reading and commenting on significant portions of this text in various stages. I'm indebted to many others connected to the EER as well: Whitney Bauman, Clayton Crockett, and Karen Bray have opened opportunities and conceptual planes. Robert Smith offered feedback at a crucial time for Chapter 3 and the Introduction. Hilda Koster and Lisa Sideris have supported this book through conversations during panel presentations and planning meetings. Along with Arnfríður Gudmundsdóttir, these members of the book series editorial board have encouraged the project from its earliest proposals and have offered close reads of chapter drafts. Hilda in particular has been remarkably generous with her time and editorial comments on all of the chapters.

This work has also been supported by older intellectual communities, especially the "Keller Collective." Alongside her brilliant and creative scholarship, Catherine Keller has fostered a supportive and engaging community of current and former grad students. I'm especially grateful for insightful comments and suggestions offered by Austin Roberts, Brock Perry, Dan Siedell, and Desmond Coleman on Chapter 2. Despite a full house of current mentees, Catherine has still found time and energy to read drafts and offer comments on this work, for which I'm profoundly grateful.

Many thanks to Storyhill for their generous permission to quote significant sections of their song, "I-90" in Chapter 1.

From early on my mom has encouraged a love of learning and reading. She redoubled this support of my scholarly pursuits by offering us refuge and childcare assistance at crucial times throughout the pandemic.

Finally, but most crucially I want to express my wholehearted gratitude to Jim for his unflagging encouragement and remarkable co-parenting. Over the past 4—and especially 2—years, he has shouldered more than his fair share of the childcare, meal prep, cleaning, bill paying, and more. This project would certainly have never been completed if it wasn't for the many hours he spent trying to get his own work done while essentially running a day care and school from home. Thank you, love. And to Mica and Bea: your curiosity inspires me every day, your antics are delightfully distracting, and your hopes for the future continue to compel my work.

Note

1 UNT Land Acknowledgement, written in collaboration with the UNT Native American Student Association, https://idea.unt.edu/land-acknowledgement.

INTRODUCTION

Ida Tarbell was already famous for her incisive reporting on John D. Rockefeller and his Standard Oil when she penned an essay on religion. Though Tarbell's reputation has developed as a remarkably strong, independent, and career-driven woman who would stand up to (and then take down) the most powerful oilmen in the world, her views on both gender roles and oil were complicated, notably, by her religious influences. For Tarbell, oil was not the enemy—and feminism not the answer.[1] Rockefeller and Standard Oil had provoked her to sharpen her pen because their means of production seemed to threaten oil's profound possibilities for her country and its people. In contrast to Rockefeller and his big business approach, Tarbell valorized independent oilmen like her father and Lyman Stewart.[2] Describing them in her *History of Standard Oil* she wrote, "Life ran swift and ruddy and joyous in these men. There was nothing they did not hope and dare."[3] As historian Darren Dochuk explains, quoting her religion essay, "[in] contrast to Rockefeller, small-producing oilmen struck Tarbell as the last hope to recreate the 'whole' and 'perfect man in the Bible sense.'"[4] For Tarbell, American independent oilmen were full of life and vigor—energized, whole, and perfected specimens of Christian masculinity.

While Tarbell's thoughts on masculinity and oil surface as quite settled and straightforward, her views on femininity seem significantly more varied and complex. Many have commended her for embodying emerging feminist ideals during her pathbreaking and influential career in journalism. It remains surprising then that she eventually denounced the women's suffrage movement, insisting that "there is no escape from the divine order that [a woman's] life must be built around . . . the child, his bearing and rearing."[5] The female ideal was still in the home with a family.[6] Consequently, from Tarbell's perspective, her particular path served as exception rather than rule for feminine aspirations.[7] In many ways, rather than symbols of feminist resistance to oil, Tarbell's life and thought emerge as emblematic of the complexities, contradictions, and entanglements of nineteenth- and twentieth-century feminism, oil, and religion.

Particularly striking in Tarbell's ready pairing of "whole," "perfect" men and oil as an idealistically materialized truth revealed in scripture is the way she treats this petro-religio-masculine amalgamation as common sense. She provided no further explanation. Tarbell seems able to assume there was no need for it. Her contemporary readers presumably would fully comprehend and accept there was something about "Bible sense" that clearly and naturally conveyed masculine fulfillment—and that oil provided an ideal medium for the aim. In making this connection Tarbell appears to be channeling some deep cultural resonance between gender, religion, and energy. Such connections were no longer self-evident to this twenty-first-century reader, but they seemed enticingly familiar, resonating with still commonly recognized alliances between the US Bible Belt and oil, a petromasculine ethos of individualistic libertarianism and domination.

If something of the historical common sense of US oil culture has been siphoned off a biblical patriarchalism, there are still more current ways that theologically inflected "imperialist white supremacist capitalist patriarchal"[8] desires and assumptions function in the framing of this time of climate crisis widely described as the Anthropocene.[9] Much has been made of the Anthropos of the Anthropocene—importantly contested for the ways it universalizes the human being of those whose practices are driving species loss, climate change, nuclear proliferation, and dispersion of plastics, while simultaneously obscuring the ways the climate crisis has rendered humans precarious in unequal measure.[10] But not nearly enough attention has been given to another way the injustices of climate change are obscured by the common framing of the climate crisis as a global "emissions problem." Phillip Usher, for example, highlights a key obfuscation in the COP21 Paris Climate Accord which frames the climate crisis as rooted in an imbalance of "emissions." The Accord uses this term ninety-eight times, while terms like "mining" or "extraction" are entirely overlooked and do not appear even once. This omission is shocking given that those emissions nearly all result from extractive practices. Usher comments that it is "as if what we burn had no origin."[11] Indeed, why skew the problem exclusively toward the global, atmospheric, meteorological, and elusively ethereal when these consequences are so tightly bound to localized terrestrial practices intimately linked to the injustices of colonialism, neocolonialism, racialization, and pollution? Evoking ejaculatory transcendence, "emissions" almost immediately directs one's perspective to that of the overview effect, a God's-eye view of the global.[12] A focus on the energy-driven climate crisis as rooted in terranean extraction, by contrast, would focus attention of care and concern to the nearly always tangible entanglements of embodied harms and intersectional oppressions.

I realized early on in my research for this book that if there was any hope of contesting the continued obfuscations of white supremacist hetero-capitalist-patriarchy functioning in the climate crisis, energy culture would need to be framed in the context of histories and continuing practices of extractivism. I came to see that the modern extractivist imaginary, as demonstrated by Tarbell and COP 21, is deeply indebted to theological anthropologies and ideals of divine power. In the current context of reemerging political authoritarianism, religiously induced climate denialism,[13] and the very real threat of over 200 years of fossil-fuel addiction culminating in "catastrophic" warming by 2050[14] only reinforcing patterns of oppression and inequality rooted in the colonial project, theologics like those functioning in Tarbell's writing and an emissions framing of climate change seem worth attending to. This book examines the current energy-driven climate crisis through the lens of intersectional-, decolonial-, and ecofeminisms, arguing that Western theo-philosophical ideals of human fulfillment and theologies of divine power have enchanted the pursuit of energy-intensive lifestyles. In particular, I will analyze the ways energy, extraction, and oil have been entwined with white Western gender constructs and Christian narratives. These analytical and ethical aims also inform an exploration of alternative embodied energies that can be attended to in the disrupted time/space of energy-intensive, extractive capitalism.

Energy Humanities and the Climate Conundrum

Beyond the problematic emissions framing of the climate crisis, concerns have been more broadly raised among humanities scholars about the ways climate change has been approached predominantly as a scientific problem with technoscientific solutions. The predominant strategy to address climate change has been exemplified by the UN's IPCC (Intergovernmental Panel on Climate Change): consolidate rigorously peer-reviewed scientific results from the best minds across the globe on the causes and pace of climate change into reports made available to policymakers and the public so they can be informed and act on their findings. The IPCC and climate scientists have provided crucial, groundbreaking, persuasive scientific evidence of anthropogenic climate change, at times acting or speaking out in the face of enormous challenges and even threats. It is imperative that this work continue, yet climate scientists and activists of the last couple of decades have increasingly had to face a profound problem. At least since James Hansen testified before Congress about climate change in 1988 and the IPCC was created as a massive international research project on climate change, trajectories of CO_2 emissions and fossil-fuel consumption have only risen.[15] In other words, the more that is *known* about the anthropogenic causes of climate change, the more fossil fuels are *consumed* and the more CO_2 is *emitted*.[16] Several theories have been posed to explain this *climate conundrum* ranging from basic human evolutionary needs for energy excess,[17] to capitalist, market-driven amplifications,[18] to imperial and anti-democratic patterns reinforced in fossil capitalism.[19]

Increasingly, scholars in the emerging field of environmental humanities (including subfields like energy humanities and petroculture studies) are emphasizing that the causes of and mitigation strategies for climate change require a broader response than what a solely technoscientific strategy can offer. Something is lacking in the strategy: increasingly accurate information, supplied by more rigorous science, communicated in summary reports with a trickle-down expectation for political change suggests a diagnosis that the problem currently faced is primarily epistemological. Besides inadequately accounting for the fact that humans rarely make decisions about their daily activities and means of sustenance based primarily on fact and reason, a purely epistemological approach to the climate crisis also overlooks the reality that an artificial separation of nature and culture, fact and value has been central to the project of modernity, modern sciences, and technologies. These nature/culture, fact/value dualisms also map onto divisions between reason and emotion, knowledge and action, and thus emerge as a key problematic of modern epistemologies currently functioning in the climate conundrum.

Encompassing but expanding beyond solely epistemologically oriented diagnoses and technologically driven solutions, environmental humanities scholars emphasize that a rise in greenhouse gasses is rooted in the persistence of culturally driven socioeconomic habits, practices, affects, beliefs, assumptions, future expectations, values, and desires. These are communicated and symbolized in cultural expressions of art, philosophy, literature, and belief structures—precisely the realm humanities scholars are trained to analyze. Environmental humanities scholars therefore emphasize that climate change is an issue deeply rooted in culture and power—and therefore requires approaches of the humanities as well as the sciences.[20] As anthropologist Dominic Boyer and cultural theorist Imre Szeman emphasize in their introductory anthology to *Energy Humanities*, "the next steps in addressing the environmental crisis will have to come from the humanities and social sciences—from those disciplines that have long attended to the intricacies of social processes, the nature and capacity of political change, and the circulation and organization of symbolic meaning through culture."[21] While climate science has been and will be crucial for tracking and understanding climate change, it cannot remain a sole strategy.

An environmental humanities approach is broadly informed by a critique of modern divisions between nature and culture, fact and value, knowledge, emotion and action which radically obscure important ways of knowing.[22] In particular, intersectional postcolonial or decolonial feminisms and womanisms often emphasize the ways dualistic hierarchies have justified the marginalization, exclusion, and oppression of feminized others, including the other-than-human world. The feminist Mayapple Energy Transition Collective, for example, emphasizes that "ecofeminists have long examined the ways in which those constructed as 'feminine' (e.g., women, nature) are oppressed in an effort to infuse investigations on a variety of topics—such as environmental racism, global economics, maldevelopment, and militarism, among others—with questions of devaluation and exploitation."[23] Donna Haraway famously pressed ecofeminist approaches to more rigorously challenge gender essentialism and nature/culture dualisms by critically attending to the porosity, not just between humans and nature, but also between humans, nature, and technology.[24] Haraway's work, acknowledged by environmental and energy humanities scholars as profoundly influential for the methodological approach of these discourses, promotes a *natureculture* analysis of relations between humans or human technosciences and the natural world.[25]

From a perspective that seeks to analyze the cuts and porosities of natureculture, petroleum emerges not just as matter with mechanistic use and technological potential, but also what feminist philosopher of science Karen Barad refers to as material-discursive entanglements.[26] Material-discursive entanglements of petro-matter and meaning-making systems emerge as a *petroculture* that has pervaded the modern unconscious. For the Canada-based After Oil Collective, petroculture refers to the sense that "postindustrial society today is an oil society through and through."[27] The influence of fossil fuels has not merely been mechanistic. It is not just something to fuel cars, machines, and industries. Petroleum has also "shaped our values, practices, habits, beliefs and feelings."[28] In particular, petroleum has shaped some of the concepts and values most associated with modernity and the Enlightenment. Autonomy, democracy, and freedom, for example, have been profoundly (and largely unconsciously) shaped by fossil fuels. Historian and postcolonial theorist Dipesh Chakrabarty emphasizes as much in his essay, influential in the initiation of energy and environmental humanities, "The Climate of History: Four Theses."[29] Chakrabarty notes a correspondence between the emergence of a modern philosophy of freedom and the "time when human beings switched from wood and other renewable fuels to large-scale use of fossil fuel."[30] While allowing for complications and contradictions between Enlightenment articulations of freedom and the manifestation of the Anthropocene/Capitalocene/Chthulucene,[31] he nonetheless concludes that "the mansion of modern freedoms stands on an ever-expanding base of fossil fuel use. Most of our freedoms so far have been energy-intensive."[32] Think, for example, of the way the affect and aesthetic of the open highway has merged with and informed the Enlightenment emphasis on freedom, or the way belief in the kind of autonomous and self-sufficient individualism Tarbell lauded has been sustained by a petroleum-fueled economy.

Such affective resonances between petroleum and modern concepts have often been aided by pop-culture. "Get your kicks on Route 66" helped merge a romanticism of the highway with a frontier aesthetic: optimism for the pursuit of a better life through better opportunities "out West" and freedom to fulfill one's potential. Even the ideal of the middle-class American vacation seems unthinkable without the autonomy of a minivan, the open stretch of the road, and an electrifying destination. This is the case even, ironically, with US national parks. Leader in petroculture studies, Stephanie LeMenager, has emphasized the strategic role roads and scenic drives played in the construction and promotion of these national parks.[33] Since national parks have played a profound role in shaping the imaginary and concept of "nature" for US citizens, consequently, even perceptions of "nature" have been profoundly influenced by and mediated through petroleum.

Analyzing such profound humanistic impacts of oil, petroculture scholars have questioned how modern society could have gone so long without really seeing oil—without being conscious of its formative power not just for technology and industry, but also for values and concepts of reality. The After Oil Collective, for example, concludes that for the most part, still "[t]he power of oil is unconscious; we cannot grasp it and we don't perceive it."[34] Flying under the radar of conscious, critical reflection, oil has been the "magic that powers modernity"[35] and, as such, has largely remained unthought.

Amitav Ghosh is widely credited with first bringing to attention the need to grasp the full imbrications of modernity and oil. Ghosh first coined the term "petrofiction" in a 1992 review of Abdelrahman Munif's novels, *Cities of Salt*. What struck Ghosh as unique about these novels was that they addressed what otherwise seemed taboo; in Western society, especially the US, the profound reliance of society on oil and the Middle East was a "matter of embarrassment verging on the unspeakable."[36]

Twenty years after Ghosh's petrofiction essay, Frederick Buell wrote "A Short History of Oil Culture: Or, the Marriage of Catastrophe and Exuberance," calling for a new kind of discourse, a new critical study of oil.[37] This essay was one of the first to focus on the *culture* of oil that had for so long gone without adequate recognition or conscious reflection.[38] Through analysis of modern literature such as Upton Sinclair's *Oil!* Buell argues that oil "remains an essential (and, to many, the essential) prop underneath humanity's material and symbolic cultures."[39] For Buell, the consequence of not examining the energy impacts of these material and symbolic cultures is none other than the current climate crisis. By ignoring oil, one fails to acknowledge reliance on it—not just techno-industrial-economic reliance, but also the ways cultural, symbolic, value, and belief systems have become infused by it. Buell concludes: "We need to ask what we start finding when we cease living in oil as if it were our oxygen and look back on its histories—material, technological, social, and cultural—from the standpoint of today's startled awareness of the fragility of the system 'Colonel' E. L. Drake and John D. Rockefeller built."[40] If we cannot see oil's current impact, we also cannot see a way beyond it. Consequently, Buell calls for a new scholarly trajectory: "Perhaps the gap between energy and culture can be bridged and made available to the traffic of a new field of study."[41] Shortly thereafter, in 2015, Imre Szeman, Dominic Boyer, Cymene Howe, Jeff Diamanti, Bob Johnson, Sheena Wilson, and others launched the Petrocultures Research Group and the After Oil Collective.

In terms of the climate conundrum, Environmental and Energy Humanities scholars emphasize the profound depth of cultural commitments to high-energy lifestyles.[42] Even as knowledge of the dangers of such lifestyles increases, cultural patterns, pleasures, goals, aims, and desires—informed by and overlaid with infrastructurally and economically enforced habits—create resistance to aligning behavior with the facts of climate science. Accordingly, for Szeman and Boyer, the task before us emerges as clear but profoundly complex: "What we need to do is, first, grasp the full intricacies of our imbrication with energy systems (and with fossil fuels in particular), and second, map out other ways of being, behaving, and belonging in relation to both old and new forms of energy. The task is nothing less than to reimagine modernity...."[43]

Gender and Energy Humanities

While feminist disruptions of nature/culture binaries have been profoundly influential for the energy humanities, it is still the case that gender and race analyses characteristic of intersectional-feminist approaches are often overlooked. Consider again the example cited earlier of the ways the open road has infused and informed modern ideals of freedom and autonomy. The example is commonly referenced among energy humanities scholars, but this freedom is rarely identified as a particularly gendered and raced white masculine human achievement. The gendered dynamics of the freedom of the open road become more clear in

Storyhill's folksy cult classic, "I-90" wherein the song's subject leaves his girlfriend crying "'cuz she don't really wanna see me leave," only to pursue the healing and actualizing character of the highway: "I-90's soothin' me/ It's movin' me to be a better man/This highway's givin' me/The time to be, to understand.... 'Cuz a while on the road can make you stronger/Ever so slightly/Soon I'll be hightailin' I-90."[44] Here the open space and freedom of the road are portrayed as an opportunity to actualize not just human self-definition, but also masculine identity.

Looking again at Buell's incisive essay, he cites several examples of the way oil became a cultural influence, particularly in the United States. One source given is Tarbell's introduction to Paul Gidden's 1938 glorified history, *The Birth of the Oil Industry*. Once again, Tarbell writes with idealism and admiration about the independent oilman: "Men did not wait to ask if they might go into the Oil Region, they went. They did not ask how to put down a well: they quickly took the processes which other men had developed for other purposes and adapted them to their purpose... It was a triumph of individualism."[45] Buell sees Tarbell constructing a narrative of oil extraction that builds on an older "epic-heroic ideology of democratic, self-reliant, community- and nation-building individualism."[46] This spirit of self-reliance and individualism, Buell notes, is also reflected in Upton Sinclair's 1926 novel, *Oil!* In the novel, written in the wake of the Teapot Dome Scandal, Sinclair's characters echo the kind of self-reliant individualism Tarbell lauded, but Sinclair adds another dimension, imbuing the character Dad with a new kind of energy. Buell demonstrates how Dad is figured as "a sufficient early example of a new kind of bio-energetics, pep, produced by oil."[47] Such high-energy ideals suffused culture, becoming expressed even through new slang: "People started (bodily and psychically) to 'rev up' and 'step on the gas.' Sometimes they operated on all their cylinders and stopped, when necessary, to refuel."[48] In the post-war high-energy United States, "men have 'pep' and Dad is a 'real guy' who has 'the stuff,' 'barrels of it.' Dad is, in short, an enlivened, positive, capable, always energetic machine himself—one that is fueled by oil. Dad thus is part of a long line of figures self-styled as 'modern.'"[49] While Buell significantly identifies the way petroleum inspired a culture of high energy, what he doesn't adequately analyze are the evident gender dynamics functioning in both Sinclair's and Tarbell's texts. Tarbell's oilmen and Sinclair's Dad are not merely self-styled moderns, but representative of a new iteration of white US American masculinity—one that, as we will see, reanimated a variously articulated but persistent Western alignment between high energy and the fulfillment of humanity.

Important work on petroculture and feminisms has been initiated especially by Sheena Wilson's "Just Powers" and "Feminist Futures" projects[50] as well as the Mayapple Energy Transition Collective.[51] Petroculture scholars more broadly have shed light on the way petro produces subjectivities. Modes of identity construction, self-expression, and culture construction now rely so heavily on fossil-fueled industry and media that LeMenager, for example, wonders whether "the category of the human [can] persist without such forms indebted to fossil fuels."[52] More specifically, Cara Daggett emphasizes that fossil fuels produce gendered and raced, "petro-masculine," subjectivities.[53] Echoing traditional hegemonic masculinities embodied by Sinclair's "Dad" or Tarbell's independent, biblically ideal, oilmen, Daggett identifies petro-masculinity as "the relationship—both technically and affectively, ideationally and materially—between fossil fuels and white patriarchal orders."[54] Analyzing post-Trump "Make America Great Again" dynamics, she demonstrates that "for many, extracting and burning fuel was a practice of white masculinity, and of American sovereignty, such that the explosive power of combustion could be crudely equated with virility."[55]

Daggett emphasizes that the complex interactions of petroculture, colonialism, racism, and sexism call for further analysis along the lines of a perspective Wilson has identified as "critical petro-intersectionality."[56] Similarly, the Mayapple Energy Transition Collective (MET Collective) emphasizes the importance of building on ecofeminist and feminist modes of analysis attuned to the ways "gender combines with other interlocking modes of oppression, including race, class, ethnicity, nationality, ability, sexuality, indigeneity, colonial history, and Global North/South divides."[57] In particular, this involves attending to the ways that "different categories of women are impacted differently by the networks of oil."[58] These modes of analysis take seriously the fusion of heterosexism with race, thus playing a key role in the "operations of colonial power."[59] Often, cisgendered white women have benefited from freedoms and privileges associated with oil. From petroleum-based make-up and plastics specifically commercialized with female domestic roles in mind, to energy-intensive freedoms consistent with bourgeois suburban lifestyles also dependent on redlining, one can plainly see how oil has both granted privilege and reinforced prescribed roles for cisgendered white women. Along these lines, Wilson and LeMenager have specifically attended to basic complexities of North American political feminism and its relationship to or debated dependence on the rise of fossil fuels.[60]

Energy is an important site of intersectional-feminist analysis particularly on account of the inequalities of energy distribution around the world and the way these inequalities reinforce histories of domination. The benefits afforded Euro-Americans through access to cheap and plentiful fossil fuels are often extracted from sites of profound energy poverty.[61] Energy poverty and exploited conditions at extraction sites, in turn, often maintain colonial-patriarchal societies.[62] Consequently, a critical petro-intersectionality seeks to illuminate the ways that current energy regimes both perpetuate and depend on race, class, and gender inequalities.[63]

Critical petro-intersectional perspectives are also key for thinking through energy transitions. Emphasizing the way gendered, colonial, and racial power structures help maintain energy systems, the MET Collective argues "that a feminist perspective on energy offers an important underacknowledged framework for understanding what keeps us stuck in unsustainable energy cultures, as well as a paradigm for designing truly just energy systems."[64] Many concerned with climate change recognize that reimagining energy values and structures will necessarily entail shifts in socio-political-economic power dynamics as well.[65] Citing Sheena Wilson, Bell, Daggett, and Labuski argue that "'energy transition is a feminist issue' because decarbonizing our energy supply 'could provide opportunities to develop more socially just ways of living that put the concerns of the most exploited—

women, people of color, and the global 99 percent—at the core of energy transition politics."⁶⁶ Consequently, in the midst of despair-inducing projections, attending to such inequalities and oppressions in the current energy regime means that the climate crisis could also present an opening to a more just, egalitarian, and democratic public.⁶⁷

Religion and Energy Humanities

While something of Tarbell's common sense can be explained by reference to gender dynamics, there is clearly a religious dimension that exceeds mere gender. Thus far, religion has been missing in our introduction to energy humanities. This is broadly reflective of the field. In the multiple volumes on energy humanities and petroculture studies published in the twenty-first century, religion has, until recently, rarely emerged as a point of focus and is only recently beginning to be addressed.⁶⁸

The importance of religious reflection on energy practices has been reinforced by studies demonstrating that attitudes about climate change as well as energy consumption are often significantly influenced by religious affiliation.⁶⁹ For example, historian of science Naomi Oreskes has written compellingly about the imbrications of religious affiliations and climate denialism. Oreskes famously demonstrated in *Merchants of Doubt* that US-based climate denialism was merely the next iteration of the strategy to create a climate of doubt about scientific consensus, inspired by the tobacco industry.⁷⁰ In her spin-off essay, "The Religious Politics of Scientific Doubt," co-written with religion scholar Myrna Perez Sheldon, the authors argued that climate denialism has emerged in the US context also as the next iteration of evangelical anti-evolutionist strategies and subjectivities.⁷¹ Oreskes and Sheldon point to key alliances between evangelicalism and the Republican Party. While much attention has been given to the ways climate denialism has been lucratively funded by oil-connected politicians and think tanks, as Amitav Ghosh suggests,

> it would be a mistake to assume that denialism within the Anglosphere is only a function of money and manipulation. There is an excess to the denialist attitude that suggests that the climate crisis threatens to unravel something deeper, without which large numbers of people would be at a loss to find meaning in their history and indeed in their existence in the world.⁷²

This "excess"—the kinds of subjectivities it produces, the affects that spill over with it, the kinds of religion, gender, and experience of the world it depends on—needs more attention.

As with climate denialism, so with hydrocarbons in particular. The need for focused attention on the imbrications of oil and religion has become particularly evident with religion historian Darren Dochuk's 2019 text, *Anointed With Oil: How Christianity and Crude Made Modern America*. This is the first compressive history of oil and Christianity in the United States, supported by voluminous research that spans the nineteenth to the twenty-first century. Key exceptions among energy humanities scholars' general lack of attention to religion—like Cara Daggett's chapter on the "geotheologies" of early modern energy scientists in *The Birth of Energy* or Michael Marder's chapter on energy theology in *Energy Dreams*—also prove to be tip-of-the-iceberg enticing.[73] Given such compelling demonstrations of the entrenched nature of Christianity, oil, and energy, one wonders, to paraphrase the After Oil Collective, how this particular story of the magic of oil has remained unthought, unexamined, and unchallenged. Perhaps the conjunction of religion intensifies a sense of oil as a "matter of embarrassment verging on the unspeakable."[74]

Religious reflection on energy ethics has actually been quite well established, even preceding widespread concerns about climate change. Yet, in religious discourses from ethics to religion and ecology or religion and science, a critical engagement with energy sciences, economies, and the materialities and technologies of petroleum has not received wide attention.

There are several important studies, edited volumes, influential figures, and ecumenical or interfaith statements on Christian energy ethics dating back to the 1970s.[75] In 2010, leading Christian environmental ethicist Larry Rasmussen joined with Normand Laurendeau, Professor Emeritus of Combustion from the Purdue School of Mechanical Engineering, to organize what may have been the first conference in the United States "to consider fully the significant connections between energy and religion."[76] In an issue of *Zygon* devoted to the proceedings, the organizers acknowledge that "little attention has been given to the fundamental religious and ethical questions surrounding the upcoming transition to renewable energy."[77] However, even as the conference organizers recognized "significant connections between energy and religion," a critical history of the convergences of energy sciences, fossil fuels, and religion was missing from the conference proceedings, as well as more widely in the discipline.

While religion and ecology scholars have done admirable and extensive research on climate change, here too, with a handful of exceptions, a critical engagement with energy cultures remains underdeveloped.[78] Religion and ecology scholars do recognize energy as a key issue of concern—many cite energy policy and the need for alternative renewable energies as issues of crucial importance. Much of the work around religion and climate change—including my own previous work—has focused on the relationship between Christianity and capitalism.[79] For example, this relationship is cited as a reason why historically Christian locales have higher carbon emissions.[80] A focus on the economic drivers of climate change is certainly not misplaced. But a closer examination of Christianity and energy culture, including its sciences and technologies, demonstrates that it does not encompass the whole picture.

Within religion and science scholarship, too, a *critical* assessment of religion and energy sciences and technologies is broadly missing.[81] Consequently, a person studying Christian energy ethics, religion and ecology, or religion and science could walk away with the impression that the mid-twentieth-century-religious environmental movement was the first time that religious folk actively and creatively engaged with energy. As we will see, this is far from the case. What have not been given adequate consideration are the ways the technologies, fuels, and sciences discussed are natureculture productions that have *already* been influenced by religion in their construction. As the After Oil Collective emphasizes, if "oil is not only something you put in your car" but also a material-discursive phenomenon, then "how we tell the story of oil... shapes how we see... the problem at its core."[82] Indeed, how we tell the story of oil and energy is crucial. Leaving certain aspects unexamined allows them to continue unaddressed, retaining their unconscious power. The critical story of religion, energy, extraction, and oil needs to be told.

Critical Petro-theologies

Given that the climate crisis is at root an energy crisis, how is it possible that within the scope of energy humanities as well as religious reflection, energy has received so little critical religious attention? I suggest that this is at least in part the case because of the ways through which the humanities and social sciences, including religious studies, have been formed and assumed what religion scholar Jason Storm calls the "myth of disenchantment": the widely held misconception that modernity is characterized by a belief that "magic and spirits had to go if the world was to be amenable to systematic and rational interpretation."[83] While the predominant religious scholarly analysis of environmental destruction has identified disenchantment at the heart of the problem, I will emphasize that modern Western energy culture has also been profoundly *enchanted* by Western theo-philosophical ideals of human anthropology, divine power, and redemption and thus is in need of a *critical petro-theology* that can analyze these entanglements.

Energy and the "Myth of Disenchantment"

At the heart of the disenchantment thesis is the "conflict thesis"—the idea, first clearly articulated in the nineteenth century, that religion and science are fundamentally incongruous, that the two have been and will remain at war with one another, that the rise of modern science and scientific epistemologies has gradually eroded the legitimacy of religion and magic.[84] The conflict thesis has been profoundly disrupted, complicated, and roundly dismissed by religion and science scholars of the twentieth and twenty-first centuries.[85] Current scholarship on the history of science and the relationship between religion and science emphasizes that the categories of what moderns call "religion" and "science" have been culturally constructed and therefore have changed significantly over time depending on the local context.[86]

A new wave of critical religion and science scholars agree with the analysis of religion and science as constructed, but emphasize that predominant scholarship in this area has not sufficiently engaged critical race, gender, decolonial and postcolonial discourses to better understand the layers of complex power dynamics functioning.[87] For example, a critical race or gender analyst would emphasize that the conflict thesis is particularly problematic in that it significantly obscures the ways that religion and science have frequently worked harmoniously to justify colonialism, slavery, sexism, and other oppressions.[88] Relatedly, postcolonial scholars influenced by Dipesh Chakrabarty look to *provincialize* the relationship between religion and science, demonstrating the ways that universalizing claims of both religion and science have been used to reinforce imperial aims.[89]

While the West is typically portrayed as secularized and disenchanted, the Global East and South are portrayed as mystical, spiritual, still enchanted, and either admirably or backwardly resistant to the march of scientific-capitalist rationalism. In spite of the persistence and pervasive acceptance of this "single most familiar story in the history of science," Storm methodically and persuasively argues that modernity, inasmuch as it is associated with this project of rationalization, desacralization, or demythologization, has never been successfully completed—even in the West. Along the lines of Bruno Latour's "we have never been modern" and drawing from postcolonial critiques of portrayals of Western science as mythless, objective, and culturally universal, Storm argues that even the heart of the enlightened secularized world—Europe and the United States—has never been disenchanted. Even from its beginnings, where many histories emphasize a religion/magic/science rupture, early promoters of the modern scientific method such as Francis Bacon explicitly framed science as a kind of purified magic while Isaac Newton articulated his scientific project in terms that presumed divine presence and the necessity of omnipotent power for the maintenance of a mechanistic cosmos.[90]

Much of the myth of disenchantment remains at the heart of the social sciences and humanities. Storm demonstrates the centrality of a disenchantment narrative for key initiating figures for these disciplines: Max Weber, who is most closely associated with the term; Marcel Mauss, and Sigmund Freud; Max Horkeimer, Theodore Adorno and other critical theorists; even founders of logical positivism like Otto Neurath. Religious studies is no exception. Often, narratives of the founding of religious studies are rearticulations of the secularization or disenchantment thesis.[91] Storm demonstrates that often the very same people, such as Max Weber, who diagnosed modernity as disenchanting were compelled by this conviction to *pursue new enchantments*.

Consequently, rather than a conflict between religion, science, and magic, Storm emphasizes a more dialectical relationship. One should not be surprised, he explains, to find that "reason does not eliminate 'superstition' but piggybacks upon it; that mechanism often produces vitalism; and that often, in a single room, we can find both séance and science."[92] Rather than suppressing "religion" monolithically conceived, new technosciences have often inspired new religious movements, affects, and expressions, while, conversely, religion, spirituality, and the occult have inspired or enticed scientific exploration. With their ready and ancient associations with light, enlightenment, vibrancy, life, liveliness, vigor, and vitality, energy sciences and technologies have been *particularly* prone to enchantment.

In religion and ecology discourses disenchantment is often assumed, with re-enchantment posed as a necessary antidote. Variations on the disenchantment thesis and claims that it lies at the heart of environmental degradation—alongside a related loss of values at the heart of Western culture—are prevalent in texts recognized as foundational to the field. From Lynn White famously identifying historical roots of the ecologic crisis in Judeo-Christian dominion corresponding to the loss of animist enchantments, to Thomas Berry's call for a "new story" in the wake of the loss of the relevance and meaningfulness of Western Judeo-Christian narratives, and Joseph Sittler's emphasis on the loss of divinity and grace in nature leading to both a spiritual and environmental crisis, these key initiating figures of religion and environmentalism have communicated a sense that spiritual and environmental crises emerge as dual consequences of Western disenchantment.[93] In addition, the framing of environmental problems in religion and ecology are often profoundly indebted to and follow the critical theory of Horkheimer, Adorno, and others. Though Storm does not explore environmental implications, the connections are evident in his succinct summary: "The primal form of critical theory's master narrative is that autonomous reason (or freedom or science or enlightenment), once yoked to the domination of nature, turns into its opposite—namely, the domination of humanity."[94] We, like Storm, may acknowledge indebtedness and retain a commitment to many of the tools and aims of critical theory while remaining vigilant about its more dogmatic forms of disenchantment.

Whether influenced by critical theory, the conflict thesis, or the myth of universalized rationality, much of the humanities and religious studies have assumed that modernity has rendered the West disenchanted. If being modern means not believing in magic, ghosts, spirits, deities, and other enchantments—that science, technology, and modern empiricisms pushed enchantment into the realm of the implausible, or at least the private and interior—how could energy and petroculture enchantments surface as anything other than a "matter of embarrassment verging on the unspeakable"?[95] The point here is not to suggest that religion and environmental thinkers have been wrong to draw connections between mechanization, instrumentalization, reductionism, and environmental crises, but to emphasize that if disenchantment remains the *only* lens through which religion and environmentalism is approached, then many existing enchantments of matter—for environmental good or ill—remain profoundly obscured.

If the crisis of energy and climate continues to be framed through lenses formed by the disenchantment thesis, then religious convergences with energy technosciences emerge as enormous blind spots—giant anomalies that just don't compute. In terms of the climate conundrum, then, I suggest that a key factor in the continual increase in energy production and consumption, even in the face of compelling climate science, is at least partially due to the fact that the Western world, particularly the US, has made not just infrastructural and economic investments in oil, but also affective—often secularized—*theological* investments in oil.

What current approaches to religion and energy ethics miss then is crucial: energy sciences, technologies, and environmental crises have not been constructed on the turf of a religious void, and religious folk have not merely reflected after the fact on the ethics of what science has rendered. As we will see consistently throughout this book, religious concepts, beliefs, values, and desires have profoundly informed these technoscientific productions. Neither religion nor energy humanities discourses have adequately accounted for the radical imbrications of Christian theology in the formation of concepts of energy science or desires for extraction. Conversely, they have also not been able to account for the significant ways extraction, electricity, energy science, and oil profoundly shaped Christian theology, practice, affect, and belief. Adequately accounting for the role of energy in Western religion and science calls for an altogether different approach.

Methodologies for Critical Petro-theologies

To more readily recognize and account for the ways energy and hydrocarbons in particular have pervaded modern religious life and how religious ideals and themes have enchanted energy calls for something like a critical petro-theology. Where energy humanities scholars have demonstrated the ways energy and petroleum in particular have been animated by cultural values, beliefs, and assumptions, religious scholars are specially equipped to analyze these modes of meaning and value production.[96] Critical petro-theologies could draw from methods of religious studies, especially analyses of religion and capitalism, prosperity gospel, and what Callahan, Lofton, and Seales have called "industrial religion."[97]

Analyzing the climate crisis as animated by a dynamism between enchantment and disenchantment rather than solely rooted in a discourse of disenchantment provides a particularly intriguing point of connection where theological and religious studies are typically bifurcated. Theological studies have historically been driven by confessional and ecclesial aims to explain, expound on, apply, or account for, the role of a particular theme or motif of religious doctrine. One of the most compelling aspects of theological studies today is in its critical turn, transforming theology into an iconoclastic tool for critically analyzing seemingly secular structures, institutions, and concepts. These approaches analyze the processes by which humans create gods and imbue seemingly secular territories with divine or sacred authority. From this perspective, the task of theology becomes identifying how seemingly secular beliefs, structures, assumptions, and values have been functioning theologically—with the kind of authority of religion or divinity.

Postsecular Energy Although they are sometimes identified as *postsecular theologies*, these scholars emphasize that "postsecular" should not be taken as a triumph of either the secular or the religious, but as a troubling of the modern binary between them.[98] Among postsecular approaches, political and radical theologians have analyzed how imperial, political, and economic power can function with the authority of a religion, imbuing empire, market, or political leaders with dominion previously associated with an omnipotent law giver.[99] Some religion and ecology scholars have already applied these approaches to analyses of climate change. For example, Michael Northcott and Catherine Keller have made important contributions to political theology by analyzing the dynamics of political subjectivities, theologies of divine power, and issues surrounding climate change.[100]

Important points of collaboration have emerged between postsecular theologies and critical religion and science approaches. For example, while J. Kameron Carter and Vincent Lloyd, among others, have taken a political theological approach to analyze the ways modern racial constructs still function with particular theological traces,[101] Terence Keel has emphasized as much and adds that even "racial sciences"—in spite of their purported secularity— retain the trace of Christian theologies.[102] Addressing scientific epistemologies more broadly, Mary-Jane Rubenstein has advocated an approach to the sciences whereby it becomes the "task of radical theology of science to unravel the tangle of human, mechanical, bacterial, technological, ideological, and elemental processes that act together to *make* any particular truth: a production Latour calls factish."[103] According to postsecular, radical, or political theologies, realms constructed as secular are not void of functioning religious or moral meaning.

Similarly, from the perspective of a critical petro-theology, environmental degradation and resource exploitation would be diagnosed less as a way modern Westerns fill a void of spiritual meaning, less as a loss of shared values or morals, and more as the function of a *theological overflow*—an enduring but transformed enchantment—on to economic and imperial practices. Such an approach would call for closer attention to the kinds of theologies functioning in extraction or the particular divine characteristics informing and infusing technology and the sciences. Critical, postsecular theological approaches have become particularly adept at analyzing absent presences and present absences, following the trace of signifiers even as they are rendered unconscious. Where an "energy unconscious"[104] is functioning, or where petroleum emerges as the "magic that fuels modernity,"[105] a critical petro-theology is called for.

Petro-theology Affects While analysis of a theological trace in texts, reasonings, values, and ideals will remain imperative for a critical petro-theology, when dealing with something like an energy unconscious there will invariably be limits to its conscious, linguistic, and textual expression. When analyzing something like a mood of empowerment and fulfillment on the open road, authoritarian subjectivities and desires, or the evangelical tent revival atmosphere of an energy conference, we will need to attend more closely to the ways affect travels through bodies, materialities, and technologies.

Karen Bray has recently argued for the importance of affect theory for political theology—and I would argue it is also an imperative tool for analyzing energy culture and religion.[106] Affect theory tracks the kinds of lessons our bodies teach our minds by mapping, as Donovan Schaefer emphasizes, "how discourses attach to bodies" making them "move without being told."[107] It disrupts key assumptions often made about sensation and cognition. First, affect theory emphasizes that its focus is not individualized, privatized emotion. This is no turn toward individualism or an interior, privatized space. In fact, affect theorists resist a focus on interiority or individualism by emphasizing that affect often exceeds linguistic, symbolic expression or the cognitive functions of the liberal sovereign subject.[108] Influenced by critical traditions of queer theory, feminism, and postcolonial theory, affect theorists focus on the intersection of bodies and discourses/systems/institutions of power, viewing the body as a particular locus where systemic and intimate power converge.

The second common assumption about cognition and feeling that affect theory calls into question are enlightenment-influenced conclusions that cognition always precedes the sensory. Religious and theological studies have been dominated by textual and logical approaches that assume human actions and decisions flow from rationality or a theologically ordered cosmos which subsequently influences values, beliefs, and emotion. An affect approach reverses this, challenging linguistic and textual approaches to religion and culture by demonstrating that often human don't think first and then feel. Often, preconscious affective responses influence the kinds of reasonings employed and the decisions made.[109] In this way, as Schaefer has argued, an affective approach to religion "dovetails with contemporary feminist science studies and research into embodied cognition that have insisted on understanding the operations of knowledge production as driven by bodies, rather than transcendent, immaterial 'reason.'"[110]

For Schaefer, affect allows for an approach to religion that resists a cognitive-linguistic framework associated with J. Z. Smith in which religions manifest primarily as cosmologies that function as a kind of text that informs bodily action and sensory experience. For Smith, religions form cosmologies which function as a kind of bodily text through which bodies move, create, and make sense of their worlds. While power analysis remains a debt affect approaches to religion owe to Smith's linguistic shift, it departs from Smith's "neo-Kantian assumption that power is directed by language" and retains a phenomenological emphasis on embodiment.[111] Informed by affect theory, Schaefer suggests that perhaps we don't start with cosmologies, with "the need to write the world differently." Perhaps embodied practice begins before concepts that are "driven by forces outside of language."[112] In other words, an affect approach to religion seeks to analyze those moments when practice or bodily orientations inform a rational sense of the world, when bodies teach our minds lessons.

Lisa Sideris, Whitney Bauman, and Laura Hobgood Oster have independently emphasized that the study of religion and ecology has been broadly informed by, and frequently remains entrenched in, the linguistic cosmological approach to the study of religion.[113] Accounting for the enchantments of energy requires closer attention to the imbrications of affects, concepts, ideals, and desires. Affect theory helps put a finger on those elusive and enchanted points of connection between energy, gender, and religion—particularly those historical convergences that may have thrown off their religious language, yet still retain affective resonances between masculine mechanistic power and transcendence.

As William Connolly has emphasized in his affect-influenced analysis of the relation between "cowboy capitalism" and US evangelicalism, often alliances between seemingly unrelated phenomena do not rely so much on expressed or rationally conjoined beliefs, creeds, or doctrinal agreements, as on the ways affects associated with them resonate, blend, fold into, and often amplify one another.[114] Such relations defy modes of linear causality. Here, "causation as resonance between elements . . . morphs into energized complexities of mutual imbrication and interinvolvement, in which heretofore unconnected or loosely associated elements *fold, bend, blend, emulsify, and dissolve into each other,* forcing a qualitative assemblage resistant to classical models of explanation."[115] Attending to extra-cognitive registers or nonlinear influences and imbrications of affect emerges as all the more important when dealing with something like secularized theologies or technoscientific enchantments such as an energy or oil unconscious. Such religio-secular entanglements do not always register on a conscious linguistic level before influencing drives, desires, alliances, and actions. Postsecular affect approaches can get at the importance of the livedness, the everydayness of something like an energy culture where neoliberal narratives of redemption are functioning, conveying that "to be productive, efficient, and happy is to be free."[116]

That is to say, this book aims to draw affects of care and concern as well as attention from the ethereal universalizations of climate emissions and techno-savior climate solutions to the terranean imbrications of theological and material extractions. Doing so will involve attending to places where the desire for alternative embodied energies merges with movements to resist the universalizing fulfillments of Man, making room for ways of living and habits of daily life that have persisted in extractive zones or at the margins of extractive capitalism.

Overview of Chapters

The postsecular affect approach of this critical petro-theology broadly informs the following chapters that follow a trajectory from theological anthropologies to doctrines of God to grace and redemption. The first chapter, "Energy," engages theological anthropologies to demonstrate how energy concepts, values, and practices in the West have been communicated at the nexus of religion and gendered, racialized bodies. Imbrications of energy, masculinity, and divinity have been so consistent that their alignments could show up, articulated by Tarbell, as common sense, or even communicated on an affective level in current technoscientific encounters with masculine energy. Given the way Western theologies and philosophies have disproportionately impacted modern energy practices, the focus of this chapter—and the book in general—will retain a primary focus on these trajectories. Since Aristotle's neologism, *energeia*, energy concepts in the West have been consistently but variously aligned with the fulfillment or completion of humanity. An alignment between *energeia* and Christian divinity was, furthermore, inspired as early as St. Paul who again reinforced a connection between *energeia* and human fulfillment. Consistently, "fulfilled humanity" in the West has been measured by high-energy production and consumption, a theo-philosophical trajectory that has informed a predominant sense, unquestioned until recently, of the necessity of energy excess for individual and civilizational fulfillment.

Chapter 2, "Extraction," explores the implications of significant shifts in late medieval Western doctrines of God for emerging concepts of political power, human subjectivity, and racialization. The chapter engages decolonial, critical race, and political theological perspectives to analyze the ways these emerging concepts and theologies are interconnected in what I will identify as a modern extractive imaginary.

A theo-political ideal of power as sovereign infuses not only modern extraction but modern energy and economy as well. Doctrines of grace are the theological locus of Chapter 3, "Capital." This chapter reexamines Max Weber's famous Protestant work ethic by focusing on the particular dynamics of *extractive* capitalism. While grace and work—free gift and economy or exchange—are commonly seen as opposing terms in modernity, this chapter demonstrates that the free gift has been *internal* to extractive capitalism. The chapter traces free gift concepts in three key moments of extractive capitalism: (1) the beginnings of modern extraction in Saxony during the Reformation, (2) the explicitly theological framing of Presbyterian Scottish energy scientists of modern energy as a divine free gift, and (3) the framing of oil magnates like Lyman Stewart of petro as a free, even omnipotent, divine gift. These references to divine gift/chance/grace both *rely on* and profoundly *disrupt* the Protestant work ethic as traditionally conceived—a symptom that is becoming more prevalent in twenty-first-century finance capitalism.

Where modern extraction has resonated with an ancient Western conception of matter as passive, dead, and inert, feminists, womanists, new materialists, and ecotheologians have compellingly argued for the re-animation of matter. However, through theological loci of Christ and redemption, Chapter 4 will demonstrate how these animating aims emerge as uniquely complicated when one focuses on a particularly potent form of matter: "Oil." In late-nineteenth-century pro-petro writings, oil was framed as animated, agential, and redemptive—at times even taking on Christ-like figuration or portrayed as a theophany. Facing the problematic Storm outlines between the perils of both enchantment and disenchantment, I suggest that the Christian animation of oil in the context of the US oil discoveries demonstrates the need for a critical new materialism that not merely resurrects "dead" matter, but critically attends to the gendered and racializing delineations between life and death, inert and vibrant, passive and active, organic and inorganic, sacred and profane. As a de/animated trickster figure, oil emerges as an ever ambivalent—never animated savior, certainly not inert—disrupter of Western dualisms on which modern religion and extraction culture have been built.

The concluding chapter, "Alternative Energies," traces how, on the way to becoming the world's highest energy consumers, US Americans dealt with early energy crises, resiliently overcoming energy anxieties by subsuming them into strengths through various bodily energy-enhancement techniques. These energy crises—as well as their solutions—were profoundly gendered, racialized, and theologized, and they continue to inform desires for new "alternative energies." Where the time of extractive capitalism has depended on subsuming limitation, loss, and crisis into renewed (energy-intensive) life, proposals for alternative energies will need to recognize the ways energy traumas continue to interrupt and haunt the fullness of the present and thus restrict energy imaginaries of the future to more of the same.

From within a culture that has been energized by the imaginaries of resurrection triumph over death, something like Holy Saturday time/space is needed to recognize that true alternatives need not be "discovered" but require time/space to remain.

In spite of its modern turns and supposed disenchantments, modern energy concepts, technologies, and sciences retain the traces of divine power, white supremacy, and heteropatriarchy. These continue to draw on divine sovereignty where they are framed and function as exceptions to a natural order that yet set the necessary conditions of the every day. Though energy has been approached as disembodied, delocalized, and universal, its ties with histories of embodied, localized extractivism demonstrate that the current climate crisis requires a full-scale reimagining of social and environmental relations rather than an exchange of alternative energy inputs. True alternatives, then, will depend neither on the determined march of the ordinary nor the exceptionality of the irruptive new, but will draw attention to and call for solidarity with embodied energy cultures that have persisted in the face of extractive capitalism's annihilations.

Notes

1. Robert Stinson, "Ida M. Tarbell and the Ambiguities of Feminism," *The Pennsylvania Magazine of History and Biography* 101 (1977): 217–39.
2. A deeply religious man concerned with the liberalization of Christianity in America at the time, he also provided the vision and funding for the publication of *The Fundamentals* which initiated US American Fundamentalism. See Chapter 3 for more on Stewart.
3. Ida B. Tarbell, *History of the Standard Oil Company*, 2 vols (New York: McClure, Phillips and Company, 1904), 6–37.
4. Darren Dochuk, *Anointed with Oil: How Christianity and Crude Made Modern America* (New York: Basic Books, 2019), 151. Quoting a draft of Tarbell's "My Religion" essay. A revised version of this essay appears in Kochersberger (ed.), *More Than a Muckraker* (Knoxville: University of Tennessee Press, 2017), 217–21.
5. Ida B. Tarbell, "The Business of Being a Woman," in *More Than a Muckraker*, 118–28 (118).
6. Ibid.
7. Cf. Stinson, "Ida M. Tarbell and the Ambiguities of Feminism."
8. bell hooks, *Writing Beyond Race: Living Theory and Practice* (New York: Routledge, 2013), 4.
9. Paul Crutzen and Eugene Stoermer, "The 'Anthropocene'," *IGBP Newsletter* 41 (2000): 17–18.
10. See, for example, Kathryn Yusoff, *A Billion Black Anthropocenes or None* (Minneapolis: University of Minnesota Press, 2018) and Donna Haraway, *Staying with the Trouble: Making Kin in the Chthulucene* (Durham: Duke University Press, 2016).
11. Phillip John Usher, *Exterranean: Extraction in the Humanist Anthropocene* (New York: Fordham UP, 2019), 1.
12. Usher does not emphasize the ways an emissions interpretation obscures environmental justice concerns as I've done here, but later in the text, does, with reference to Bruno Latour, emphasize the way it assumes a transcendent perspective.

13 Myrna Perez Sheldon and Naomi Oreskes, "The Religious Politics of Scientific Doubt," in *The Wiley Blackwell Companion to Religion and Ecology*, ed. John Hart (Hoboken: Wiley Blackwell, 2017), 348–67.

14 Yangyang Xu and Veerabhadran Ramanathan, "Well Below 2C: Mitigation Strategies for Avoiding Dangers to Catastrophic Climate Change," *Proceedings of the National Academy of Sciences of the United States of America* 114 (2017): 10315–23. Xu and Ramanathan conclude that "with unchecked emissions, the central warming can reach the dangerous level within three decades, with the LPHI ['low probability high impact'] warming becoming catastrophic by 2050" (10315).

15 "In the 1990s, the annual increase in global CO2 emissions stood at an average 1 percent; since 2000, the figure has been 3.1 percent—a tripled growth rate, exceeding the worst-case scenarios developed by the IPCC and expressing a trend that still does not show any signs of reversal" (Andreas Malm, *Fossil Capital: The Rise of Steam Power and the Roots of Global Warming* (Brooklyn: Verso, 2016), 3).

16 P. Friedlingstein, R. Andrew, J. Rogelj, et al., "Persistent Growth of CO_2 Emissions and Implications for Reaching Climate Targets," *Nature Geoscience* 7 (2014): 709–15. See Malm for a more complete outline and history of this problem, 2+.

17 Leslie A. White, "Energy and the Evolution of Culture," *American Anthropologist* 45 (1943): 335–56.

18 Malm, *Fossil Capital*; Richard York, "Do Alternative Energy Sources Displace Fossil Fuels?" *Nature Climate Change* 2 (2012): 441–4.

19 See Amitav Ghosh, *The Great Derangement: Climate Change and the Unthinkable* (Chicago: University of Chicago Press, 2017), 138, and Timothy Mitchell, *Carbon Democracy: Political Power in the Age of Oil* (New York: Verso, 2011) on democracy and imperialism in fossil capitalism.

20 Poul Holm, et al., "Humanities for the Environment—A Manifesto for Research and Action," *Humanities* 4 (2015): 977–92.

21 Imre Szeman and Dominic Boyer (eds), "Introduction," in *Energy Humanities: An Anthology* (Baltimore: Johns Hopkins University Press, 2017), 1–14 (3). See also ecotheologian Sallie McFague, who similarly comments on the problem: "what is needed is not more information but the will to move from belief to action, from denial to profound change at both personal and public level" (*Blessed are the Consumers* (Minneapolis: Augsburg Fortress, 2013), 5). McFague notes that this issue is regularly recognized by scientists as well. She reports that "In studies of the contributions by the sciences and technology, the closing sentence is often something like the following: 'But of course it is really a spiritual [or moral] problem—a problem of changing hearts and minds so that people will live differently,'" (Ibid., 6).

22 See, for example, Val Plumwood, *Feminism and the Mastery of Nature* (London: Routledge, 1993) and Donna Haraway, *The Companion Species Manifesto: Dogs, People, and Significant Otherness* (Chicago: Prickly Paradigm Press, 2003).

23 Shannon Elizabeth Bell, Cara Elizabeth Daggett, and Christine Elizabeth Labuski, "Toward Feminist Energy Systems: Why Adding Women and Solar Panels Is Not Enough," *Energy Research & Social Science* 68 (2020): 1–13 (1).

24 Donna J. Haraway, *Primate Visions: Gender, Race, and Nature in the World of Modern Science* (New York: Routledge, 1989). See also, Stacy Alaimo, "Cyborg and Ecofeminist Interventions: Challenges for an Environmental Feminism," *Feminist Studies* 20 (1994): 133–52.

25 Imre Szeman and Jeff Diamanti (eds), *Energy Culture: Art and Theory on Oil and Beyond* (Morgantown: West Virginia University Press, 2019), 1.
26 Karen Barad, *Meeting the Universe Halfway: Quantum Physics and the Entanglement of Matter and Meaning* (Durham: Duke University Press, 2007).
27 Imre Szeman et al., "Introduction," in *After Oil* (Edmonton: Petrocultures Research Group, 2016), 9–12 (9). See also, Sheena Wilson, Adam Carlson, and Imre Szeman (eds), *Petrocultures: Oil, Politics, Culture* (Chicago: McGill-Queen's University Press); Szeman and Boyer, *Energy Humanities*; Szeman, *On Petrocultures: Globalization, Culture and Energy* (Morgantown: West Virginia University Press, 2019).
28 Szeman et al., *After Oil*, 50.
29 Dipesh Chakrabarty, "The Climate of History: Four Theses," *Critical Inquiry* 35 (2009): 197–222.
30 Ibid., 208.
31 See Haraway, *Staying with the Trouble* for debates about the moniker for this new geological time period we seem to have entered.
32 Chakrabarty, "The Climate of History," 208.
33 Stephanie LeMenager, *Living Oil: Petroleum Culture in the American Century* (New York: Oxford University Press, 2014), 79.
34 Szeman and Petrocultures Research Group, *After Oil*, 48.
35 Ibid., 50.
36 Amitav Ghosh, "Petrofiction," *The New Republic* 2 (1992): 29–33 (29).
37 Frederick Buell, "A Short History of Oil Cultures: Or, the Marriage of Catastrophe and Exuberance," *Journal of American Studies* 46 (2012): 273–93.
38 Buell contrasts his natureculture approach to energy and oil with that of Vaclav Smil. Smil is widely held as a key authority on energy and energy history. Bill Gates, leading his Gates Foundation to come up with technoscientific solutions to climate change, regularly refers to Smil's work as a key influence and resource. Yet Smil emphasizes that energy and culture have remained independent, uninfluenced by one another. Rather than analyzing the ways culture has influenced oil consumption and energy practices, Smil cites "timeless literature" that has "no correlation with advances in energy consumption" (Vaclav Smil, *Energy in World History* (Boulder: Westview Press, 1994), 252).
39 Buell, "A Short History of Oil Cultures," 274.
40 Ibid., 275.
41 Ibid.
42 Szeman and Diamanti, *Energy Cultures*, 3.
43 Szeman and Boyer, *Energy Humanities*, 3.
44 Storyhill, "I-90," Recorded 2001, Track 28 on *Reunion*, Story Hill Records.
45 Paul H. Giddens, *The Birth of the Oil Industry* (New York: Macmillan Co., 1938), xxxix.
46 Buell, "A Short History of Oil Cultures," 281.
47 Ibid., 286.
48 Ibid., 287.
49 Ibid., 286.
50 "Just Powers," *Just Powers*. Available online: https://www.justpowers.ca/about/ (accessed June 2021).
51 The Mayapple Energy Transition Collective is the name of the collective, collaborative, non-hierarchical work. Collective participants include Cara Daggett,

Shannon Bell, and Christine Labuski Cf. Bell, Daggett, and Labuski, "Toward Feminist Energy Systems."

52 LeMenager, *Living Oil*, 6.
53 "Coal and oil do more than ensure profit and fuel consumption-heavy lifestyles. If people cling so tenaciously to fossil fuels, even to the point of embarking upon authoritarianism, it is because fossil fuels also secure cultural meaning and political subjectivities" (Cara Daggett, "Petro-masculinity: Fossil Fuels and Authoritarian Desire," *Millennium: Journal of International Studies* 47 (2018): 25–44 (27). These privileged subjectivities, she continues, are "oil-soaked and coal-dusted" (28)).
54 Ibid. Daggett further argues that petro-masculinity emerges especially "when agents of genetic masculinity feel threatened or undermined, thereby needing to inflate, exaggerate, or otherwise distort their traditional masculinity" (Ibid., 33).
55 Ibid., 32.
56 Sheena Wilson, "Gender," in *Fueling Culture: 101 Words for Energy and Environment*, ed. Imre Szeman, Jennifer Wenzel, and Patricia Yaeger (New York: Fordham University Press, 2017), 177. On intersectional feminism, see Kimberle Crenshaw, "Demarginalizing the Intersection of Race and Sex: A Black Feminist Critique of Antidiscrimination Doctrine, Feminist Theory and Antiracist Politics," *University of Chicago Legal Forum* 1 (1989): 139–67.
57 Bell, Daggett, and Labuski, "Toward Feminist Energy Systems," 2.
58 Sheena Wilson, "Energy Imaginaries: Feminist and Decolonial Futures," in *Materialism and the Critique of Energy*, ed. Brent Ryan Bellamy and Jeff Diamanti (Chicago: MCM Publishing, 2018), 377–412 (398).
59 María Lugones, "Heterosexualism and the Colonial/Modern Gender System," *Hypatia* 22 (2007): 186–209 (186).
60 LeMenager writes, "I became frustrated while writing *Living Oil* by how much of what I think of as progressive modernity—feminism, environmentalism even, as it has been expressed in the U.S. in particular—is actually tied to assumptions, but also objects and paths, that have been created by fossil fuel energy" (Bellamy et al. 2016, n.p., cited in Szeman and Boyer, *Energy Humanities*, 12). Sheena Wilson has also acknowledged the ways that "the histories of feminism and oil are intertwined," echoing such historical corollaries between the rise of petroleum and Enlightenment-style freedom. Wilson outlined chronological overlaps between oil and feminism: "The age of oil in the West is virtually synchronous with the women's rights movement: after similar periods of development, both the oil industry and the Western women's rights movements had gained significant momentum by the early twentieth century" (Sheena Wilson, "Gendering Oil: Tracing Western Petrosexual Relations," in *Oil Culture*, ed. Ross Barrett and Daniel Worden (Minneapolis: University of Minnesota Press, 2014), 244–63 (248). The footnote attached to this claim focuses on a correlation of timing: Seneca Falls in 1848, first commercial oil well in 1858 (Canada), PA oil in 1859) (Ibid., 281–2). From this Wilson concludes that the "age of oil in the West is virtually synchronous with the women's rights movement: after similar periods of development, both the oil industry and the Western women's rights movements had gained significant momentum by the early twentieth century" (Ibid., 273).
61 Nigeria is commonly cited as an example of a fossil-fuel-rich country with a high percentage of the population living without electricity.
62 Cristina Cielo and Nancy Corrión Sarzosa, "Transformed Territories of Gendered Care Work in Ecuador's Petroleum Circuit," *Conservation and Society* 16 (2018):

8–20; Francisca Isi Omorodion, "The Impact of Petroleum Refinery on the Economic Livelihoods of Women in the Niger Delta Region of Nigeria," *JENDA: A Journal of Culture and African Women Studies* 6 (2004): 1–15.
63   Wilson, "Gender," 177.
64   Bell, Daggett, and Labuski, "Toward Feminist Energy Systems," 2.
65   Naomi Klein emphasizes the interconnection of social power structures and the injustices of climate change. She emphasizes that in order to address climate change, these socio-economic-political power structures must change as well (*This Changes Everything: Capitalism Vs. the Climate* (New York: Simon & Schuster, 2014)).
66   Bell, Daggett, and Labuski, "Toward Feminist Energy Systems," 2, citing Wilson, "Energy Imaginaries," 387.
67   Catherine Keller, *Political Theology of the Earth* (New York: Columbia University Press, 2018).
68   *After Oil* recognizes religious studies as part of the humanities, but does not address religion, divinity, or sacrality. *Energy Humanities* contains a section on energy and philosophy where religion, faith, theology, or deity emerges as a minor element in Allan Stoekl, Martin McQuillan, and Reza Negarestani's work. *Petrocultures* includes mentions of religion, faith, and sacred, but these are not a main theme in any of the contributions.
69   Mark Morrison, Roderick Duncan, and Kevin Parton, "Religion Does Matter for Climate Change Attitudes and Behavior," *PLoS ONE* 10, no. 8 (2015): e0134868. doi:10.1371/journal.pone.0134868; Willis Jenkins, Evan Berry, and Luke Kreider, "Religion and Climate Change," *Annual Review of Environment and Natural Resources* 43 (2018): 9.1–9.24.
70   Naomi Oreskes and Erik M. Conway, *Merchants of Doubt: How a Handful of Scientists Obscured the Truth on Issues from Tobacco Smoke to Global Warming* (New York: Bloomsbury Press, 2010).
71   See Sheldon and Oreskes, "The Religious Politics of Scientific Doubt." See also Antony Alumkal, *Paranoid Science: The Christian Right's War on Reality* (New York: New York University Press, 2017). Especially chapter 1 on anti-evolution movements and intelligent design, and chapter 4 on anti-environmentalism in evangelicalism.
72   Ghosh, *The Great Derangement*, 138.
73   Cara New Daggett, *The Birth of Energy: Fossil Fuels, Thermodynamics, and the Politics of Work* (Durham: Duke University Press, 2019) and Michael Marder, *Energy Dreams: Of Actuality* (New York: Columbia University Press, 2017). We could also include Rochelle Raineri Zuck's essay, "The Wizard of Oil: Abraham James, the Harmonial Wells, and the Psychometric History of the Oil Industry," in *Oil Culture*.
74   Ghosh, "Petrofiction," 29–33 (29).
75   See especially, Dieter Hessel (ed.), *Energy Ethics: A Christian Response* (New York: Friendship Press, 1979) where several National Council of Churches studies starting in 1974 are outlined. See also the US Catholic Bishops 1981 statement on energy, "Reflections on the Energy Crisis" (Washington: United States Catholic Conference, 1981) and the Pontifical Academy of Sciences, "Mankind and Energy: Needs, Resources, Hopes," in *Mankind and Energy: Needs, Resources, Hopes*, ed. André Blanc-Lapierre (Amsterdam: Elsevier, 1982). For a good overview of Catholic energy ethics since 1981, see Erin Lothes Biviano et al., "Catholic Moral Traditions and Energy Ethics for the Twenty-First Century," *Journal of Moral Theology* 5 (2016): 1–36. For a literature review of religious energy ethics (among energy ethics in

general), see Giovanni Frigo, "Energy Ethics: A Literature Review," *Relations* 6 (2018): 173–214.
76   Larry Rasmussen, Normand Laurendeau, and Dan Solomon, "Introduction to 'The Energy Transition: Religious and Cultural Perspectives," *Zygon* 46 (2011): 872–89 (873).
77   Ibid.
78   In the Bron Taylor (ed.), *Encyclopedia of Religion and Nature* (London: Continuum, 2008), for example, there are entries on science and religion with a section on physics, but energy science is not a focus in this entry. There are entries on topics like religion and rubber, but no entries on religion and energy, thermodynamics, or oil. Willis Jenkins et al. (eds), *The Routledge Handbook of Religion and Ecology* (New York: Routledge, 2017) has sections on climate change, oceans, food, water, animals, population, and consumption but no section devoted to energy science, technology, or extraction. In Ernst Conradie and Hilda Koster (eds), *The T&T Clark Handbook on Christianity and Climate Change* (London: Bloomsbury, 2020), a text to which I proudly contributed, there are sections on engaging with policymakers, geoengineers, artists, and ecological economists, but no section devoted explicitly to energy, fossil fuels, electricity, and so on. Energy and fossil fuels as a key reason for climate change are certainly identified, but the crucial convergence of Christianity and fossil fuels is overlooked. For example, Willis Jenkins identifies a key problem with climate denialism in the context of US politics. He correctly identifies the imbrication of white nationalism as a factor in climate denialism. But he breaks this down and asks, "Is it the whiteness, the US citizenship or the Evangelicalism that is more explanatory?" (71). Fossil fuels, and a history of Christianity enchanting energy sources, sciences, and ideals is not addressed.

There are a handful of noteworthy exceptions. For example, Marion Grau provides a key point of departure from the avoidance of oil in her essays "Petro-eschatology," in *Eschatology as Imagining the End: Faith Between Hope and Despair*, ed. Sigurd Bergmann (New York: Routledge, 2018), 45–60, and "From Refiner's Fire to Refinery Fires: Reflections on the Combustive Element of Fire," in *Bloomsbury Handbook of Religion and Nature: The Elements*, ed. Laura Hobgood and Whitney Bauman (New York: Bloomsbury Academic, 2018), 159–72. Evan Berry and Robert Albro emphasize the significance of religion and oil in economic and political struggles in Latin America, *Church, Cosmovision and The Environment: Religion and Social Conflict in Contemporary Latin America* (New York: Routledge, 2018). Hilda Koster addresses gender, oil, and Christianity in "Trafficked Lands: Sexual Violence, Oil, and Structural Evil in the Dakotas," in *Planetary Solidarity: Global Women's Voices on Christian Doctrine and Climate Justice*, ed. Grace Ji-Sun Kim and Hilda P. Koster (Minneapolis: Fortress Press, 2017), 155–78. Michael Northcott addresses hydrocarbons, though not in a comprehensive way, in his *A Political Theology of Climate Change* (Grand Rapids: William B. Eerdmans Publishing Co, 2013).

Clayton Crockett and Donna Bowman's edited volume (*Cosmology, Ecology, and the Energy of God* (New York: Fordham University Press, 2012)) focuses in particular on energy and theology, though here the historical connections between Christianity and energy sciences/technologies are not addressed and fossil fuels are not an area of focus. Stoyan Tanev's *Energy in Orthodox Theology and Physics: From Controversy to Encounter* (Eugene: Pickwick, 2017) is also an exception in that the author explicitly engages energy science from an Eastern Orthodox perspective. The clear aim of his work, though, is apologetical—to demonstrate consonance between Eastern Orthodox theologies of *energeia* and modern energy science. This current book will demonstrate why that's an historically complicated move to make, and also one that emerges as highly problematic rather than triumphal.

79 Terra Schwerin Rowe, *Toward a Better Worldliness: Ecology, Economy, and the Protestant Tradition* (Minneapolis: Fortress Press, 2017).
80 Ernst Conradie, "Christianity," in *Routledge Handbook of Religion and Ecology*, 70–8 (71). Again, my own previous work also fits into this gap—identifying the problem of capitalism but not seeing the deeper connections with oil as well.
81 In Ian Barbour's influential and discipline-defining text, *Religion and Science: Historical and Contemporary Issues* (San Francisco: Harper Collins, 1997) for example, the entire chapter on the nineteenth century is focused on evolution, with no focused attention on electricity or thermodynamics which was the predominant science before evolution took center stage in the 1870s. Alister McGrath's popular textbook, *Science and Religion: A New Introduction*, 3rd ed. (Hoboken: Wiley Blackwell, 2020) does not mention thermodynamics; Richard Olson's *Science and Religion (1450–1900): From Copernicus to Darwin* (Baltimore: Johns Hopkins University Press, 2004) contains chapters on evolution, conflict thesis, and geology without a single mention of energy sciences; Gary Ferngren's *Science and Religion: A Historical Introduction*, 2nd ed. (Baltimore: Johns Hopkins University Press, 2017) includes sections on geology, biology, and cosmology from 1650 to 1900 without a single mention of energy sciences; Phillip Clayton's *Religion and Science: The Basics*, 2nd ed. (New York: Routledge, 2019), has chapters on physics and science, technology and ethics, without a mention of energy sciences; and finally James Haag et al. (eds), *Routledge Companion to Religion and Science* (New York: Routledge, 2012) contains mentions of thermodynamics in chapters on biological evolution, but not as a topic of ethical consideration in energy practice and policy.
82 Szeman et al., *After Oil*, 29.
83 Jason A. Josephson Storm, *The Myth of Disenchantment* (Chicago: University of Chicago Press, 2017), 10.
84 See David Lindberg and Ronald Numbers (ed.), "Introduction," in *God & Nature: Historical Essays on the Encounter between Christianity and Science* (Berkeley: University of California Press, 1986), 1–18.
85 Ian Barbour's work has been profoundly influential in distinguishing religion and science as an independent field of study. *Religion and Science*, based on his Gifford Lectures has been especially influential. Even as more recent scholarship has emphasized the need for further complication, complexification, and critical analysis of the historical ways "religion" and "science" have been variously constructed over time, his four categories of religion and science interaction—conflict, independence, dialogue, and interdependence—have themselves profoundly disrupted the conflict thesis merely by demonstrating that conflict is not the only way science and religion have interacted with historically or currently.
86 Peter Harrison, *The Territories of Science and Religion* (Chicago: University of Chicago Press), 2015.
87 Myrna Perez Sheldon, Ahmed Ragab, and Terence Keel (eds), "Introduction," in *Critical Approaches to Science and Religion*, (New York: Columbia University Press, forthcoming 2023).
88 Nancy Tuana, *The Less Noble Sex: Scientific, Religious, and Philosophical Conceptions of Woman's Nature* (Bloomington: Indiana University Press, 1993), and Terence Keel, *Divine Variations* (Stanford: Stanford University Press, 2018).

89   Dipesh Chakrabarty, *Provincializing Europe: Postcolonial Thought and Historical Difference* (Princeton: Princeton University Press, 2000). See also Keel, "Introduction," in *Divine Variations*.
90   Storm is building on vast stores of literature on the religious influences on and of Bacon, Newton, and other early modern scientists commonly taken to be eradicating the world of divine agency and magic.
91   In chapter 4, Storm offers an analysis of the roots of disenchantment in religious studies and suggests an alternative narrative that "shows how a putative opposition between religion and science, combined with fears of despiritualization and mourning for the death of God, motivated the rise of spiritualism and occult movements, and contributed to the birth of religious studies as a discipline" (Josephson Storm, *The Myth of Disenchantment*, 19).
92   Ibid., 3.
93   Lynn White, "The Historical Roots of Our Ecologic Crisis," *Science* 155 (1967): 1203–7; Thomas Berry, "The New Story," in *Teilhard in the 21st Century: The Emerging Spirit of Earth*, ed. Arthur Fabel and Donald St. John (Maryknoll: Orbis Books, 2003), 77–88; and Joseph Sittler, "Called to Unity," *The Ecumenical Review* 14 (1962): 177–87. Even the nature transcendentalists Emerson and Thoreau articulate versions of the disenchantment thesis in their diagnosis of the environmental crisis and how it is tied to a loss or lack in Western Spirituality.
94   Josephson Storm, *The Myth of Disenchantment*, 9.
95   Ghosh, "Petrofiction," 29.
96   Evan Berry emphasizes that "This transmutation of values and meaning into social fact is a core concern in religious studies and is a useful theoretical explanation of the 'invisibility' of oil in modern life and of the other energy sources that remain obscured from view within their own sacred contexts," Evan Berry, "Religion and Energy," in *The Routledge Handbook on Energy Humanities*, ed. Janet Stewart and Graeme Macdonald (London: Routledge, 2022).
97   Richard Callahan, Jr., Kathryn Lofton, and Chad Seales, "Allegories of Progress: Industrial Religion in the United States," *Journal of the American Academy of Religion* 78 (2010): 1–39.
98   Beatrice Marovich and Alex Dubilet, "Negotiating Terrain: Gender and the Postsecular?" *Journal for Cultural and Religious Theory* 16 (2017): 109–25.
99   Clayton Crockett, *Radical Political Theology: Religion and Politics after Liberalism* (New York: Columbia University Press, 2013). Carl Schmitt, *Political Theology: Four Chapters on the Concept of Sovereignty* (Chicago: University of Chicago Press, 1985).
100 Keller, *Political Theology of the Earth*; Northcott, *A Political Theology of Climate Change*.
101 J. Kameron Carter, *Race: A Theological Account* (New York: Oxford University Press, 2008); Vincent W. Lloyd (ed.), *Race and Political Theology* (Stanford: Stanford University Press, 2012).
102 Keel, *Divine Variations*.
103 Mary-Jane Rubenstein, "Science," in *The Palgrave Handbook of Radical Theology*, ed. C. D. Rodkey and J. E. Miller (New York: Palgrave, 2018), 747–56 (751).
104 Patricia Yaeger proposed the term "energy unconscious," inspired by Frederick Jameson's political unconscious. Patricia Yaeger, "Editor's Column: Literature in the Ages of Wood, Tallow, Coal, Whale Oil, Gasoline, Atomic Power, and Other Energy Sources," *PMLA* 126 (2011): 305–26.
105 Szeman et al., *After Oil*, 50.

106 Karen Bray, *Grave Attending: A Political Theology for the Unredeemed* (New York: Fordham University Press, 2020).
107 Donovan Schaefer, *Religious Affects: Animality, Evolution, and Power* (Durham: Duke University Press, 2015), 35 and 14, respectively.
108 Cf. Ibid., 23.
109 Melissa Gregg and Gregory J. Seigworth (eds), "An Inventory of Shimmers," in *The Affect Theory Reader* (Durham: Duke University Press, 2010), 1–25.
110 Schaefer, *Religious Affects*, 12.
111 Ibid., 11.
112 Ibid.
113 Lisa Sideris, *Consecrating Science: Wonder, Knowledge, and the Natural World* (Oakland: University of California Press, 2017); Laura Hobgood and Whitney Bauman (eds), "Introduction," in *Bloomsbury Handbook of Religion and Nature*.
114 William Connolly, *Christianity and Capitalism: American Style* (Durham: Duke University Press, 2008).
115 William Connolly, "The Evangelical-Capitalist Resonance Machine," *Political Theory* 33 (2005): 869–86 (870).
116 Bray, *Grave Attending*, 11.

Chapter 1

ENERGY

On a Sunday morning during the first pandemic lockdown, I stepped out of the house for the first time in weeks. Biking the trail circumnavigating my hometown of Sioux Falls, South Dakota, I remember the feeling of the lockdown being close to the surface: a deprivation of social, emotional, cultural, intellectual connection; a need to be moved, to experience more than the everyday plane of existence. The trail follows the unfortunately named Big Sioux River which at one point quietly flows past the Sioux Falls airport. Approaching the Maverick (yes, literally) wing of the airport, I noticed folks camped out in lawn chairs along the bike trail facing the river—a perfect vantage point from which to view the airstrip. Continuing along, the trail curves to run perpendicular to the runway. Crossing this portion of the trail, a SD Air National Guard fighter jet approached on the runway and took off, passing directly overhead. The power of the engine was more felt than heard—the kind of all-encompassing sound that penetrates your body. The experience stopped me cold along the trail. I was surprised at first and then increasingly disgusted to find I was moved to tears. What was this unexpected and inexplicable feeling of awe, wonder, fear, and admiration—quickly followed by disgust, loathing, and shame?

My body knew before I was conscious of it—the close encounter with such raw penetrating power was not something I instinctively interpreted as a violation, but something more like a *mysterium tremendum*, a mysterious, fearful, yet awe-inspiring feeling of boundary bursting freedom. The disgust and shame arose as I became conscious that the encounter with the power of human technoscientific might and masculine Maverick bravado had landed on that affective gap of longing for an experience outside the mundane isolation of a pandemic lockdown and immediately registered not as problematic, but as transcendent. I suddenly realized why there were other folks sitting out alongside the trail. It was Sunday and this was the best bit of church available.

I should have known better. I did know better—I was in the midst of having studied the consistent Western alignments of masculinity, energy, and transcendence for the past three years. I *knew* better, but my body—molded by decades of life in a predominantly Christian petroculture—*felt* differently. Such disjunction between thought and feeling, knowledge and action is precisely the kind of problem that animates environmental humanities approaches to the climate conundrum. As knowledge of the anthropogenic causes of climate change increase while carbon emissions continue to rise, the importance of analyzing affective associations and unconscious alliances that motivate behavior, even in spite of better knowledge, becomes clear.

This chapter and the broader themes of this book bring to attention the ways theologies of energy have functioned in the West, the ways they have informed what it means to be human, what it is to live a good life, what redemption means, and what is held as sacred. I want to emphasize how commitments to exuberant fossil fuel–dependent energy systems take the form of theological—and not just monetary, economic, or infrastructural—investments, and indeed, how these mutually inform and infuse one another. This is the case even, and especially, in contexts that are no longer overtly religious, and recognizing their influence will be an important step not just in consciousness raising, but in removing obstacles for imagining alternative energies.

In the twentieth century, US Americans became the highest energy consumers in the world. Even when compared to other "developed" nations, US energy consumption dwarfed others: 40 percent more than Germany, 200 percent more than Sweden, 300 percent more than Japan and Italy. In the twentieth century, this 5 percent of the world's population accounted for 25 percent of the world's oil and 22 percent of carbon emissions.[1] A continued rise in fossil-fuel consumption and CO_2 emissions even in the face of increased knowledge of the anthropogenic causes of climate change is certainly due to the convergence of multiple and complex factors. Economic systems and energy infrastructures do not change overnight and many entities retain vested interests in maintaining current predominant energy practices. International as well as domestic political agreements on climate change have been thwarted time and again by disagreements, misdirection, and climate denialism. High-energy consumption is often justified by a reigning economic logic that links increased energy consumption to increased GDP and human well-being. While this logic remains entrenched among political, economic, and engineering decision makers, it is increasingly being challenged.[2] Seeking to build momentum, this project calls into question the basic logic that more energy is better, that increased energy production and consumption leads to more cultural development, and that cultural evolution follows technological advancement.

The current chapter will develop a basic claim of this book: that energy—even modern energy science—has been profoundly enchanted and that often-unconscious theological investments play a key role in maintaining high-energy lifestyles even as mounting evidence demonstrates their danger. This chapter will focus in particular on the ways that related energy concepts from Aristotle and St. Paul's *energeia* to *vis viva* and modern energy have come to define human fulfillment such that gender and racial distinctions have been drawn along lines of energy variance. From a decolonial feminist perspective, exuberant fulfillment has defined what Sylvia Wynter has identified as overrepresented Man.[3] The energy dreams and values of overrepresented Man continue to be exported, imposed, and violently obtruded on diverse cultures and energy systems. More measured, moderate, or fluctuating patterns of life, speech, and thought, and contemplative activities, restful states, or meandering modes are treated in energy-intensive economies and societies as pathological, immoral, deficiencies of a fulfilled healthy human body.[4] A drive for completion over process, activity instead of contemplation, or a destination rather than a journey all emerge as embodied energies and habits of life carefully promoted through positive associations with fulfillment, completion, and wholeness.

Energy values, gender distinctions, racial hierarchies, and conceptions of divinity have been mutually informed and constructed in the West. Even as the authority of natural philosophy and theology waned in early modernity, ancient connections between divinity, *energeia*, and the full development of humanity were mapped onto civilizational and human aims. Such historical alignments between divinity and human fulfillment have infused and informed the enthusiastic reception and euphoric interpretation of "energy resources" like coal and oil, energy technologies involving electricity and magnetism, and energy sciences like thermodynamics. With Ida Tarbell's commonsensical association of masculinity and the vigor of life such that the oilman represented the perfected, completed, even divinely ordained man, this seems to be the tradition she and her readers were tapped into. Reciprocally, in the play between enchantment and disenchantment, the seemingly miraculous discoveries and functions of electricity and oil have infused new religious expressions and been leveraged as evidence of theological truths in conflicts with a perceived rise in atheism. Man, energy, and divinity have formed something of an unholy trinity, perichoretically weaving in and out of one another, informing, infusing, amplifying one another—all circling around a modern Western exuberance that has brought a planet to the brink of disaster and derangement.[5]

Pervasive assumptions that human well-being requires excessive energy are currently being challenged and rethought, as we will see, with empirical support by ecological economists. Yet, historical alliances and mutual enchantments between divinity, Man, and energy have thwarted the imaginaries of alternative energies and obscured the sense that more energy consumption does not necessarily lead to better life quality, that though energy poverty remains a key issue in the majority of the world, the high-energy consumption of a relatively small group of humans is not an ideal goal either. Consequently, this whole line of reasoning, this whole theology of the energy of Man must be reexamined, its racial, colonial, and gender legitimations exposed. More than identifying "roots" or "origins" of the current energy crisis, this kind of analysis is an important step in coming to terms with all that modernity has implied as a way of beginning to think it otherwise, to reimagine the relationship between humanity and energy so that it is not geared toward the aims and goals of the domination of Man but reimagined for multiple mutually sustaining and enriching forms of human and more-than-human life.

Brief Introduction to the Modern Energy
Synthesis: Energeia, Work, and Heat

To understand how Man, energy, and divinity have infused one another we first need to see how the concepts of work and heat became fused to Aristotle's *energeia* in modern thermodynamics. What were diverse or loosely connected concepts in ancient thought, *energeia*, work, and heat converge in modern energy science. In modernity each of these—*energeia*, work, and heat—has retained ancient associations with the completion or fulfillment of humanity idealized in the rational masculine form. From these traditions modern energy has assumed the logic of human fulfillment arising from high—even excessive—heat and energy.

From Aristotle's *energeia* to nineteenth-century thermodynamics, Western energy concepts have been rooted in a Greek preoccupation with the relationship between change and stasis. As early as Parmenides, Western thinkers had perceived that beneath the seemingly constant surface-level change of the material world, something was retained or remained the same.[6] The law of energy conservation associates this constant, static remainder with energy. Historically, though, Western thought has consistently associated the constant amidst all (presumably surface-level) changes with divinity. In natural philosophy and science this constant has often retained an explicit link to divinity, identified variously as *energeia*, ether, force, *vis viva*, and, then, modern energy.

Though current scholars trace the concept of energy conservation back as far as Parmenides, there was no shared and coherent sense of what in particular was conserved until modernity. And though the term *energeia* was introduced by Aristotle, it differs in significant ways from modern "energy"—a term introduced in the nineteenth century. Modern energy emerged as an overarching term that united several physical sciences from physics to electricity and magnetism. Most importantly for our current purposes, though, modern energy synthesized three different concepts that had previously been distinct. *Energeia*, work, and heat converged from diverse historical trajectories to form thermodynamics in the nineteenth century.

German philosopher Gottfried Wilhelm Leibniz made the connection between ancient *energeia* and an emerging modern concept of energy explicit in his response to a debate in the seventeenth century about what was transferred and conserved in moving bodies.[7] Based on Galileo's findings, French philosopher Rene Descartes concluded in his *Principles of Philosophy* (1644) that all bodies possess a force. When a moving object impacts another its motion is transferred, causing it to move. Descartes' text is often cited as a key initiating text in the theory of energy conservation—yet the content of what was transferred was still debated and the term "energy" was still a couple of hundred years on the horizon. Leibniz disagreed with the Cartesian interpretation that motion itself was transferred between objects and conserved. He argued that the Cartesians had conflated two kinds of force that should be distinguished: dead force (*vis mortua*)—because the phenomena of motion did not yet exist—and living force (*vis viva*)—because it was active force in motion.[8]

Leibniz fortified his new science of "power and action" or "dynamics" with an ancient pedigree, framing these forces in terms of Aristotle's distinction between *energeia* and *dunamis* (Latin: *potentia*). The living force, *vis viva*, he associated with Aristotle's *energeia* or entelechy (later called kinetic energy) and *vis mortua* he associated with Aristotle's *dunamis*. Describing Aristotle's *energeia*, Leibniz wrote, ". . . the entelechy of Aristotle, which has made so much noise, is nothing else but force or activity; that is, a state from which action naturally flows if nothing hinders it."[9] It was not a quantity of motion itself, as Descartes had theorized, that was conserved but *vis viva* transferring to *vis mortua* and vice versa. As such, *dunamis* is integrated into *energeia* as merely a different form that force takes. Conversely, *energeia* was reinterpreted as activated potential for movement within things. Liebniz's *vis viva* and his distinction between active and potential force remained authoritative through the eighteenth century.

Thomas Kuhn has noted the remarkable way that the principle of energy conservation emerged nearly simultaneously from as many as twelve scientists working independent of one another in the 1840s.[10] The law of conservation, though, is frequently associated with Hermann von Helmholtz. A German physicist, Helmholtz was influenced by Kantian metaphysics of nature in conceptualizing force (*Kraft*) as a conserved substance rather than an activity.[11] In 1847 he wrote "The Conservation of Force" where he concludes that "Whenever bodies act upon one another by forces of attraction and repulsion which are independent of time and velocity, the sum of their *vires vivae* and tensional forces must be constant."[12] For Helmholtz, this universal force is the great constant: in, among all living, moving, changing things, it may change forms but cannot be destroyed. Energy humanities scholars Brent Ryan Bellamy and Jeff Diamanti emphasize that it wasn't just *Kraft* (power/force) that Helmholtz identified, but specifically *Arbeitskraft*—labor power. Helmholtz thus introduces the concept of work by identifying "objective consistency between the worker's caloric output, the coal power expressed in the machinery, and the abstraction of both forms of *Arbeitskraft* by the value form of capital at a more general level."[13]

While Leibnitz's *vis viva* and Helmholtz's *Kraft* are now considered roughly synonymous with what became identified as "energy," the science of dynamics had not yet envisioned any transfer of *vis viva* into heat. It wasn't until the work of Sadi Carnot, unappreciated during his own lifetime, and then James Joule that heat would become associated with the ability to do work. With Carnot's understanding of motive power, Joule's view of heat, and the remarkable reconciliation between them in 1850 by Rudolf Clausius we see an integration of the *vis viva* tradition with concepts of heat and the assertion of an equivalence between heat and work.[14]

The first law of thermodynamics would eventually be articulated as a version of the law of energy conservation. Clausius is credited with its earliest explicit statement in 1850: while energy can transfer from heat to work, it can neither be created nor destroyed. The optimism and dependability infused into the principle of energy conservation drew on the history tracing back to Parmenides of a preference for constancy consistently aligned with a divine, sustaining, ruling force in creation that could create change but which itself could neither be created nor destroyed.

The optimism of energy conservation, though, was quickly interrupted by the principle of energy dissipation or entropy in the following decade. Clausius himself had concluded that heat "always shows a tendency to equalize temperature differences and therefore to pass from hotter to colder bodies."[15] Yet, while Clausius had concluded, based on experiential evidence, that the reverse—colder to hotter—could not be true, such irreversibility was not a key point of concern as it was for William Thomson (ennobled in 1892 as Lord Kelvin). Thomson played a key role in formulating the second law of thermodynamics—the law of entropy or heat loss—anticipated by Carnot and articulated as well by Clausius. In closed systems, the amount of energy available for use will degrade—entropy will increase—as it crosses energy gradients (from mechanical to heat, for example) while the total amount of energy, consistent with the first law, remains stable. For Thomson then, not only is energy indestructible, but its irreversibility also suggested to him that nothing in the physical world will remain in its present form but remains transitory.[16]

For Thomson in particular there were not just scientific, but—as I will demonstrate more fully later in this chapter—key theological concerns at stake as well. The term "energy" was not widely introduced until Thomson began to employ it, according to historian Crosbie Smith, for two key reasons. First, he used the term to encompass a range of terms from *vis viva*, force, mechanical effect, animal magnetism, and work and so "to avoid terminological confusion."[17] In avoiding terminological confusion, Thomson brought together previously dispersed insights of physics, theories of motion, light, heat, electricity, and magnetism. This synthesis resulted in a profound shift of power and influence among the sciences. As Philip Mirowski argues, "Only after 1850 did physics become the king of the sciences, usurping the throne from physical astronomy. Energy was the reason."[18] Second, and according to Smith "more importantly" for Thomson, he began to employ the term "energy" in order "to signify the special status assigned to *vis viva* and its related concepts" as something that can be conditioned only by the kind of power possessed by a deity.[19] Thomson interpreted the laws of thermodynamics through the lens of a voluntarist theological worldview. He objected to the reigning deist or atheistic mechanism of natural philosophy that viewed the natural orders as self-sufficient and self-sustaining, requiring no divine intervention or sustenance. For Thomson, a world ordered by an omnipotent creator would surely not be self-sufficient, but continually reliant on divine power. Consistent with the law of conservation, Thomson emphasized that no destruction of energy could take place "without an act of power possessed only by the supreme ruler."[20] Yet, while energy could not be destroyed outside of divine action, the material world remained fallible. In a draft of his famous "Dynamical Theory of Heat" (1851), he cited biblical support for the idea that post-Fall creation was constantly degrading. While energy could not be created or destroyed, it was continually "lost to man irrecoverably"[21]—thus Thomson felt the practical *and theological* weight of finding more efficient ways to not lose energy, but put it to work for the good of humanity.

Smith concludes that "energy" attained primary status within the context of scientific discovery and debate and *concurrently* within the assumed worldview of a voluntarist deity. Energy—the modern term and concept—thus synthesized not only *energeia*-cum-*vis viva*, heat, and work, but also a newly revived and legitimated voluntaristic theological world view *through* a modern science.

Human Fulfillment through Energeia, Work, and Heat

Modern energy thus brings together diverse sciences, ancient concepts, observed phenomena, and theological worldviews. It is important to emphasize, though, that *energeia*, work, and heat had remarkably diverse ancient trajectories that did not make their synthesis inevitable. However, what they did share would be monumentally consequential. Despite diverse and even divergent ancient uses, a shared theo-philosophical association with fulfillment resonated between them, smoothed their eventual synthesis, and amplified an eventual modern sense that high-energy production and consumption is necessary for full individual and collective human development.

Energeia

In the current context energy is most commonly defined as the ability to do work. The ancient descent of this particular definition is seemingly supported by Joe Sachs' commonly referenced translation of Aristotle's neologism, *energeia*, "being-at-work."[22] Yet, this translation suggests too much and simultaneously not enough. Translating *energeia* in this way rightly highlights the fact that *energeia* is the result of Aristotle's lexical synthesis of *en*, meaning "in" or "within" and *ergon*, which is often translated as "work." Yet, to translate *ergon* as work can be misleading in that it suggests reading the modern synthesis of work with energy onto an ancient concept where, as we will see, it was excluded.

Unlike the ancient Stoics or the modern Western positive assessment of work, Aristotle did not embrace labor as a moral good.[23] Following Plato, Aristotle held that perfecting a manual skill required a kind of deadening and degrading effect on the mind that would make it unfit for contemplation, which was the true and most actualized use of the human mind.[24] For Aristotle, therefore, the repetitive action and progressive activity of work was *explicitly excluded* from the contemplation of *energeia*.

Philosopher David Bradshaw has traced the development of Aristotle's use of *energeia*, beginning with influences from Plato's distinction between the mere possession of a thing and the use of a thing. Aristotle identified *energeia* as the use of a thing in action—more specifically, an activity that is the "exercise of a capacity in contrast to its mere possession."[25] Something possessed so that it *could* be used is *potentia* (Latin) or *dunamis* (Greek). To this he contrasted *energeia* as something like a capacity that was not just possessed, but also in use. *Energeia* eventually took on the sense for Aristotle of actuality—completion, fulfillment, consummation.

In this sense, *energeia* became synonymous for Aristotle with *entelecheia*, which indicates an aim, goal, purpose, completion, full actuality, or full realization.[26]

The distinctiveness of *energeia* was helpfully illustrated by Aristotle in reference to two kinds of activities. While modern definitions would identify multiple forms of energy (muscle power, machine power, etc.) required to build a home, for Aristotle these efforts would fall under *kinesis* (motion or change) on the grounds that while work was being done, it was not fully completed or actualized in the act. By contrast, Aristotle gave the examples of thinking, seeing, understanding, living well, and flourishing as proper examples of *energeia* since these actions encompass their own ends—they are fulfilled in the act. Aristotle suggested a tense test to determine the difference: when one is *building* a house, it is not at the same time *built*, but when one *sees* one at the same time has *seen*.[27] Sight is an example of *energeia* in that, unlike the action of building a house, it is complete in its activity. *Energeia* is activity that is fulfilled or completed and not incomplete or in process.

In key ways, then, the modern association of energy with work is a departure from—or even, as philosopher Michael Marder emphasizes, a reversal of—Aristotle's *energeia*.[28] Marder's energy philosophy is fueled by concerns with the current climate/energy crisis. While other twentieth- and twenty-first-century philosophers like Heidegger and Derrida have dismissed *energeia* as irredeemably metaphysical, merely another example of "invariable presence" (Derrida), or a "misnomer for being" (Heidegger), Marder has emphasized the inherent instability, ambiguity, and indeterminacy of the term. He argues that in the context of a climate-induced energy crisis, such dismissals only abandon the concept to be defined and determined by industry.[29] That *energeia* is neither necessarily metaphysical nor determined, but a "term in crisis, divided against itself," suggests the ambiguity may be an "opportunity rather than an obstacle, for thinking."[30] Marder aims to reclaim a certain unrealized possibility from Aristotle's thought, emphasizing that what moderns call "energy" actually functions in a manner that is "more intensely metaphysical" than ancient *energeia*.[31] While modern definitions of energy are often synonymous with power—the power to effect a change or power to do work, as we've noted—Aristotle's *energeia* was, in important ways, characterized by the absence of power, potency, *potentia*. Where *potentia* is characterized by work, striving, and the power of activity in progress, ancient *energeia* was characterized by fulfillment that no longer has need of power: "Aristotle's energy is thus markedly powerless and incapable, not by way of deprivation, but because it is beyond the vicissitudes of *dunamis*, which names an incompletion to be overcome."[32] Rather than power to effect change, Marder associates ancient *energeia* with the active passivity of contemplation, the powerlessness of accomplishment, and the fullness of consummation and happiness. From an ancient sense, these states—and not power—are characteristics of the "most intense energetic state imaginable."[33] Contrasted with the contemplative powerlessness of *energeia*, modern energy functions as more intensely metaphysical in that it "presents itself as the sole possible reality . . . that excludes other alternatives as unrealistic, utopian, unproductive."[34]

Where modern energy "is precisely, not actuality"—not ancient *energeia*—Marder diagnoses that moderns are not *energeia*-occupied but *potentia*-obsessed.[35] It is this insatiable preoccupation with potentiality that makes the current energy crisis so volatile: "The greatest enemy of contemporary humanity, of our planet, and of material existence as such is thus unbridled possibility that more and more renders the world impossible."[36] For Marder, the modern *potentia* obsession involves the evacuation of actuality, a reckless dissatisfaction with *energeia* and its plenum. Marder argues, "we are so enthralled with the possible that we've ceased caring about the actual and forfeited the energy of the latter."[37] In short, the modern love of potentiality has become a desire for the "ruinous force of means devoid of an end."[38]

Consequently, Marder proposes ancient *energeia* with its satiated contemplation as an important *disruption* of the modern *potentia*, work-energy preoccupation. Transcending binaries between work and rest, activity and passivity, temporality and eternity, this *energeia* of contemplation emerges as an "inexhaustible energy in every instant that fleets by solely according to the perspective of those who are, themselves, rushing without noticing its inimitable singularity."[39] This allows Marder to make fascinating and disruptive alliances between energy and contemplative practices ranging from Eastern Orthodox Hesychasm to a Buddhist attentiveness to the fullness of the present, the completeness of the self in attention to each moment.

I find Marder's reading of ancient *energeia* fresh, insightful, and an inspired way of working out the profound philosophical and theological implications of energy practice and policy. Indeed, consistent with Marder's thesis, I will emphasize a shift in the next chapter in early modernity where *potentia*, as the root of potency (*potestas*), emerges as a key obsession of modern political theo/philosophy that comes to infuse modern extraction.

Yet, I can't get past a sense that moderns are still also *energeia*/actuality obsessed. While *energeia* is emphasized in Marder's thought as a satiated fulfillment to the exclusion of *potentia*, I'm skeptical that the two can be separated so cleanly. They only find their meaning—and more significantly, their desirability—in relation to one another. *Potentia* emerges as so appealing in modernity precisely because it promises (no matter how indefinitely) to actualize. And *energeia* emerges ultimately as a fulfillment of power and potency which is precisely its modern as well as ancient appeal. *Energeia* remains enticing for moderns in its self-reliant satisfaction and it can rest in its fullness precisely because it has conquered all other *potentia* pretenders. Just as in the ancient world, moderns desire *energeia* above all because in its plenum there is no lack, no need for dependence, no need for anything outside of itself. This Charlton Heston, true grit, blue-jean-capitalist-cowboy *energeia* can be satisfied in as much as it transcends the vicissitudes of *potentia* and remains whole and complete by itself. This is expressed most pointedly by Aristotle's unmoved mover which, on account of its completeness, has no need of—indeed, remains unmoved by—anything outside of itself.[40] Moderns are not just potentiality-occupied, but also actuality-obsessed because of its ability to convey precisely what Marder lifts up: completion, fulfillment, wholeness, consummation.

Related to this self-sufficient fulfillment, *energeia* also remains tied to possession in important ways. Recall that Aristotle was building on Plato's distinction between the mere possession of a thing and its active use. Aristotle distinguished *energeia* from something that was merely possessed and articulated it as something possessed but also in use. *Energeia*, therefore, remains rooted in and assumes possession. Though ancient *energeia* does not yet assume an imaginary of a subsurface, Lockean possession, or modern race, the ancient employment of the term already entwines possession and human fulfillment, anticipating or smoothing the way for a modern sense of human fulfillment tied to possession or "whiteness as property."[41]

I'm also not convinced that the modern sense of energy is pure *potentia*, obsessed only with the production of more *potentia*, void of any end, value, or goal. To his credit, Marder is remarkably tuned into the importance of the continuing role of theology. He devotes an entire chapter to the theological influences and implications of *energeia* and notes that "Rather than doctrinaire hairsplitting, irrelevant to the secular world, the study of theology may explain the axiological and epistemological patterns that prevail in actuality."[42] In this sense, Marder's emphasis on the contemporary importance of theology is remarkably consonant with the one emphasized here. Yet, in spite of Marder's succinct and persuasive argument for the ongoing postsecular role of theology, he succumbs to the disenchantment view of modernity as empty striving in his framing of *potentia* as void of an end or goal. To argue that modernity is merely *potentia*-obsessed "without an end and to no end" suggests that moderns face a void of value that gets translated into an endless desire for consumption—*potentia* for its own sake. This view of modernity as valueless and aimless, stuck on a nihilistic treadmill of consumption driven by the need to distract from life emptied of meaning is part and parcel of the disenchantment thesis. For those of us who were introduced to environmental issues with films like *Affluenza*[43] and early ecotheological arguments that crucially aimed to increase the engagement of religious folk by arguing that the environmental crisis was simultaneously a spiritual crisis of modernity's loss of meaning,[44] aspects of this argument will surely ring true: wanton consumption of modern capitalist societies is fueled by the need to fill the modern void of meaning, purpose, and value that, nonetheless, material consumption can never fill. However, I argue that this view of environmental problems as emerging primarily from disenchanted modernity profoundly obscures the ways that energy—even modern energy science—emerges not only from a vacuum of religious content or moral meaning, but also as a theo-philosophical overflow or a play between enchantment and disenchantment. Rather than driven blindly to fill a void, modern compulsions for accumulation and consumption can be seen as profoundly informed by old aims, drives, and meaning that have not been evacuated, but have merely taken on new form in modernity. Rather than a mere striving to fill a void of meaning, I think moderns are also compelled toward high-energy lifestyles by a desire for fulfillment, completion, wholeness, and perfection that has been associated with a certain mode of divinity and what Sylvia Wynter calls overrepresented Man.[45] Viewing environmental problems merely from the perspective of the disenchantment thesis obscures, in particular, the ways energy concepts and practices emerge at the nexus of gendered, racialized, and theological idealizations of human being.

Indeed, the entire scope of Western thought could be characterized as an extended occupation with actuality and actualization, with certain "genres" of the human coming to count as more fully human than others. At least since Aristotle, what it has meant to become a biologically, spiritually, intellectually fully developed human entails a kind of self-mastery that is fully actualized only in rational man. In an essay aptly titled "On Not Becoming Man," Claire Colebrook demonstrates the entwinement of potentiality and actuality in Western philosophical definitions of human being. In this trajectory, "man's proper potentiality—that which defines the human as *human*—is what the human soul achieves when it actualizes its utmost power."[46] Aristotle concludes in *Protrepticus* among other places that thinking or reasoning is the proper work of the soul.[47] The one who most fully actualizes this proper potentiality of the soul emerges as the height of humanity: "Now if living is, alike for every animal, its true being, it is clear that the one who will be in the highest degree and the most proper sense is the thinker, and most of all when he is in action and contemplating the most knowable of all things."[48] The use of the capacity for reason, above the exercise of any other capacity, distinguishes the human from other animals, and certain ways of being human from others. As I will demonstrate in the next chapter, eventually this will allow Man—a particular expression of humanity that becomes overrepresented as *the* expression of humanity[49]—to become exceptional, the exception that exceeds or transcends an undifferentiated feminized matter of blackness, thereby justifying his law-giving, mastering role.

In reference to the proper functioning of the soul, Aristotle's articulation of *energeia* already entails spiritual-theological implications. An alignment between human fulfillment, *energeia*, and divinity gets more explicitly mapped onto Christian theology in particular as early Christian thinkers, starting with St. Paul, took on Aristotle's neologism and confined it to divine and spiritual agencies.

St. Paul's Energeia *Energeia* and energy have been more internal to Christian history and thought than has been accounted for by twentieth-century Christian ethicists and scholars of religion and science. As we will see, St. Paul interpreted *energeia* in influential ways, and from this perspective, different interpretations of divine *energeia* can be seen at the heart of theological divides between Eastern and Western Christianities.

Early Christian theologians embraced Aristotle's *energeia*, maintaining the original sense of a capacity that, when exercised, results in a fulfillment or actualization, while adding distinctive emphases. St. Paul, in particular, relied on Aristotle's neologism, applying it in a way that Bradshaw deems "unprecedented" in ancient thought.[50] Paul's use of *energeia* was remarkable for its singular focus. Unlike others who applied the term more broadly, Paul restricted it to spiritual agents: God, Satan, Christ, angels, or demons. Bradshaw notes that "there was no similar restriction [in the application of *energeia* to spiritual agents] in non-Biblical Greek or the Septuagint."[51] He furthermore suggests that "Paul's restriction of *energeia* and *energein* to supernatural action was so striking that it apparently established a precedent for subsequent Christian literature."[52] Of the occurrences of the term in the writings of Apostolic Fathers—from the Shepherd of Hermas to the Epistle of Barnabas, First Clement, and Justin Martyr—"all refer to the action of God, Christ, angels, or demons."[53] According to Bradshaw, this indicates the profound influence Paul's restriction of the term had on later generations of Christian thinkers.

In addition to applying *energeia* exclusively to spiritual agents, Paul used the term to build on a key theology expressed in the Hebrew Bible: the sense of the human becoming fully human by embracing the divine. Paul took this belief and, in an entirely new way, applied the language of *energeia* to express a sense of human fulfillment through the embrace of the divine.[54] *Energeia* took on a sense of "a capacity for action or accomplishment"[55] associated with both divine action and divine presence. This Pauline usage of the term also became widely influential for early Christians. As such, for these early Christians *energeia* was not just the activity or the exercise of a capability, but a capacity associated with the presence of the Judeo-Christian God and associated with human fulfillment.

Bradshaw emphasizes that the Eastern Christian understanding of deification has its roots here. From Paul to the Cappadocians to Gregory Palamas (*c.* 1296–1357), deification is understood as an "ongoing and progressively growing participation in the divine energies."[56] Eastern Christian *theosis* also, however, makes clear that the divine energies are not just any activity, but acts "that manifest the divine character,"[57] articulated specifically by the Cappadocians as wisdom, being, power, life, love, holiness, beauty, virtue, immortality, eternity, infinity, and simplicity.[58] Eventually, this tradition would be articulated in Palamas' divine energy/essence divide. Palamas emphasized a distinction between divine essence (*ousia*) and divine energies (*energeia*), or the ways God manifests Godself in divine action. While God remains unknowable in God's essence, God is knowable in God's energies, or manifestations of divine action. Similarly, while God's essence remains unchanged and unmoved by human actions, divine energies retain a reciprocal relation with and can be moved by creaturely agencies. Importantly, this allows for a sense of human cooperation or participation with divine energies in *theosis* while the divine essence remains unchanged.

While conflicts and tensions had remained high between the East and West churches for centuries, Bradshaw argues that the Eastern Church's embrace of Palamas' energy/essence distinction and the West's rejection of it formalized the theological break between these expressions of Christianity. In contrast to Palamas, the West—Aquinas in particular—emphasized the necessary oneness of divine energy and essence, fearing a slide into polytheism. Where divine essence and activities/energies remain undifferentiated, Aquinas' conclusion that God's essence is pure act remains the logical conclusion.

Marder is particularly critical of Aquinas' interpretation of *energeia* restricted to "pure act" which he sees as solidifying the Western departure from Aristotle's sense of *energeia* as a kind of powerless passivity in completion and fulfillment. Indeed, where the West has come to embrace a sense of necessary forward movement, progress, and activity as essential to human actualization and integral to modern definitions of energy, Marder's point is well taken. Yet, while Aquinas' emphasis on *energeia* as pure act rather than the completion of something like contemplation surely contributed to a Western embrace of the activity of progress, both Aquinas and Palamas continued to share a sense of the important role of divine *energeia* in human fulfillment. Moreover, as we will see throughout the following chapters, what often resonates between energy sciences, technologies, or resources and divine ideals is a sense that energy does what God does, that energy acts in ways that correspond with divine actions: electricity seems divine for the ways it vivifies, oil emerges as divine for the ways that it animates, transforms, and seems to redeem. Therefore, even more than resonance with an *essence* of divinity, energy emerges as divine in the West because it manifests as divine action (*energeia*)—it seems to do what God does.

With Paul's influential use of *energeia* applied exclusively to supernatural agents, synthesizing the term in a new way with a Hebrew understanding of the human becoming fully human by embracing the divine, his theological trajectory amplified a consistent Western philosophical and religious alignment between the pursuit of energy and the full development of humanity. Furthermore, as I will emphasize in the following sections, even if Aquinas departed from Aristotle's contemplative rather than active sense of *energeia*, Aristotle's close association of heat and *energeia* is retained in the West through embryology and biological theories of human development.

Work

So Aristotle excluded work from *energeia* in his embrace of effortless completion, and Paul clearly emphasized the important role of divine *energeia* in human fulfillment. Yet, in modernity, energy became nearly synonymous with the ability to do work. In spite of these ancient exclusions, what eventually resonates between *energeia* and work is their shared commitment to human fulfillment.

Identifying work as a basic characteristic of human life has a long history in Western thought. More often than not, it has been taken as not just a requirement for living that must be endured, but a gift, something that positively contributes to human being, forms human character, and even defines what it means to be human in contrast to animality. In contrast to Aristotelian and Platonic diminishment of work, positive assessments of work were, according to anthropologist Herbert Applebaum, first proposed in the West by the Stoics.[59] Stoics embraced work as granting a sense of the human role or place in the order of things. Stoics therefore moralized work and introduced the idea of a calling, conveying a sense that even the lowliest person has a mission in life to fulfill. An embrace of work as a moral calling to a particular role in the order of creation strongly resonated with the Judeo-Christian tradition and its belief in a deity whose work includes the act of creation. With God as divine laborer and humans created in this image, humans are seen to fulfill their divine image by engaging in work.[60]

Positive assessments of work were intensified into the Middle Ages through Benedictine monasticism. Contrary to Aristotle, St. Benedict did not see contemplation and work as mutually exclusive, but as complementary. For Benedict the highest form of spiritual life would be expressed in overcoming the division between contemplation and action. In creating his Rule of monastic life, he ordered saintly life around *ora et labora*, prayer and work. Social critics like Karl Marx have long noted the broad cultural and economic significance of both the medieval monastic perception of work and the Protestant transformation and expansion of vocation as the religious calling of every Christian (not just a monastic few) into a secular world.[61] In response, Max Weber insightfully argued that what capitalism needed was not just for work to be sacralized (as in Marx's analysis of Luther's *bereuf*, vocation) but to become an end in itself.[62]

For all the differences that distinguish Adam Smith and Karl Marx, they are joined with the majority of modern Western thinkers in valuing work and its role in fulfilling humanity. Smith emphasized the importance of everyday work—of one's ability to produce and be a productive member of society—in identity formation, believing that a "man's character was formed by his 'work functions.'"[63] While Marx struggled against the ways capitalism alienated humanity from their work, his critique was premised on the assessment he shared with Smith of the importance of work for human self-understanding, meaning, and identity formation. For Marx, capitalism was particularly problematic not because it placed undo emphasis on work, but because it alienated humans from this essential aspect of human being.

In addition to the ethos of a work ethic, John Locke's theory of property further solidified the role of work in society as a justification for property rights. Locke argued that claims of property were legitimate when human labor was mixed with *terra nullis*, or unclaimed material or land. Where any full citizen with voting rights must be a property holder, work literally creates Man in civic society. In performing work, a male becomes, indeed creates, his actualized human self with full rights and responsibilities in society.

Such positive evaluations of work were articulated by influential religious figures in the nineteenth century, resulting in what is commonly referred to as the Gospel of Work. In England, Thomas Carlyle and William Morris praised its virtues. In the United States, the influential preacher Henry Ward Beecher, along with Thoreau, Melville, and Hawthorn, articulated versions of a work gospel.[64] Into the twentieth century, Pope John Paul II addressed the value of work for human meaning and fulfillment in his encyclical *Laborem Exercens* (*On Human Work*), arguing that it is what distinguishes humans from other species: "Only man is capable of work, and only man works."[65] In a comprehensive analysis of late twentieth- and early twenty-first-century theologies of work, religion scholar Jeremy Posadas confirms that remarkably few have questioned the basic purpose of work for constructing human value and meaning. For theologians of work, this "is part of what it fundamentally means to be a human; there is an aspect of work that is intrinsically good, because it reflects God's work."[66] In this theo-economic nexus, work becomes associated with human actualization, conceptually paving the way for a synthesis with energy concepts despite its initial exclusions from *energeia*.

Heat

By the modern period, work, divinity, masculinity, and—as I will emphasize here—heat come to form a constellation of resonating reason and affect around human fulfillment. Human completion or actualization is the shared aim that resonates between *energeia*, mastery, masculinity, heat, work, and divinity resulting in a modern, seemingly "secular" concept of energy that nonetheless remains rooted in this shared theo-philosophical desire for human fulfillment.

We've noted that one of the key shifts initiated in thermodynamics—differentiating it from ancient *energeia*, Galileo's and Newton's force, and seventeenth- to eighteenth-century *vis viva*—is the application of heat to the theory of dynamics. Yet, for Marder as well as other energy humanities scholars where *energeia* is acknowledged or analyzed, it is not sufficiently recognized that the modern concept of energy was also synthesizing *vis viva* with concepts of heat that were still reverberating with ancient associations with full human development. Indeed, physicist Robert Bruce Lindsay emphasizes that the "historical evolution of the concept of energy is inextricably connected with the problem of the nature of heat."[67] Despite the dramatic shifts of modern sciences, Aristotelian concepts of heat are retained particularly in biological development distinctions articulated in modern embryology, biology, and evolutionary theory. Consequently, Aristotle's views on the role of heat in the full development of humanity emerge as particularly important for modern energy analysis.

While Aristotle attributed actuality to the exercise of rationality and the mastery of matter, heat played a related role. The active agent in the formation process of material life, the process by which undifferentiated matter is mastered and given order or form, is heat. The formative or mastering role Aristotle gave to heat was informed by an already long-existing tradition in Greek thought associating fire with divine ordering properties. Presocratics had long associated fire with the *logos*. Heraclitus (sixth century BCE), for example, is thought to be the first to use *logos* in a philosophical sense, associating it with both fire and *logos* as the formative or ordering principle of all matter.[68] This history of thought influenced the formative role Aristotle granted to heat as well as its traces of divinity. For Aristotle, heat, the fourth element was pervasive, a "life-endowing substance" and the highest element—a terrestrial derivative of celestial ether.[69]

Aristotelian scholar Gad Freudenthal argues that the role of heat in Aristotle's thought has been overlooked. Aristotle gave to vital heat the power of not just warming, but also of in-forming, of giving form through concoction. For Aristotle, concoction was the process of heating a moist substance, making it more dense, compact, and dry, thereby transforming "indeterminate," passive, feminine matter into its "mastered" form. "Generally speaking," Freudenthal explains, "concoction is the process through which a loose heat is 'worked up' into a unified and organized whole" (*Metaph* 7. 16, 1040b8-10).[70] The process of concoction by vital heat eventually attains a "stable logos" such that the substance acquires its proper form.[71] Aristotle gives the example of the coagulation of milk by rennet. In the same way, concoction works on a formless, fluid substance, "setting" it into its form.

This gives heat a particularly important role in human formation and gender construction since, for Aristotle, sexual difference was not primarily or fundamentally based on biological organs, but on heat variance that subsequently determined sex. In his theory of concoction whereby vital heat transformed unformed elements into formed substance, Aristotle linked heat, masculinity, in-forming, mastery, and perfection. Heat clearly played a key role in mastery that was synonymous for him with formation and masculinity. Semen's capacity for mastery/formation, for example, was due to its vital heat—its ability to concoct, and thus to give form. This is exemplified in his embryology where semen was given the power of mastery/formation: "If [the semen] gains the mastery, it brings [the material] over to itself; but if it gets mastered, it changes over either into its opposite [i.e., female] or else into extinction" (4. 1, 766b16 f).[72] The power to give form through concoction was evident not just in semen but also in other forms of vital heat. The role of vital heat in forming matter through concoction remained consistent throughout an organism's development.

With varying levels of vital heat come varying levels of concoction, formation, and, thus, perfection. Karen M. Nielsen builds on Freudenthal's reading of Aristotle, addressing gender and the associated "degrees of perfection" more explicitly. Aristotle assumed a kind of equivalence between male semen and female menstrual fluid, with semen more fully developed or perfected because it is fully concocted. Menstrual fluid, then, was "semen not in a pure state, but in need of working up" (GA I, 20, 728a26).[73] In humans with sufficient levels of vital heat, menstrual fluid was properly, or fully, concocted into semen. Differences in vital heat between semen and menstrual fluid are passed on in the formation of an embryo. In the *Generation of Animals* Aristotle concludes:

> It will perhaps be now clearer for what reason one embryo becomes female and another male. For when the first principle does not bear sway and cannot concoct the nourishment through lack of heat nor bring it into its proper form, but is defeated in this respect, then must the material change into its opposite. Now the female is opposite to the male, and that insofar as the one is female and the other male.[74]

Greater amounts of vital heat led to the actualization of the potential of matter in the form of the male. Consequently, as Nielsen emphasizes, for Aristotle the female was defined by a lack or "natural deficiency"[75] in vital heat which subsequently led to a lack in physical and intellectual development.

Philosopher Nancy Tuana also emphasizes the importance of heat in Aristotle's gender distinction, tracking the differences Aristotle marked in the brain development of males and females.[76] Aristotle concludes that males develop larger brains with more "suture configurations" primarily because of their higher levels of vital heat. Male brains are the largest "because the heat in man's heart is purest . . . [and man's] intellect shows how well he is tempered for man is the wisest of animals" (*GA*, 744.a, 25–30).⁷⁷ In addition to having smaller brains, even in proportion to their size, female brain sutures take on a different structure than that of men's. Where female sutures are circular, he claimed, men's brains have three sutures that meet at a point. Again, he attributed this difference to varying levels of heat, claiming that the female circular sutures cool the brain more quickly, while the male sutures better retain heat (*History of Animals*, 653.a.37–65 3.b.3).⁷⁸ Tuana concludes that for Aristotle, feminine tendencies toward passion, emotionality, and less rationality are, in the end, due to a less developed rational soul in accordance with lower levels of vital heat.⁷⁹

Where vital heat played a key role in the development of both biological organs and the soul, "it will emerge that vital heat defines the *scala naturae*, that is, the scale of being as an ontological hierarchy."⁸⁰ For Aristotle, gender difference emerged as a result of heat variance which played a key role in the actualization or exercise of the capacities (*energeia*) of matter. Furthermore, since heat was seen to be a terrestrial derivative of divine ether, Aristotle also understood vital heat to be a form of *pneuma* with spiritual as well as biological implications for gender that Western thinkers and Christian theologians in particular would also assume.⁸¹

In as much as modern energy emerged in the nineteenth century as a science of thermodynamics—of heat and work—it diverges significantly from Aristotle's *energeia*. Yet, the shared commitments of heat and work to human fulfillment also retain key resonances with Aristotle's *energeia* as completion or perfection, resonances which proved particularly attractive to Paul and other early Christians. From this perspective, a key problem in modern energy does not necessarily lie with a modern obsession with potentiality to the exclusion of actuality, but with the Anglo-masculine-divine values ascribed to actuality that continue to fuel the dreams of potentiality.

Gender and Race in Energy and Development

Even if one considers modern energy to be a complete reversal of Aristotle's *energeia*, excluding continuity with modern energy's *potentia* obsession, the fact remains that historically feminized humans have not fared well in political, domestic, economic, or biological relations organized by actualization, fulfillment, or the threshold of consummation. In the Western tradition, for centuries after Aristotle and even, despite the modern shift away from Aristotle's authority, into modernity, gender and race come to be distinguished and defined according to heat/energy variance. From this perspective, energy transitions have not just been marked by science and technology, they've also been marked on bodily practices of gendering and racialization.

The continuing impact of ancient *energeia* on gender differentiation emerges primarily in terms of the extended influence of Aristotle's developmental biology. The ancient Greek philosopher-physician Galen of Pergamon (130–210 CE) remained a leading medical authority in the West for the next fourteen hundred years and accepted Aristotle's conclusion that the female was less developed than the male on account of lower levels of heat, differing from Aristotle only in giving further anatomical explanation for female deficiency.[82] Even as Aristotle's natural philosophy lost favor in modernity, the association between energy, heat, and full masculine development remained. Sixteenth-century biologist Ambroise Paré, often credited with initiating modern surgery, fully accepted Galen's ancient interpretation of the equivalence between male and female reproductive organs which differed only by the females' inferior supply of internal heat, resulting in their lesser development.[83] Biologists Patrick Geddes and John Arthur Thomson demonstrate the persistence of this theory of gender differentiation by heat in 1889 when they argue, regarding avian gender, that "temperatures are known in some cases to be decidedly higher than those of the females."[84]

The persistence of a correlation of higher heat/energy with further biological development intensifies rather than fades with the advent of modern energy science, particularly where thermodynamic and evolutionary theories converged. Darwinist Herbert Spencer (1830–1903), for example, applied the second law of thermodynamics to the closed energy system of a human body. Spencer theorized that with the body as a closed system of finite energy, an expenditure of energy for one function necessitated a loss of energy for another. Such zero-sum energy logic resulted in competition among organs. Spencer identified the reproductive organs and the brain as the most powerful organs in the human body, placing them in direct competition for energy. An excessive draw of energy for reproductive organs meant a lesser amount of energy for the full development of the brain.[85] Therefore, differences between males and females were due to the "somewhat earlier arrest of individual evolution in women than in men, necessitated by the reservation of vital power to meet the cost of reproduction."[86] Where a female's reproductive organs necessitated an excessive draw of energy, her full intellectual development was impeded.[87]

In the US context, arguments depending on assumptions of a feminine lack of biological or psychic energies have been used to bar feminized humans from public spheres such as voting booths, universities, and pulpits. In the nineteenth century, Harvard University, among other schools, was debating whether women should be accepted as undergraduates. Edward Clarke, Harvard medical department faculty, wrote an influential and popular book, *Sex in Education, or a Fair Chance for the Girls* (1873), wherein he concluded that a university education fails to give a woman a fair chance because the mental energy required would drain excessive energy from her female reproductive organ, thus cutting off her chance to develop fully into a woman.[88]

Such requisite vital energies retained a sense of both inherent masculinity and divinity. With a similar energy logic, females were seen as unfit for ordained ministry in the twentieth century. An Episcopal bishop of California, for example, ruled against the ordination of women, citing a lack of capacity for the "'initiative' that represents the 'potency' of God."[89] The "muscular Christianity" movement of the nineteenth and twentieth centuries can also be seen in the wake of these heat/energy/development logics and affects. This movement which gained popularity in the United States and Britain among Protestants and Catholics has emphasized, like Ida Tarbell, an oftentimes implicit or commonsense connection between strong, muscular, energetic, and self-sufficient men and Christian values.[90]

Historians emphasize that muscular Christianity was a response to changes not only in gender but also in social dynamics due to industrialization and racialized fears that white men were losing their power and influence. With the emergence of the modern concept of race, it became possible to place not just individuals or genders, but also purported racial groups on a hierarchical scale of development associated with high heat and energy. While a comprehensive sketch of the impact of energy distinctions on modern racial categories has yet to emerge, as nineteenth-century historian Jürgen Osterhammel emphasizes, "the racism of the age did not end with skin color: it classified the human 'races' on a scale of potential physical and mental energy."[91] For example, in addition to Herbert Spencer's application of energy variance to describe gendered biological development, Spencer also theorized correlating developmental differences among races according to energy variance. Spencer saw a "direct connection between the complexity of organisms, from protozoa to hydra to crustaceans" and the complexity of human societies. "Bushmen" tribes he associated with the "protozoa" level of complexity, aboriginal tribes were associated with the "hydra" and industrial European societies were associated with the most complex organisms.[92] Charles Lyell similarly concluded that even given the best climactic conditions for full human development, the energies of the African race would still lag behind those of the Caucasians. In 1845 he wrote, "it would be visionary to expect that, under any imaginable system, this race could at once acquire as much energy, and become as rapidly progressive, as the Anglo-Saxons."[93] Such logics served the conclusion, as philosopher Achille Mbembe has argued, that "Only the White race possessed a will and a capacity to construct life within history. The Black race in particular had neither life, nor will, nor energy of its own,"[94] or in Edward Said's summary, African and Asian populations were denied full humanity on account of their apparent inability "to either mine their own resources or inventively use them."[95]

The valuation of high energy as a mark of full human development was applied to evaluations of religions as well. In the West, religions associated with pantheism commonly evoked what philosopher of religion Mary-Jane Rubenstein identifies as a fear of "collective, racialized unmanning."[96] Rubenstein examines the writings of New England Episcopal Reverend Nathaniel Smith Richardson (1810–83), who articulates his worry of a seduction of "'rosy,' Western men into passivity and inertia, until they become like the 'earth-born Indian sage.'"[97] Rubenstein describes Richardson's characterization of these sages as those "who allegedly dreamed his life away in womanly passivity, in that inactive contemplation which he considered the highest of all states."[98] Richardson, of course, was not alone. Other anti-pantheist writers of the time similarly denigrated the teachings of the Buddha for promoting a restful, inactive "quietism" and "beatific inaction."[99]

Consequently, a key distinction emerged between Black or Oriental energies (collectively less developed, best suited for manual labor) and white energy (fully actualized in rationality and thus naturally suited for ordering or mastering other less developed energies) and was used to justify a natural line of distinction between master and slave, colonizer and colonized. In this embodied, gendered, racialized sense, energy thus emerged in modernity not merely in industrial and technological forms, but as a measure of human and social civilizational fulfillment.

Enchanted Electricity and Energy Science

In addition to the evaluation of human development according to heat/energy variance, associations between high energy, divinity, and the full development of society also significantly impacted the reception and interpretation of energy "resources" and technologies in the West. Rather than a slow march toward disenchantment since the seventeenth century, electricity, magnetism, coal, aspects of energy science, and then, oil, emerged in the seventeenth, eighteenth, and nineteenth centuries profoundly enchanted. Barbara Freese, for example, explains that in the nineteenth century, coal was commonly associated with divine purpose, racial superiority, and full human development. At the time, the vast majority of coal deposits had been found in England and America, a fact that was interpreted as proof of the divine role God had granted to the world's most energetic peoples to bring about the full development of humanity. Freese, for example, cites an 1856 edition of the *Christian Review* wherein an US American writes of

> a race of men energetic and enterprising; fitted by their natural characteristics, by their mental and moral culture, and by their hold on the pure gospel of Jesus Christ, to be leaders in the onward march of humanity, have had thrust into their hands, unlooked for and unexpected, a treasure, which if used aright, must secure to them a controlling influence on the affairs of the world.[100]

We will see in Chapter 4 how, given the narrative of oil's first "discovery" in the United States, oil too seemed to verify American exceptionalism—the special, divinely ordained role of the United States in the divine plan for creation. And while other industries and resources such as cotton, railroads, and gold have also certainly been interpreted as divine gift or blessing, the long history of associations between masculinity, human development, divinity, and energy resulted in a distinctive resonance between oil and Christianity.

Interpretations of electricity, too, were energized by ancient associations of heat, *energeia*, divinity, and full human development. Historians of the time period emphasize that it was common in the eighteenth and nineteenth centuries to attribute god-like powers to electricity as a source of all animation and life.[101] In the 1780s Italian physician and professor of anatomy Luigi Galvani and his wife Lucia identified what they called "animal electricity" when they found that an electric current could make a dead frog's leg kick. Evoking divine properties of animation and life creation, Galvani identified electricity as "life force itself."[102]

Virility—with its ancient associations of life force, energy, strength, and vigor—was also consistently used to describe electrical properties.[103]

At the convergence of ancient assumptions about masculinity and divinity with mysterious new energy technologies, historians identify a full-blown "electrical theology" functioning by the eighteenth and nineteenth centuries.[104] Historian Carolyn de la Peña defines electrical theology as a "belief that electricity was a spiritual triumph of mysterious power with unlimited potential."[105] Historian Carolyn Marvin emphasizes that electrical theology emerged at the intersections of constructed concepts of electricity and gendered bodies, connections smoothed over by religious assertions. For many, "electrical science was treated as an extension of religious revelation," a conclusion upheld by a belief that "electricity contained the divine power to bestow life."[106] Religion historian Brett Malcom Grainger demonstrates that this influence was felt not just in more progressive or experimental forms of Protestantism, but also in conservative evangelical Protestantism. Eighteenth- and nineteenth-century US Protestant evangelical electrical theologies were profoundly incarnational, communicating a compelling sense of God's presence within the natural, material world, made evident and put to work for the betterment of humanity through electricity.[107]

Both Grainger and Ernst Benz emphasize that while religion influenced the reception of energy technologies, these new technologies inspired new religious practices and affects as well. In his extensive analysis of electrical theologies, Benz argued that the influence of electricity and magnetism on Western Christianity was so strong that the main metaphor for divinity shifted from associations with the transcendent sun to a more immanent association with electricity and magnetism. What's more, he demonstrates that electricity emerged as highly gendered and divinized primarily on account of the ways medieval alchemy (with key Aristotelian influences) was employed in describing these phenomena.[108]

Religion scholar Darryl Caterine has affirmed Benz's conclusion that alchemy played a significant role in interpreting electricity, noting that this took on a particularly significant form in US nineteenth-century Spiritualism. Caterine explains that "despite its name, Spiritualism was essentially a metaphysics of materialism, admitting differences in degree, but not in essence, between matter and spirit."[109] Influenced by alchemical principles, Spiritualists considered mind and spirit to be more subtle forms of matter. A goal of Spiritualism, then, was to resolve any such dualisms through transformations of lower forms of matter to their higher forms.

Spiritualism was widely popular and endorsed by many well-known and highly respected public figures.[110] It gave US Americans a profound sense of the intimate connections between the material and more-than-material worlds. Andrew Jackson Davis' work is an influential example of the ways Spiritualism imbued industrialism and technology with cosmic meaning. In his *Principles of Nature* (1847) Davis articulated a cosmic vision of devolution and subsequent refinement of matter. Davis asserted a primordial reality, the Sensorium, with a series of concentric planes of reality. As creation unfolded, matter became less refined and more diffuse, causing more and more separation between spiritual and material forms: a "cosmic alchemical process in reverse."[111] Davis posed technology as a kind of antidote to the spirit/material devolution of Nature. Properly employed in a process Davis called "progression," technology (along with social reforms) could function as a new kind of alchemy, refining matter, unifying opposites, returning all things to their original source and unity, and thus actively reversing the process of devolution and dissolution.

For Davis and other Spiritualists, the value of modern technology was not solely or even primarily economic. Its true value was as "a metaphysical teaching tool."[112] Electricity was of particular interest to Spiritualists as "the very principle of motion itself, an immanent dynamism that raised all matter to higher states."[113] Electricity and magnetism, like spirit and mind, were more subtle forms of matter, and as such, they offered a kind of bridge between the unseen spirit and visible material worlds. In Davis' work especially, the electric machine functioned as a "kind of sacrament" through which humans could "come to know the indwelling power of the universe directly."[114] If used properly to resolve spirit/matter, male/female, mind/body dualisms, electricity could function alchemically to raise matter—and society—to a higher state.[115] Consequently, as Caterine argues, the electrification and industrialization of America merely "represented the latest phase in a cosmic process of progression that encompassed all aspects of life in the refinement of their society into a more spiritualized state."[116] Through nineteenth-century Spiritualism and other variously articulated electrical theologies, energy was reaffirmed as divinely given and essential for the full development of humanity. Through energy-intensive technologies, this influential group of humans felt they were coming to a deeper appreciation and knowledge of a divine and indwelling animism.[117]

A Theological Apologia for Energy Science

Links between divinity and electricity informed the shape of modern energy science as well. Historians Crosbie Smith and Norton Wise have dedicated significant research to analyzing the sociocultural and commercial influences on the rise of modern energy science. Their work focuses on the life and thought of not only William Thomson (Lord Kelvin), introduced earlier, but Thomson's close associates and interlocutors as well: his brother James Thomson, William Rankine, Peter Guthrie Tait, and James Clerk Maxwell. These Scottish scientists who played key roles in the formation of modern energy science were also committed Presbyterian evangelicals with religious views that profoundly informed their pursuit of and framing for modern energy science. Rather than conflict between modern energy science and Protestantism, Thomson and his fellow evangelicals perceived in energy science a strategic way to *combat* a growing tide of reductionist materialism, disenchantment, and atheism. Religion and ecology/science scholars have widely overlooked this key *synthesis* of nineteenth-century religion and science which Cara Daggett identifies as a "geotheology of energy."[118]

In his analysis of influences on energy science, Smith emphasizes the shared theological assumptions of this group of Scottish evangelical energy scientists.

Energy, as they conceptualized it, presupposed a sovereign, voluntarist deity. In particular, Thomson and others saw in the first law of thermodynamics scientific support for a view of the world "completely dependent on divine choice."[119] Given the law of conservation's emphasis on energy's indestructibility, omnipresence, and constancy, energy became "the new primary concept related to the immutability of God."[120] For these Scottish scientists, God was seen not just as a distant, watch-maker creator, content to step back and let creation run. God was clearly emphasized as both creator and continuous sustainer, actively ordering and maintaining the universe either directly or through divinely ordained natural laws.

The second law of thermodynamics, with its emphasis on entropy, might have been interpreted as a threat to the theological interpretation of energy conservation. Headlined as "heat death," such revelations led to increased anxieties about energy limits on all levels from the cosmic, to the national, to the bodily. Remarkably, rather than rejecting such scientific conclusions as a fundamental disruption of a sovereign, beneficent, sustaining deity supported by the principle of energy conservation, influential evangelicals like Thomson embraced this more pessimistic scientific advance for theological reasons as well.

To understand the theological role entropy played for these evangelical energy scientists, Smith closely follows the writings of Thomas Chalmers, professor of moral philosophy and evangelical preacher at St. Andrews in 1823 and then chair of divinity at Edinburgh in 1827. Chalmers became an influential preacher among faculty and students alike, counting William Thomson and his brother James as personal friends and influencing other contemporary energy scientists as well. Chalmers embraced the science of entropy just as enthusiastically as the law of conservation, for while the first law seemed to confirm a sovereign force pervading all of life, the second law seemed to reaffirm a Calvinist sense of the depravity creation was subject to on account of original sin. For Chalmers, energy science confirmed that not only humans but also all of creation was subject to loss, decay, and death after the Fall.

Chalmers' embrace of the second law of thermodynamics was politically strategic as well as theologically influenced. Placing Chalmers' embrace of entropy in relation to contemporary evangelical interests in resisting various forms of atheism, Smith concludes that "any materialist or deist creed that the laws of nature were self-sufficient and eternal, was undercut by the claim that these laws [...] were themselves subject to processes of decay and derangement."[121] For evangelicals like Chalmers, then, while the conservation of energy confirmed a hidden force disrupting any reductive mechanism, entropy did not overturn the beginnings of an evangelical/energy alliance, but solidified it by seemingly providing scientific evidence of the particularly Protestant doctrine of original sin and creation's full reliance on a gracious deity rather than self-sufficiency.

Smith and Wise go on to emphasize the surprising and underrecognized theological influences on the Scottish scientists' articulation of modern energy including its omnipotent character lacking limitation, its progressive trajectory, and the moral weight placed on the proper acceptance (and use) of energy as divine gift.[122] Consequently, while ancient *energeia*, work, and heat consolidated around human fulfillment, resulting in energy variance as a measure of full human development, these same connections made possible a variety of energy theologies that resulted in a profound sense of the enchantment of energy and energy resources in modernity. In associating energy with virility, divinity, and life force, it became widely assumed that more energy consumption and production would lead to higher levels of civilizational and human development. That electrical currents could give life and—as we will see in Chapter 5—that bodies could overcome energy limits through it, are strategies that depend on a deep, culturally assumed energy theology where divinity, life, high energy, and virility are associated.

Energy Fulfillment and the Climate Crisis

Persistent, though variously articulated, associations of high-energy production/consumption with the fulfillment of human potential in Western religion and philosophy continue to reverberate into the twentieth and twenty-first centuries. Take, for example, Lewis Mumford's conclusions about the relation between energy and fully developed civilization in his famous *Technics and Civilization* (1934). Mumford describes a four-step process in the role of energy and societal development: (1) Conversion, (2) Production, (3) Consumption, and (4) Creation. Mumford concludes that society cannot meet the criteria for full development without an energy excess: "Not until the economic process reaches the stage of creation—not until it supplies the human animal with more energy than he needs to maintain his physical existence" can we expect any civilizational gains.[123] Philosophy, art, architecture, and literature are acts of creation that define a civilization as such, and these achievements can be realized only through an excess of energy.

Remarkably similar assumptions can be found in anthropologist Leslie White's thesis in his influential essay, "Energy and the Evolution of Culture" (1943). White articulates what has, in the twenty-first century, taken on an aura of common sense or even dogma: increased energy production positively correlates with sociocultural development. White concludes with what he calls "*the* law of cultural evolution: *culture develops when the amount of energy harnessed by man per capita per year is increased; or as the efficiency of the technological means of putting this energy to work is increased; or, as both factors are simultaneously increased.*"[124] In nineteenth-century views such as Spencer's hybrid Darwinian-thermodynamics of gender difference, the human body became seen as a site of energy conservation and exchange where energy excess was identified as a requirement for full human masculine development. Mumford and White expand such conclusions beyond the individual to the social, concluding that the full development or fulfilled potential of society requires energy exuberance. While the importance of creative pursuits for individuals and collectives is not in dispute here, note especially the unsupported assumption Mumford and White make that meaningful, creative acts can emerge only through energy excess. Yet, creative artifacts and practices of meaning production have clearly been produced in a variety of energy cultures from subsistence economies with low-energy consumption to high-energy–consuming capitalist economies.

Arguments citing the developmental necessity of energy excess are regularly referenced by pro-hydrocarbon voices in the twenty-first century. According to Alex Epstein's *Moral Case for Fossil Fuels*, increasing or maintaining high-energy lifestyles is a matter not just of practicality or economy, but morality since fulfilled human potential is at stake.[125] The ecomodernist Breakthrough Institute report, *Our High-Energy Planet* (2014), makes the argument more extensively. The report's authors call for policymakers to "embrace a high-energy planet" even in the face of an energy-driven climate crisis. Unlike climate denialists, ecomodernists acknowledge the very real concerns of anthropogenic climate change, yet argue that only by "using expanded access to energy" will human needs be met while also enabling technological advancements necessary to address the climate crisis. The authors argue that continued and increased expansion of energy resources is necessary "to unleash human ingenuity" in order to meet the challenges of climate change.[126] While significant philosophical and political differences remain between ecomodernism, Epstein, White, and Mumford, each continues to reiterate the ancient theo-logic that human actualization ("unleashed ingenuity") depends on high—indeed, excessive—energy production/consumption.

To be sure, biological life depends on energy transfer and exchange. And inequitable access to energy resources remains a key justice issue with clear embodied consequences for much of the world's population.[127] While Mumford, White, Epstein, and ecomodernists assert the continual necessity of energy excess for full human and societal development, they rarely acknowledge limits to energy expansion and often argue against energy conservation or reduction even for currently high-energy–consuming populations. Yet, recent studies challenge the value of exuberant lifestyles, demonstrating an upper limit to the benefits of energy consumption for human well-being.[128] For example, Vaclav Smil emphasizes that there is an upper limit to the correlation between energy consumption and human well-being (measured according to the Human Development Index (HDI)). Up to about 100 gigajoules (GJ) per year, per capita there is a correlation, but beyond that they start to diverge—and energy consumption beyond 200 GJ per year, per capita is even counter-productive to human well-being. To put these numbers in perspective, in 2017 US residents consumed 316 GJ per capita which far exceeds the outer limit of a productive correlation between energy consumption and human well-being.[129] Clearly a mismatch has developed between US Americans' desire for energy consumption and the amount of energy that actually contributes to multi-species health and sustainability. Smil emphasizes that low to moderate access to energy is, indeed, vital, but after a certain point, moderate- to high-energy consumption shows diminishing returns and then even negative effects for well-being. To understand such incongruence between the United States' unlimited energy desires and the demonstrated ceiling for the value of energy, it will be important to attend to the historical ways human fulfillment or perfection have been consistently defined in terms of high-energy production and consumption and an overcoming of, rather than attending to, energy limits.

While the possibility of decoupling associations of high energy from ideals of human fulfillment may seem idealistic and nearly impossible to enact, current research among ecological economists demonstrates its real material possibility. Building on evidence of an upper limit to a positive correlation between human well-being and increasing energy consumption, ecological economists Julia Steinberger and J. Timmons Roberts conducted a massive study, published in 2010, analyzing correlations over the past seventy years between energy consumption, traditional markers for economic growth such as GDP, and markers for human development. The researchers found evidence of a previously unidentified decoupling of energy use from markers of human development during this time.[130] Specifically, they note that, while "economic activity is becoming more tightly coupled to energy and carbon emissions," at the same time, "human development parameters like life expectancy and literacy are becoming decoupled."[131] In other words, while economic growth continues to be highly dependent on ever-increasing energy consumption, we should not assume that high energy leads to high economic development which leads to markers identified with "high human development." Indeed, it is possible to achieve high markers for human well-being with low to moderate levels of energy consumption. For example, Steinberger and Roberts' research identifies places in the world like Costa Rica where low or moderate energy-consumption habits are high markers for human well-being. Though they do not trouble the aim of "high human development," they conclude that it can be "achieved at moderate energy and carbon levels" because "increasing energy and carbon past this level does not necessarily contribute to higher living standards."[132] Such results not only support long-standing concerns over the inadequacy of GDP for measuring human well-being,[133] but also have key implications for the ways potential impacts of climate change mitigation are accounted for.[134]

If new energy imaginaries are to be assembled, current energy values and assumptions, along with how they were maintained, must be recognized. Further analysis of the kinds of narratives and values that sustain dreams of an inherent link between energy excess and an ideal of human perfection is needed. Given the historical ways divinity, masculinity, and whiteness have been aligned in the West with high-energy consumption/production, the humanistic and theological aspects of energy—and extraction, as we will see in the next chapter—need closer attention.

Notes

1 David E. Nye, *Consuming Power: A Social History of American Energies* (Cambridge, MA: MIT Press, 1999), 6.
2 Even in 1976, ecological economist Herman Daly explains the beginning breakdown of the logic that has typically tied together high energy with GDP and human welfare. Cited in Hessel, *Energy Ethics*, 4.
3 Sylvia Wynter, "Unsettling the Coloniality of Being/Power/Truth/Freedom: Towards the Human, After Man, Its Overrepresentation—An Argument," *CR: The New Centennial Review* 3 (2003): 257–337.

4   For further reflections on problematic valuation of wholeness, completeness, in human bodies, see Robert McRuer, *Crip Theory: Cultural Signs of Queerness and Disability* (New York: New York University Press, 2006); Sharon Betcher, *Spirit and the Politics of Disablement* (Minneapolis: Fortress, 2007); Jack Halberstam, *The Queer Art of Failure* (Durham: Duke University Press, 2011), Bray, *Grave Attending*.
5   Ghosh, *The Great Derangement*.
6   For this particular reading of energy science, connecting to Parmenides, even before Aristotle, see Robert Bruce Lindsay, *Energy: Historical Development of the Concept* (Stroudsburg: Dowden, Hutchinson, and Ross, 1975); and Phillip Mirowski, *More Heat than Light* (Cambridge: Cambridge University Press, 1989), who are building from Emile Meyerson's philosophy of science, *Identity and Reality* (1908).
7   This section is influenced by Mirowski, *More Heat Than Light*, 11–98, and Crosbie Smith, *The Science of Energy: A Cultural History of Energy Physics in Victorian Britain* (Chicago: University of Chicago Press, 1998).
8   This distinction he makes in 1695. The first distinction, in the 1694 writing, he makes between moving power (*potentia*) and moving force (*vis motrix*).
9   Gottfried Leibniz, "On the Doctrine of Malebranche: A Letter to M. Remond De Montmort, Containing Remarks on the Book of Father Terte Against Father Malebranche," in *The Philosophical Works of Leibniz* (New Haven: Tuttle, Morehouse & Taylor, 1890), 233–7 (234).
10 Thomas S. Kuhn, "Energy Conservation as an Example of Simultaneous Discovery," in *The Essential Tension*, (Chicago: University of Chicago Press, 2011), 66–104.
11 P. M. Heimann, "Helmholtz and Kant: The Metaphysical Foundations of 'Über Die Erhaltung Der Kraft,'" *Studies in History of Philosophy and Science* 5 (1974): 205–38.
12 Quoted in Mirowski, *More Heat than Light*, 46.
13 Brent Ryan Bellamy and Jeff Diamanti, *Materialism and the Critique of Energy* (Chicago: MCM, 2018), xiv.
14 Crosbie Smith, "Natural Philosophy and Thermodynamics: William Thomson and the 'Dynamical Theory of Heat,'" *The British Journal for the History of Science* 9 (1976): 293–319 (309).
15 Quoted in Ibid., 310.
16 A third law of thermodynamics was identified in the early twentieth century, but will not be of primary focus here as it did not have the kind of sociocultural impact as the first two. The third law roughly states that entropy approaches zero as temperature approaches 0C.
17 Ibid.
18 Mirowski, *More Heat than Light*, 35.
19 Ibid. See also, Smith, *The Science of Energy*, 309–18. Thomson was using energy in a new way, but cited Thomas Young's earlier usage—according to Smith, in order to give the term a more authoritative pedigree.
20 Smith, "Natural Philosophy and Thermodynamics," 311.
21 Quoted in Ibid.
22 Aristotle, *Nicomachean Ethics*, trans. Joe Sachs (Newbury: Focus, 2002), viii.
23 See Mirowski, ch.1, *More Heat than Light*, and Herbert Applebaum, "The Concept of Work in Western Thought," in *Meanings of Work: Considerations for the Twenty-First Century*, ed. Frederick C. Gamst (Albany: State University of New York Press, 1995), 48. A less anachronistic translation proposed for *ergon* is activity or actuality.
24 Applebaum, "The Concept of Work in Western Thought," 46–78 (49).

25 David Bradshaw, *Aristotle East and West: Metaphysics and the Division of Christendom* (New York: Cambridge University Press, 2004), 3.
26 Aristotle confirms he means for their meanings to intersect: Aristotle, *Metaphysics* 1047a30 (trans. Joe Sachs; Santa Fe: Green Lion Press, 2002), 171.
27 *Metaphysics*, Book IX, ch. 6 (Sachs, 174–5).
28 Marder, *Energy Dreams*.
29 "Distance from energy at the theoretical level silently sanctions the most ecologically detrimental methods of procuring it" (Ibid., 5).
30 Ibid., 3.
31 Ibid., 28.
32 Ibid., 8.
33 Ibid., 24.
34 Ibid., 27.
35 Ibid., 7.
36 Ibid., 10.
37 Ibid.
38 Ibid., 13.
39 Ibid., 11.
40 See, for example, Catherine Keller's feminist reading of the Aristotelian influence on Christian theology in *From a Broken Web: Separation, Sexism and Self* (Boston: Beacon, 1986), 37.
41 Cheryl I. Harris, "Whiteness as Property," *Harvard Law Review* 106 (1993): 1707–91.
42 Ibid., 38.
43 John De Graaf, Vivia Boe, and Scott Simon, *Affluenza* (Oley: Bullfrog Films, 1997).
44 Joseph Sittler, "The Care of the Earth," in *Evocations of Grace: Writings on Ecology, Theology, and Ethics*, ed. Steven Bouma-Prediger and Peter Bakken (Grand Rapids: Eerdmans, 2000), 51–8; Berry, "The New Story."
45 Wynter, "Unsettling the Coloniality."
46 Clare Colebrook, "On Not Becoming Man: The Materialist Politics of Unactualized Potential," in *Material Feminisms*, ed. Stacy Alaimo and Susan Heckman (Bloomington: Indiana University Press, 2008), 52–84 (57). Emphasis in original.
47 See, for example, Aristotle, *Protrepticus: A Reconstruction*, trans. Anton-Hermann Croust (Notre Dame: University of Notre Dame Press, 1964), 21–2.
48 *Protrepticus*, B86. Translated in Bradshaw, *Aristotle East and West*, 5.
49 Wynter, "Unsettling the Coloniality."
50 David Bradshaw, "The Concept of the Divine Energies," *Philosophy and Theology* 18 (2006): 93–120 (101).
51 David Bradshaw, "The Divine Energies in the New Testament," *St. Vladimir's Theological Quarterly* 50 (2006): 189–223 (191). Passages with *energeia* in the NT—all in Paul: Ephesians 1:19–20; 3:7; 4:16, Philippians 3:21; Colossians 1:29; 2:12, 2 Thessalonians 2:9; 2:11 (Ibid., 193).
52 Bradshaw, "The Concept of the Divine Energies," 101.
53 Ibid.
54 Ibid., 106.
55 Ibid.
56 Ibid., 111.
57 Ibid., 114.
58 Ibid., 112.

59 The Stoics first transformed the understanding of work. Applebaum, "The Concept of Work in Western Thought," 50.
60 Ibid., 52.
61 Ibid., 52, citing Ovitt, Weber, Benz, Mumford, LeGoff.
62 Max Weber, *The Protestant Ethic and the "Spirit" of Capitalism*, trans. and ed. Peter Baehr and Gordon Wells (New York: Penguin Books, 2002). See Kathryn Tanner's insightful reading, analysis, and reinterpretation of the Protestant work ethic in *Christianity and the New Spirit of Capitalism* (New Haven: Yale University Press, 2019). See Chapter 3 of this volume for more on this topic and text.
63 Applebaum, "The Concept of Work in Western Thought," 58.
64 Ibid., 61. Applebaum explains that in the nineteenth-century United States, the work gospel was "above all, the gospel of the Protestant bourgeoise, the middle classes, and among the independent craftsmen, farmers, merchants, ministers, professionals, and nascent industrialists" (Ibid.).
65 Pope John Paul II, "*Laborem Exercens*," (1982): 3, cited in Applebaum, 65.
66 Jeremy Posadas, "The Refusal of Work in Christian Ethics and Theology," *Journal of Religious Ethics* 45 (2017): 330–61 (330).
67 Lindsay, *Energy*, 174.
68 Later the Stoics would build from Heraclitus and Aristotle, emphasizing the role of *logos* seeds, *seminal logoi*, which permeate all things, causing growth, development, and action. Christian logos theologies would build from these influences as well. Diogenes Allen and Eric O. Springsted, *Philosophy for Understanding Theology*, 2nd ed. (Louisville: Westminster John Knox Press, 2007), 48.
69 "[V]ital heat took over some of the roles of the former divine heat. Aristotle's physiological concept of vital heat emerged, as it were, from the de-theologization of a Presocratic-type cosmology and metaphysics" (Gad Freudenthal, *Aristotle's Theory of Material Substance: Heat and Pneuma, Form and Soul* (New York: Oxford University Press, 1995), 5).
70 Freudenthal, *Aristotle's Theory of Material Substance*, 23.
71 Ibid., 22–3, citing *Meteorologica* 4. 2, 379b25 ff.
72 Ibid., 25.
73 Cited in Karen M. Nielsen, "The Private Parts of Animals: Aristotle on the Teleology of Sexual Difference," *Phronesis* 53 (2008): 373–405 (376). Similarly, Nancy Tuana concludes, "women's menstrual fluid is the blood that would be turned into potent semen if she had sufficient heat to concoct it" (Tuana, *The Less Noble Sex*, 131).
74 GA IV, 1, 766a16–22.
75 GA 755a15–16.
76 See Tuana, "Misbegotten Man," in *The Less Noble Sex*.
77 Cited by Tuana, *The Less Noble Sex*, 55.
78 Cited in Ibid.
79 Ibid., 59.
80 Freudenthal, *Aristotle's Theory of Material Substance*, 4.
81 Cf. Abraham P. Bos, *Aristotle on God's Life-Generating Power and on Pneuma as Its Vehicle*. SUNY (Albany: State University of New York Press, 2018), who also argued for this connection between Aristotle's theology and biology.
82 See Galen, *Galen on the Usefulness of the Parts of the Body*, trans. Margaret Tallmadge May (Ithaca: Cornell University Press, 1968) and Tuana's gender analysis in *The Less Noble Sex*, 21–2, 133–6.

83 Paré asserts this inferior internal heat is evidenced by the organs' lack of protrusion from the body: "What man hath apparent without, that women have hid within, both by the singular providence of Nature, as also by the defect of heat in women, which could not drive and thrust forth those parts as in men" (Paré, *Collected Works*, 128, cited in Tuana, *The Less Noble Sex*, 25).

84 Geddes and Thomson, *The Evolution of Sex*, 26. Even as late as the 1930s Sigmund Freud would claim that "portions of the male sexual apparatus also appear in women's bodies, though in an atrophied state" (Freud, "Femininity" (1933): 114, cited in Tuana, *The Less Noble Sex*, 24–5).

85 See Herbert Spencer, *Study of Sociology*, cited in Tuana, *The Less Noble Sex*, 47. Spencer was well known and widely read at the time.

86 Spencer, "Psychology of the Sexes," 32, cited in Tuana, *The Less Noble Sex*, 47.

87 See Tuana, *The Less Noble Sex*, 90–1.

88 According to Tuana, "Influenced by Clarke's speculations, numerous studies were published at the turn of the century documenting the increase of insanity among educated women." (Ibid., 78).

89 Rosemary Radford Ruether, *New Woman, New Earth: Sexist Ideologies and Human Liberation* (New York: Seabury Press, 1975), 4.

90 Clifford Putney, *Muscular Christianity: Manhood and Sports in Protestant America, 1880–1920* (Cambridge, MA: Harvard University Press, 2001). See Chapter 5 for more on this topic.

91 Jürgen Osterhammel, *The Transformation of the World: A Global History of the Nineteenth Century*, trans. Patrick Camiller (Princeton: Princeton University Press, 2015), 658.

92 Cited in Daggett, *The Birth of Energy*, 117–8.

93 Quoted in Yusoff, *A Billion Black Anthropocenes or None*, 78.

94 Achille Mbembe, *Critique of Black Reason*, trans. Laurent Dubois (Durham: Duke University Press, 2017), 42.

95 Edward W. Said, *Orientalism* (New York: Vintage Books, 1978), 38.

96 Mary-Jane Rubenstein, *Pantheologies: Gods, Worlds, Monsters* (New York: Columbia University Press, 2018), 8.

97 Ibid.

98 Ibid., citing Richardson.

99 Ibid., 9, citing Bayle.

100 Barbara Freese, *Coal: A Human History* (Cambridge: Perseus Pub, 2003), 12.

101 Brett Grainger, *Church in the Wild: Evangelicals in Antebellum America* (Cambridge: Harvard University Press, 2019), 168.

102 Cited in Carolyn Thomas de la Peña, *The Body Electric: How Strange Machines Built the Modern American* (New York: New York University Press, 2003), 9. The first appearance of the term "electricity" was in 1650 in an updated translation of John Baptista van Helmont's writing on the effects of magnetism.

103 Carolyn Marvin, *When Old Technologies Were New* (New York: Oxford University Press, 1988).

104 See Marvin, *When Old Technologies Were New*; de la Peña, *The Body Electric*; Darryl Caterine, "The Haunted Grid: Nature, Electricity, and Indian Spirits in the American Metaphysical Tradition," *Journal of the American Academy of Religion* 82 (2012): 371–97; and Bret Michael Grainger, "Electrical Theology," in *Church in the Wild*.

105 de la Peña, *The Body Electric*, 105–6.

106 Marvin, *When Old Technologies Were New*, 127.

107 Grainger, "Electrical Theology," in *Church in the Wild*. Grainger's work demonstrates that it was not just that religion influenced the reception of electrical science; these technosciences also infused religious affect, practice, and logic. It was not uncommon, for example, for early evangelicals to explicitly describe their conversion experiences in terms of electrified affect, suggesting as Storm has emphasized, that these new technosciences were not banishing religiosity in the mode of disenchantment, but creating new forms of it (Cf. Josephson Storm, *The Myth of Disenchantment*).
108 Ernst Benz, *The Theology of Electricity: On the Encounter and Explanation of Theology and Science in the 17th and 18th Centuries*, trans. Wolfgang Taraba, ed. Dennis Stillings (Eugene: Pickwick Publications, 1989).
109 Caterine, "The Haunted Grid," 382.
110 Ibid., 381. Two key influences on US American Spiritualism were the upstate New York Fox sisters' demonstrations of communication with the dead in 1848 and Andrew Jackson Davis' *The Principles of Nature, Her Divine Revelations, and a Voice to Mankind* in 1847. Rochelle Raineri Zuck cites the wide range in estimates of Spiritualist adherents: anywhere from half a million to eleven million (Zuck, "The Wizard of Oil," 20).
111 Caterine, "The Haunted Grid," 376.
112 Ibid.
113 Ibid., 377.
114 Ibid.
115 Ibid., 383.
116 Ibid., 382.
117 Ibid.
118 Daggett, *The Birth of Energy*.
119 Smith, "Natural Philosophy and Thermodynamics," 301. Smith uncovers this overlooked theology by gaining access to mainly unpublished writings and personal letters. Take, for example, an unpublished version of Thomson's influential 1851 essay, "The Dynamical Theory of Heat." While the published version does not reference theological assumptions, the unpublished version frequently emphasizes the omnipotence of God and God's eternal and immutable nature.
120 Ibid., 313.
121 Smith, *The Science of Energy*, 19.
122 More on these in Chapter 3 of this volume.
123 Lewis Mumford, *Technics and Civilization* (New York: Harcourt, Brace and Company, 1934), 376. Mumford is here taking aim at capitalism in particular because in the capitalist ethos and system, surplus energy does not get directed toward cultural creation but is, instead, reinvested for increased production.
124 White, "Energy and the Evolution of Culture," 338. Emphasis in original.
125 Alex Epstein, *The Moral Case for Fossil Fuels* (New York: Portfolio/Penguin, 2014).
126 Mark Caine et al., *Our High-Energy Planet: A Climate Pragmatism Project* (Breakthrough Institute, April 2014). Available online: https://sites.tufts.edu/cierp/files/2018/02/Our-High-Energy-Planet_DOC.pdf (accessed May 21, 2019), 4.
127 Yannick Oswald, Anne Owen, and Julia K. Steinberger, "Large Inequality in International and Intranational Energy Footprints Between Income Groups and Across Consumption Categories," *Nature Energy* 5 (2020): 231–9.
128 D. M. Martinez and B. W. Ebenhack, "Understanding the Role of Energy Consumption in Human Development Through the Use of Saturation Phenomena,"

Energy Policy 36 (2008): 1430–5. Vaclav Smil, *Energy at the Crossroads: Global Perspectives and Uncertainties* (Cambridge, MA: MIT Press, 2003). For a summary, see Julia K. Steinberger and J. Timmons Roberts, "From Constraint to Sufficiency: The Decoupling of Energy and Carbon from Human Needs, 1975–2005," *Ecological Economics* 70 (2010): 425–33.

129 Vaclav Smil, "Science, Energy, Ethics, and Civilization," in *Visions of Discovery: New Light on Physics, Cosmology, and Consciousness*, ed. R. Y Chiao et al. (Cambridge: Cambridge University Press, 2010), 709–29. Cited in Daggett, *Birth of Energy*, 2. See also: Julia K Steinberger's UN Human Development Report, "Energising Human Development": "Here we see a high correlation between lower energy and lower HDI [Human Development Index]: a small increment of energy use corresponds to a relatively large increase in HDI. As energy use increases, we witness what economists would call 'diminishing returns' in human development outcomes. And at higher energy use, there is no statistically significant dependency: the relationship shows evidence of saturation. The best-fit curve shows high human development (HDI above 0.7) was attainable at 50 GJ of primary energy per person in 2012." Available online: http://hdr.undp.org/en/content/energising-human-development) (accessed January 2020).

130 Using the HDI, Human Development Index, regularly relied on by the UN.

131 Steinberger and Roberts, "From Constraint to Sufficiency," 425–33 (428).

132 Ibid., 425.

133 Herman E. Daly, John B. Cobb, and Clifford W. Cobb, *For the Common Good: Redirecting the Economy Toward Community, the Environment, and a Sustainable Future* (Boston: Beacon Press, 1994).

134 The IPCC, for example, has assumed that human well-being is tied to economic growth which is tied to energy production and consumption. The organization has assumed that economic growth depends on "cheap and plentiful energy." In a 2016 Report to the UN Development Program, Steinberger demonstrated that economic growth, indeed, depends on energy increases, but if energy use is being decoupled from human well-being but not from economic growth as her 2010 study concluded (Steinberger and Roberts, "From Constraint to Sufficiency"), continuing to make decisions about climate mitigation based on effects on economic growth will keep us chained to high-energy societies without necessarily improving human well-being.

Chapter 2

EXTRACTION[1]

In emphasizing the entanglements of *energeia*, work, and heat with divinity we see that rather than wholly departing from ancient *energeia*, modern energy has continued with the fulfillment of Man as one of its main aims and key contributions. In focusing on energy concepts and science, though, we have not yet accounted for a key distinguishing characteristic of modern energy practice. In the current petro-capitalocene, energy is rarely thought of in terms that are not inherently extractive. Moreover, energy "resources" are seldom brought to the global market without extractive practices that recapitulate histories of slavery, colonization, and domination.[2] The predominant diagnosis of the climate crisis as primarily an emissions problem radically obscures these entanglements.[3]

In exploring ancient roots of *energeia* it becomes evident that concepts of energy have not always been so closely connected to the imaginary of a subsurface.[4] Modern energy marks a key shift toward viewing energy as a substance that, like minerals, must be brought to the surface. In modern energy science, particularly with the first law of thermodynamics, energy becomes omnipresent but hidden behind every material surface, lying in wait for human grasp. Here energy emerges as eminently extractable—every living being, every form of material life contains energy that, given the right methods, can be removed and put to human use. For Heidegger, this perspective characterized a fundamental shift in how moderns view the world through the lens of a challenge (*Herausfordern*) placed to nature. The specific example he gave is that of energy: *Herausfordern* "puts to nature the unreasonable demand that it supply energy that can be extracted and stored as such."[5] In this sense, as Michael Marder has rightfully emphasized, modern energy emerges as *potentia*—a potential that must be "snatched from the interiority of things."[6] Marder continues, arguing that while extractive energy practices may seem shocking to environmental advocates, they also are to be expected as mere materializations of predominant Western epistemologies. Where knowledge is gained by looking beyond the surface, by cracking open the sensory world to perceive the reality and truth beneath or beyond the surface we should not be surprised that our energy practices follow suit: "Our epistemologies, too, acquiesce with the ambition to disclose the marrow of reality, usually by shattering and discarding the outward 'mere' appearances that occlude it. Thinking has assumed the shape of mental fracking."[7] Unless they are phenomenologically oriented,

Western epistemologies and spiritualities alike are generally not satisfied with the givenness of things—they seek to lay bare truth or insight by stripping away layers of surface.[8]

Feminist and ecofeminist scholars have long emphasized the problematic ways modern scientific epistemologies and methodologies have taken on a form of unveiling and revealing covered secrets. Unlike Heidegger, they have attended to the particular embodied effects of modern epistemologies and technologies. Carolyn Merchant, for example, has emphasized the important imaginary of revealing or unveiling subsurface secrets for early modern scientists like Francis Bacon. Bacon placed a new emphasis on the importance of uncovering secrets, of moving from the secretive knowledge of alchemists, magicians, witches, and midwives to the open knowledge of the scientists.[9] This was made possible by the long-standing practice, traced back to Aristotle, of applying human anatomical analogies—like mineral veins—to descriptions of the earth.[10] As Merchant has emphasized with reference to Kathrine Park's work on the gendered dynamics of early modern extractive dissection practices, the democratization of knowledge is not the only dynamic at play. A masculinist desire to penetrate, dominate, and control wild nature—aligned with the unruly, feminized, "uncivilized" peoples encountered in the colonial project—is also functioning.[11] With Merchant and Park, then, we begin to see the ways that the body of the earth and bodies of feminized others overlap in extractive imaginaries.

From feminist environmental perspectives it is already clear that mineralogical extraction is fully entwined with fleshly extractions. In analyzing such imbrications, it will be crucial to attend to the ways modern extraction does not just construct a gendered subject, but also a racialized modern subject. In the binary logics so frequently functioning in Western modern thought, extraction not only produces the autonomous white masculine subject, but also its obverse and lack. As Mbembe asserts, "[e]xtraction . . . produced the Black Man."[12] This chapter therefore takes on the extractive construction of overrepresented Man (Wynter) to foreground the ways that, for many, gender has consistently been constructed as a "genre" of their in/humanity. As Wynter emphasizes, unless gender critique also seeks to dismantle the racializing genres of humanity it has been attached to, it will not be truly emancipatory.[13]

Therefore, building from Kathryn Yusoff's remarkable work in *A Billion Black Anthrpocenes or None* (2019), this chapter will emphasize the ways that racialization has been constructed in and through imbricated mineralogical and human extractions. Yusoff attends to the spatial, geological formations of race, and so emphasizes the role of extraction in constructing this new in/humanism. Yusoff notes that these new formations emerge as a function of fungible energy exchange: "the movement of energy between enslaved bodies in plantations, plants, long-dead fossilized plants, and industrial labor is a geochemical equation of extraction in the conversion of surplus." Yet, Yusoff emphasizes that "this racialized equation of energy is located in a larger field of production and semiotics of extraction."[14] The historical constitutive entanglements of extraction and race account for the continuing ways Black and brown bodies are employed as sacrifice or buffer zones, sheltering white bodies from the immediate and localized environmental harms of extractive endeavors. What has not yet been adequately examined, though, are the profound *theological dimensions linking extractivism to white exceptionalism*.

In this vein, building from critical theologies of race articulated by J. Kameron Carter, Willie James Jennings, Kelly Brown Douglas, and Terence Keel, this chapter will emphasize that modern race has not been constructed in a void left by a modern evacuation of Christian identity, but as a theological surplus or overflow into racializing theologics. These scholars emphasize how Christian theologics continue to function in seemingly secularized rationality, practices, and assumptions in order to construct modern race—and even, as Keel especially emphasizes, racial science. They identify roots of modern race in ancient patterns of Christian anti-Semitism, connecting racialized human hierarchies with early Christian desires to distance themselves from Jewish identity, correlated with materiality and the limits of the flesh. I will argue that these racial theologies continue to function through extractivist tendencies of modernity and modern science.

Merging insights of political theology with the spatial orientation of Jennings' critical theology of race in particular, I will argue that together a modern spirit of extraction and universalized white exceptionalism were informed by key shifts in the idealization of power during the late Middle Ages—divine, political, and gendered. While political theologians have commonly recognized the significance of theological shifts in power ideals for the rise of modern political sovereignty, I want to also emphasize their role in extractive ideals and material practices.

Yet, in emphasizing the late Middle Ages shift to an extractive divinization of will I am not interested in laying out a linear chain of causality beginning in thought imposing itself on materiality. Instead, I am identifying what Max Weber called "elective affinities," or what William Connolly, inspired by Weber, identified as part of a "resonance machine" between religious ideals and material economic structures.[15] Similarly, in the vein of Karen Barad, I am identifying material-discursive entanglements of matter and meaning.[16] From this perspective, divine ideals of extractive divine-cum-political power and material extractive practices inform one another—they link up, reverberate in, activate, excite and energize one another. Modern Man vibrates with the power of divine will extracted from mutual constitutive ties of belonging and accountability, cut free from material constraints of land and matter, empowered for extractive acts of domination and control that both draw on and reinforce a theological idealization of will removed from constitutive ties.

Far from a purely technoscientific construct, extractivism inscribes itself in anthropo-geologic formations, resonates through constructs of race, and reverberates within political theologies of creation, sovereignty, and modern master masculinity. In particular, we will analyze a significant theological shift folding idealized displacement and the external application of sovereign force into political, extractive, gender, and racial dynamics alike—in other words, how modernity becomes enamored with an unlimited *potentia* that infuses *potestas*. In order to understand the emergence of the concept of extraction—much less how it functions today—we need to focus not just on the extraction of minerals and natural resources, but also on the ways the extraction of natural resources resonated with and amplified similar concepts of divine and human extraction.

Modern Extractive Imaginary

Various modes of extraction have frequently been perceived as natural, essentially human, or inevitable. In mining literature, as well as Western thought in general, even up to recent times, it is common to come across glorified claims like "mining is a pillar of civilization."[17] Francis Bacon argued as much—informed on this point by Georguis Agricola.[18] Typically, assertions like this are followed by archaeological evidence demonstrating that mining practices have been in place since the Neolithic period.[19] It would be more precise, however, to state that mining is a pillar of the current iteration of Western civilization and to recognize that not all mining and extraction can be conflated. Neolithic quarrying is not synonymous with Appalachian mountaintop removal; Indigenous surface retrieval is not the ancient counterpart of fracking; and Bavarian independent mining supported by professional guilds and a rich mining culture is not the equivalent of deep-water oil extraction.

Similarly, in a biological and evolutionary sense the very act of eating and growing food might be interpreted as extractive—taking energy from one source to give life to another. Again, in this sense extraction might be portrayed as tragic but inevitable, as essential and basic to the sustenance of life. While certain forms of energy exchange do constitute basic necessities of life, and while these may emerge as sacrificial, violent, or tragic, they are not necessarily instances of modern extraction. Mezzandra and Nielson, for example, emphasize that agriculture took a distinctively extractivist turn with the intensification of the "green revolution."[20] For this reason, Hubert Alain argues in his analysis of extractive logics of corn monoculture that the Anthropocene is more extractivist-centric than anthropocentric.[21]

Indeed, in discourses overlapping with petroculture studies and energy humanities, extractivism has been posed by some as "the dominant paradigm of contemporary capitalism and neoliberalism at large."[22] Yet, Ecuadorian economist Alberto Acosta, often credited with initiating the designator, places extractivism within a much broader historical scope. Acosta emphasizes the inherently modern, explicitly colonial character of extractivism, describing it as "a mode of accumulation that started to be established on a massive scale 500 years ago."[23] As such, extractivism encompasses more than just mining to include an ethos of economic exploitation, domination, and "colonization of nature"[24] and peoples. Consequently, I want to emphasize that modern extractivism is in no way "necessary," "natural," or "inevitable," but rooted in a particular relation to land, the "separation of human beings from their origins and birthplaces,"[25] and remains tied to energy ideals and distinctive theologics.

As Mezzandra and Neilson emphasize, "one of the problems . . . with the notion of extractivism is that all too frequently it remains associated with a narrow and literal sense of extraction."[26] Such literal focus obscures the ways that extraction works as an imaginary, a conceptual approach, or worldview. An imaginary functions as an entire worldview of what is desirable and can be possible.[27] In a conversation with Michi Saagiig Nischnaabeg scholar, writer, and artist, Leanne Betasamosake Simpson, Naomi Klein emphasizes that extraction is a "mindset." More than mere material practices like mining and drilling, "it's an approach to nature, to ideas, to people" that "encapsulates the dominant economic vision."[28] Simpson adds, "extraction is stealing. It is taking without consent, without thought, care or even knowledge of the impacts on the other living things in that environment."[29] Clearly, for Simpson extraction is distinct from the kinds of exchanges of energy that constitute the sustenance of life or anciently practiced forms of Indigenous mining. There is no sense here of extraction as inevitable, natural, or necessary.

Emerging at the intersection of the forced removal of humans or minerals and a theologic newly idealizing the external and arbitrary use of force, extractivism emerges as a particularly potent imaginary. Identifying an extractive imaginary allows us to see the ways extraction as a material/discursive entanglement of matter and meaning, theology and political power, mining and modern in/humanism, travels across disciplinary and material/ideological divides, defies linear causation, and relies on resonances and reverberations between disparate ideologies, logics, affects, and material practices. Such an approach can allow us to better analyze the still materializing links between race and environmental degradation and between settler colonialism and energy extraction.

Throughout this chapter I will highlight two characteristics of the distinctively modern extractive imaginary: a reliance on displacement (or a new relationship to space/place) and the application of an external sovereign force. Attending to both means looking closely at theological shifts as we will see shortly. At least initially, key conceptual shifts can be identified by closely attending to linguistic changes. The term extraction is derived from the ancient Latin *extraho, extrahere, extraxi, extractus*, meaning to drag (*traho*) out (*ex*).[30] Something of this ancient usage certainly continues to reverberate in modern definitions of the term: "The action or process of drawing (something) out of a receptacle; the pulling or taking out (of anything) by mechanical means; withdrawal or removal (of a person)."[31] Yet, implied in *modern* definitions of extraction is a more recent dynamic of idealized power as purely external and transcendent, resulting in a distinctive dynamic of unilateral removal by force.

The necessary use of violent, externally applied, often mechanical, force is a key characteristic of a modern sense of extraction. Take, for example, Webster's often repeated, primary contemporary definition: "To draw out or forth; to pull out; to remove forcibly from a fixed position, as by traction or suction, etc."[32] External force distinguishes extraction from a more general sense of *extraho* which could be associated with mere removal, pulling out, or withdrawal. This theme is even more consistent in the ancient and medieval Western world than a perception of matter as inert. Through the sixteenth-century mineral production was theorized as an organic process.[33] Minerals were animated, growing, and regenerative. This is not yet a case of passive and inert matter being removed from a dead place of origin, but a case of animate parts removed from a whole (Terra).[34]

Shifts in usage of the term are also significant. The year 1477 marks the earliest recorded employment of the term "extraction" (in French, *extraccion*).[35] Interestingly, this earliest usage did not reference minerals, but human origins and lineage: as in a person being of Dutch or British, noble or servile extraction. Here, surprisingly, extraction does not carry a connotation of displacement or removal from a "receptacle" or place of origin, but its seeming opposite. In such references, extraction emerges as a condensation, distillation, or contraction of a particular place or people. Though infrequently used today with regard to humans and always listed as a secondary definition in current dictionaries, it is still applied with regard to chemicals, essences, teas, or perfumes. One source describes this usage as "a concentration of the principles or elements of anything; a condensed embodiment or representation."[36] Employed in this way, extraction does not carry the implication of an active/passive dynamic, a unilateral, sovereign, and external imposition exerting force to remove something from passive matter. Rather, it emerges as distillation of something to "its essential and characteristic virtue."[37] Implied here is a profound sense of emplacement, as if a human "of Dutch extraction" emerges as a condensation or *expression* of its geography and people.

The first recorded usage of the term applied to minerals is much later. According to the *Oxford English Dictionary*, not until J. Morse, the first North American geographer, and his *American Geography* in 1794 is the term used with regard to minerals.[38] Between the older usage of extraction in reference to human origins and the more recent in reference to minerals, we can note two key shifts: (1) displacement of a sense of the condensation of place and people and (2) an active/passive binary taking new form in an external sovereign force or power. While these dynamics are functioning in mineral extraction, they are imbricated with human and divine extractions.

Extractivism in the modern sense is more than simply the removal (*extraho*) of natural resources from the earth. It is distinct from ancient—and even much of early modern—mining in that it has integrated into it a secularized theologic of divine exceptionalism and an interconnected idealization of external force. This aspect of extraction emerges only in modernity and it is what links it also, and as we will see not accidentally, with the exceptionalism of white privilege and modern masculinity.

Divine Extraction/Sovereign Exception

Political theologians and historians have long emphasized the significant role medieval shifts in the doctrine of God played in the modern concept of sovereignty and political exceptionalism.[39] It is a mark of the impact of these debates on modern political concepts that contemporary thinkers need to be reminded that a Christian understanding of sovereignty was not primarily rooted in the sphere of politics but in the doctrine of creation—with dominion. Catherine Keller has persuasively analyzed the beginnings of the *creatio ex nihilo* doctrine as the solidification of what she calls an "amoral" doctrine of omnipotence that strictly divided between corporeal and incorporeal, almighty and powerlessness. A modern doctrine of political sovereignty, then, builds on this earlier *ex nihilo* doctrine of creation that solidified as orthodoxy in the second century.[40]

When early Christians professed God as the "Father Almighty, Maker of Heaven and Earth," they were articulating a doctrine of creation that invoked a direct link between divine rule and the divine act of creation.[41] Drawing from classical *logos* philosophies of the Stoics and Philo, for whom the *logos* was a rational ordering principle of the material world, ancient Christians readily recognized that confessing God as creator entailed an acknowledgment of God playing the key role in the rational ordering of the material world. For early Christians like Justin Martyr and Origen, from Augustine through Aquinas in the Middle Ages, affirming God as *logos* "guaranteed the intelligibility of the world."[42] For Augustine and Aquinas there were limits to how far rationality could take a person in discerning divine reason and both acknowledged that human reasoning, particularly in discerning divine characteristics, was never unaided by grace. But an inherent connection between divine power to order creation and divine reason meant that rule and power—even divine power—was not unchecked. So while imbrications of divine and political power were by no means new in modernity,[43] key shifts took place in the late Middle Ages wherein divinity became an *exception to* rather than *model for* the rational laws of nature and workings of the cosmos.

The shift to an external, exceptional, rule by force also had broad implications for the way human selfhood and materiality was thought of in relation to space/place. While wide-ranging and significant insights have been offered by political theologians regarding the exceptional character of modern sovereignty, the implications of this political theological medieval narrative of sovereign force as influential in a shift toward displacement—and in particular, in gendered and racialized extractivism—has yet to be extensively analyzed. Keller, again, offers key insights in her *Political Theology of the Earth*, remarking that "the deep intersections of injustice and unsustainability expose themselves . . . in an extravagant exceptionalism. Its absolute investment in the extractivism and exterminism that pump the global economy works in tandem with the American exceptionalism that lets us (US) use or abuse the global at 'our' sovereign will."[44] This chapter will build on Keller's insights, as well as Marder's argument, that modern energy is distinctly infused and informed by *potentia*.[45] Here we will see how an external sovereign will as *potestas* became understood in a new way in Western thought as unlimited *potentia*. I want to emphasize that there are logical, historical, and theological links between extractivism and modern theo-political exceptionalism, that debates in the late medieval world about the nature of authority or rule—both worldly and divine—resonated with material mining and colonial practices, and reverberated in transatlantic slavery, race, and gender ideals.

Theological Extractions

In the centuries leading up to the colonization of the Americas through the extraction of humans and minerals, significant theo-philosophical shifts were taking place in Europe. These shifts were shaped by an interscholastic debate and informed by a centuries-long power play between popes and emperors along with more recent heightened anxieties about the political and theological influences of Islam. Many scholars now recognize that debates around papal and monarchical power led not only to a crisis in medieval law, but also the opening of a problematic that would frame modern concerns and debates.[46]

Debates about divine and political power took place with increasing intensity and organization following Aquinas' synthesis of faith and reason and centered on the ontological status of universals (Platonic Forms or Aristotelian generals/common natures). Some, like Aquinas and Bonaventure, held that there were real universals (forms or common natures) present in particulars (this specific tree, that particular cat). Others argued against this classical tradition of identifying universals in particulars, claiming that individual particulars were the only reality. This left universals as mere names (arbitrary as in nominalism) or mental constructs (as in the conceptualism of Ockham) given to things that connected individual particulars. This difference marked the key divide between two main approaches: the *via antiqua* (universals are real and inform particulars) and the *via moderna* (universals are mere concepts or ways of mentally organizing particulars).

These debates are most often characterized by current scholars as a shift from the ancient primacy of *logos* to the modern primacy of *voluntas*—from intellectualism to voluntarism.[47] Intellectualism gave philosophical and theological primacy to divine reason, while voluntarism gave primacy to the will. Theologians of the *via moderna* shifted from the position that the world emanates from a principle of divine reason to a position that the world emanates from divine will. Where *logos* theologians had emphasized a divine rational ordering of the world, the orders could be studied to come to some knowledge of God because God had created universals and thereafter was constrained or committed to act within the bounds of the universals or orders God had established. Nominalists or voluntarists, on the other hand, emphasized God's omnipotence as unconstrained by God's past acts or laws and unbound by reason. Universals were not real and therefore could not constrain God's freedom.

Characterizing these debates as a shift from a priority of *logos* to *voluntas* is not unfounded. Yet, in the case of certain particularly influential thinkers, I will argue that the trend we see is not so much a swap of the primacy of one divine characteristic for another, but a shift from mutually constitutive and conditioning divine characteristics to an extraction of one characteristic from the others. In this way, extraction sets the conditions for divine (and then white) exceptionalism.

For Augustine and Aquinas, divine authority was bound to the ordering of creation: the doctrine of God and doctrine of creation mutually informed one another. Thus, for early Christians, unlike those who came to articulate a doctrine of political sovereignty as absolute unmitigated power as a force of will, their doctrines of God emphasized that characteristics like divine will were expressed only in relation to other divine characteristics. This is demonstrated most intelligibly in Gregory of Nyssa's (335–95 CE) "Address on Religious Instruction." In this treatise overviewing basic aspects of Christian belief, Nyssa addresses what seems to have been a common objection to Christian faith at the time. He suggests Christians were commonly faced with the question from nonbelievers of an apparent incongruence between the Christian claim of God's power and the means by which God chose to redeem humanity: why should a God who claims omnipotence have had to trouble with the weakness of human flesh in an incarnation if it was possible to save humanity "by a mere command" or "by some sovereign and divine act of authority?"[48] Could such a God not have remained "free from weakness and suffering?"[49] Nyssa answered that the incarnation was, indeed, necessary because it is not within the divine character to act by power alone as sovereign will. God's character is one of excellence, virtue, and perfection. As such, divinity is not just powerful "but also just and good and wise and everything else that suggests excellence."[50] He continues, explaining the important interconnection of God's characteristics: "not a single one of these sublime attributes by itself and separated from the others constitutes virtue. What is good is not truly such unless it is associated with justice, wisdom, and power. *Power, too, if it is separated from justice and wisdom, cannot be classed as virtue. Rather it is a brutal and tyrannical form of power.*"[51] Nyssa here emphasizes that the doctrine of God that he takes as basic to the Christian faith is decidedly not characterized by the prioritization of one characteristic over all the others, but by the crucial mutual perfection and conditioning of multiple divine characteristics such that wisdom is not divine without also being just, and justice is not divine without also being powerful, and power is not divine without also being just and wise.

This co-constitutive or mutually perfecting aspect of God's attributes is a core aspect of Nyssa's doctrine of God and can be seen as influencing his doctrine of the Trinity as well.[52] Contrary to the current common characterization of a shift from a *logos* dominated *via antiqua* to a *voluntas* dominated *via moderna*, for Nyssa divine character is not constituted by the absolute of any single attribute, but their mutual perfection. He makes this quite explicit: "We must not attribute to him one transcendent attribute, and then exclude another which equally befits him. But our faith must certainly include every sublime and devout thought of God, and these must be properly related to each other."[53] For Nyssa, then, divine power may be perfect, but not absolute inasmuch as it is only truly divine power *if it is bound or conditioned* by divine justice, mercy, and wisdom.

In her analysis of theological and political sovereignty, Jean Bethke Elshtain emphasizes that this sense of a proper or perfecting binding of divine characteristics, including power, was the norm through the early Middle Ages. Jerome (d. 420 CE), for example, wrote what would become a famous letter after the fall of Rome in 410 CE. In the letter, Jerome asserts that God can do all things, but is limited in undoing what has been done. God's power was bound by what God had already ordained (natural laws, laws of reason, human free will), so was not absolute.[54] Similarly upholding divine power as ordained and not absolute,

Anselm (1093–1109 CE) would later assert that God's dominion was restricted by what God had already ordained, including the free will of humans.[55]

Even into the thirteenth century, Thomas Aquinas (1225–74) echoes Nyssa, confirming a sense of God's power, properly bound by and perfected in relation to other divine characteristics. Specifically, Aquinas emphasizes a necessary consonance between divine will and reason: God cannot will what is contradictory according to reason. As Etienne Gilson explains, summarizing Aquinas,

> The only things which God cannot will are those which, in the last analysis, are not things at all; namely, those which include in themselves a contradiction. For example, God cannot will that a man be a donkey, because He cannot will that a being be reasonable and deprived of reason at one and the same time. . . . [It] is to will that it be and that it not be at the same time.[56]

On account of this correspondence between divine reason and the orders of creation, Aquinas understood that God's power lay not in doing just anything. God's power was not absolute in the sense of sheer possibility. In other words, ideal *potestas* was not yet unlimited *potentia* and *potentia* not yet infused with *potestas*. Rather, God's power was conceptualized as action within the orders God had already established. Logos theologians like Augustine and Aquinas still maintained divine omnipotence, but affirmed that because of who God is—the height of goodness, reason, love, reason, and so on—divine power remained bound to or mutually conditioned by reason, goodness, justice, and the like.[57] This reflects an influence from earlier Christians like Nyssa who emphasized the perfection of divine characteristics in relationship to one another: God's will to act is perfected in God's reason, in God's commitment to work within the orders and rationality God had established, and thus is not unlimited *potentia*.

This sense of a proper or perfecting binding of divine power was the norm at least until the eleventh century. Francis Oakley has argued that the shift toward the unconditioned will of God is evident beginning with Peter Damian's eleventh-century response to St. Jerome's fifth-century letter.[58] Where Jerome comfortably accepted aspects of divine limitation especially according to what God had already ordained, Damian (1007–72 CE) resolutely rejected this option. He responded to Jerome through the centuries, writing that God is "[i]ncapable in his omnipotence and in his eternal present of suffering any diminution or alteration of his creative power." Even those laws and orders set in place by God cannot interfere with divine freedom and power since, as Oakley writes, summarizing Damian, "that natural order he could well replace, those laws at any moment change."[59] Here, God is not bound even by orders God had previously ordained. Creation is subject to divine whim and will, unconstrained by reason or the laws of nature.

Significantly, Damian draws particular attention to Jerome's gendered example of the limits of divine power. In his letter, written after the fall of Rome, Jerome had argued that the power of God was limited—specifically, that "although God can do all things, he cannot raise up a virgin after she has fallen."[60] In highlighting the case of a "fallen woman" to delineate the limit of divine power, Jerome's letter became a lightning rod for eleventh-century debates about the limits or limitlessness of divine power. Referring to Jerome's letter, Damian retorts, "How . . . dare we doubt that God can restore the virginity of a fallen woman?" God "can undo the past—that is, so act that an actual historical event should not have occurred."[61] Damian's ire seems all the more incited by Jerome's gendered illustration of the limits of divine power. Damian reverses the dynamic, using the contrast of a pitiful and weak fallen female to rhetorically enhance a sense of the commanding, dominating, unconstrained masculine power emanating from God. We might note that Damian had at his disposal more relevant, more convincing, and more theologically central examples from within the tradition to make the point that God could undo what had been done—the most obvious alternative being the resurrection of Jesus. But staying with the fallen female had the powerful rhetorical effect of amplifying God's power aligned with masculinity. In Damian's choice of a lesser convincing, less theologically central, but more gendered example, we get a sense that this is no mere internal theological debate about divine power. It is a debate that gets at the core issue of the concept of power, the idealized form which power may take, and an emerging preference for an unconditioned, willful kind of power as unlimited *potentia* being aligned with ideal expressions of masculinity.

Damian's objections to Jerome were written in the context of an escalating arms race between popes and political sovereigns. He anticipates what would become a full-fledged movement systematically resisting an inherent correspondence between divine reason and will, reversing Nyssa's mutually perfecting divine attributes and Aquinas' remarkable synthesis of reason and faith that followed from an ancient correspondence between the orders of creation and God's will. Following Damian, theologians of the *via moderna* began to resist a sense of a limitation—any limitation, even by reason—on divine power.

By 1270 and 1277, a list of over two hundred condemnations of Aristotelianism and Averroism were issued by the bishop of Paris and enacted at the University of Paris. The condemnations focused on propositions (several of which were Aquinas') that supposedly violated the omnipotence of God. The condemnations objected to the extent to which Aristotelian concepts of the rationality and order of nature—the existence of universals, for example—limited the freedom of God. Although dominion and omnipotence, as we have seen, were not new claims about divine nature, these condemnations were asserting in an unprecedented way that omnipotence was the "cardinal characteristic of God."[62] God's omnipotence, they held, could not be constrained by anything, even previous divine acts or principles of logic.

Such dramatic shifts in ideals and worldviews are rarely informed solely by changes in thought. In addition to responding to a power struggle between popes and emperors, Christianity and Islam, these changes took place in the context of a devastating pandemic that killed up to six out of every ten Europeans as well as climactic shifts of the Little Ice Age. British theologian and environmental ethicist Michael Northcott reminds us that "it was during the Little Ice Age that theologians began to doubt the correlation between the will of the heavens and life on earth that was central to the microcosm-macrocosm relation affirmed by

Christian Platonism and Orthodox theologians in East and West until this time."⁶³ Claiming God as loving, merciful, reasonable, *and* the one who set the patterns of the created world as ancient *logos* theologians had done becomes less tenable when the patterns of the world no longer seem reasonable, merciful, or kind to human survival. In the face of such dramatic loss of human life and changing weather patterns, a rational ordering of the cosmos corresponding to divine reason and mercy began to seem questionable—while faith in the unfettered omnipotence of God became more comforting.⁶⁴

Resonating with pandemic and climate-induced disruptions, the Franciscan Brit William of Ockham (1285–1347 CE) emphasized the absolute power of God in an unprecedented way.⁶⁵ In the context of his oppositions to papal power deemed an exception to both canon and civil law, Ockham sought to shore up the unconditioned, unshared power of God alone. In doing so, he argued against the reality of universals, systematizing his objections to limits on the freedom of God into a comprehensive metaphysics. Though there is debate about the extent to which Ockham's work was a radical departure from Thomism and it seems clear Ockham himself did not hold a nominalist position, the wake of Ockhamist influence certainly moved in this direction.⁶⁶ Like earlier Christians, Ockham still saw the world as operating in an orderly way, according to certain laws. However, he attributes this orderliness now not to divine rationality expressed in universals, but to divine will: the world operates in this orderly way because God wills it to be so, not because God ordered the world according to a rationality which humans can also access through their capacities for reasoning. Furthermore, if God has willed it to be so, God could will a change to the laws of nature as well. Consequently, rather than reason, knowledge of God comes only by revelation understood as an act of divine will. Here the Reformers will follow in Ockham's wake and, contrary to Thomism, assert that reason is divorced from revelation rather than its fulfillment.

Where God both creates the law and reserves the right to work outside the law, God becomes the sovereign exception who mandates morality from on high. Since the laws of nature were dependent on God's will rather than a rational principle, the laws continue to be contingent on God and God is not bound to limitations within these orders. God reserves the capacity and the right to change natural law at will or work outside this law. True power, ideal and ultimate power, is now portrayed as working outside the law, as an exception. Thus, as Elshtain has emphasized, a precedent for political rulers was set: "If God acts outside the laws, can an earthly sovereign act outside the established laws of a polity? Yes, say the nominalists, rulers may suspend the laws if the need arises."⁶⁷ *Potestas* becomes affirmed as exceptional and unlimited *potentia*.

Characterizing the shift from the *via antiqua* to the *via moderna* as a move from an ancient priority given to *logos* to a modern priority given to *voluntas* is clearly a well-founded portrayal. As Elshtain has emphasized, for Duns Scotus (1265/66–1308 CE), building on Damian's and others' objections to constraints on the power of God, "the will or *voluntas* moves to center stage."⁶⁸ But in light of the repeated emphases of Nyssa, Jerome, and Aquinas that divine characteristics mutually condition and perfect one another, I would argue that it is not so much a dethroning of *logos* by *voluntas* that takes place, but an extraction of *voluntas* from the ground of constitutive relations with other divine characteristics—including, but not limited to, *logos*. Scotus emphasized that God's power was not characterized by action within a sphere of possibilities of a preexisting order. Rather, God's power was exemplified in both making orders of creation and the power to suspend them to create new laws at will. Divine power, therefore, was not a "realm of possibility from which God created a physical and moral order, rather, it is the ability to act outside of an order that is already established."[69] Divine power is now sovereign inasmuch as it both makes laws and can suspend them, creates orders and can be the exception to the created order. Exceptionalism thus becomes a sanctified characteristic, a divinely idealized expression of power.[70]

Shifts in the Morality of Mining

In outlining the late medieval shift to a unique emphasis on will and by framing that not just as a shift from *logos* to *voluntas*, but as an unprecedented extraction of will from co-constitutive characteristics of divine reason, we get a sense of the way that these theological shifts also indicate changes in values and ideals. These were necessary changes for the consolidation of papal and monarchical power to have the authority necessary to initiate slavery and colonization in the Doctrine of Discovery by claiming foreign lands, peoples, and their effects.[71] They were also necessary for the moral justification of the anciently unpopular practice of mining.

Such "operation[s] of power"[72]—theological, mechanical, and political—materialized in a particularly potent manner in Potosí, in current day Bolivia. By the 1560s Spain was occupied with the project of colonizing South America through various techniques: not least of which was the extraction of mineral wealth, including the enslavement of native populations to work in mines, followed by the extraction of African peoples to replace enslaved Indigenous populations in mines. Potosí was emerging as particularly lucrative in this regard. In Potosí's *Cerro Rico* we find evidence of a particularly potent symbolic exchange between religion, extraction, and social domination.

The global significance of Potosí mines is staggering. Between 1500 and 1800, silver mines of South America produced as much as 136,000 tons of silver—what amounted to 80 percent of global production. José de Acosta reports in his *Historia natural y moral de las Indias* (1590) that "his Catholic majesty receives, year after year, a million pesos simply from the royal fifths of silver that come from the mountain of Potosí, not counting further wealth from quicksilver and other prerogatives of the Royal Treasury."[73] Yusoff discloses that four million enslaved Africans were put to work in these mines, replacing enslaved Indigenous peoples who were more prone to disease such as smallpox and typhus and were deemed weaker workers.[74] Working conditions were beyond brutal. By comparison, while a later North American plantation slave owner could expect a "working life" of eight to ten years for each enslaved person, enslaved miners in Potosí could be expected to survive the conditions only for six to eight years.[75]

One of the *Cerro Rico* mining engineer's most frequently referenced resources was the exposition of Georgius Agricola (born Georg Bauer, 1494–1555, Saxony) on mining techniques, *De Re Metallica*. Published in 1556, the tome was based on Agricola's experience in Bavarian mines.[76] For his advancements in mining methods and mineralogical knowledge Agricola is lauded as the "father of mineralogy." *De Re Metallica* in particular is recognized as the first modern resource on mining methods, with an impact comparable to that of Copernicus' *De Revolutionibus Orbium Coelestium*.[77] Shortly after its publication it gained an international reputation for granting readers a seemingly supernatural ability to locate and open metallic veins. Eventually the text would inspire Potosí priest, Padre Barba, to write the first book on American mineralogy, *El Arte de los Metales*.[78] Even earlier than that, it is clear the text was profoundly influential. Knowing how frequently the text was needed for reference, Potosí priests chained Agricola's text to the eucharistic table as a way of *continually reminding mining engineers of the sacredness of their work*.[79]

Agricola's text not only introduced practical and scientific knowledge necessary for the expansion of mining practices, it also initiated a sea change in the perception of the morality of mining. Numerous studies, including Agricola's text itself, have demonstrated that while mining was practiced in ancient and medieval Western societies, its potential was constrained by moral objections. Ancient and medieval Western thinkers seem to have agreed that while mining was at times necessary, it was not laudable and certainly not a moral good.[80] Ovid (43 BCE–*c*. 17 CE) depicts mining as a violation of Mother Earth, and Seneca (4 BCE–*c*. 65 CE) deplored mining. Pliny's (23–79 CE) *Natural History* warns that gold leads to avarice and iron leads to war. Earth is a bountiful mother and minerals obscured from view have been hidden for a reason. In Agrippa's *The Vanity of the Arts and Sciences* (1530), he argues for moral constraint of mining practices, repeating ancient arguments against mining.[81]

That moral restrictions had been a key impediment for the development of mining is furthermore supported in Agricola's text. Agricola was one of the first—certainly the most influential—to shift this negative perception. He devoted the entirety of the first book of *De Re Metallica* to combatting this deeply rooted moral suspicion. He outlines many of the ancient arguments outlined previously, singling out Pliny's in particular. In citing Pliny, he demonstrates the lasting authority of the perception of earth as beneficent mother, bringing forth fruits and vegetables for the good of humanity, but keeping concealed minerals that lead to vice.[82] Consistent with the *logos* philosophy of the *via antiqua*, Pliny roots his argument for the immorality of mining in the expectation that the orders of the world correspond with divine reasoning: what God had covered should remain covered.

Agricola's arguments for the morality of mining, on the other hand, demonstrate the influence of key shifts of the nominalist, voluntarist, or Ockhamist schools of thought. Agricola argues that mining is not an immoral disruption of the divine ordering (*logos*) of the world. Rather, the morality of mining depends on human *will*—how humans decide to use it. Agricola argues, "In truth, if there is a bad use made of [metals], should they on that account be rightly called evil? For of what good things can we not make an equally bad or good use?"[83] He goes on to give other examples of wine (good in moderation, but evil if used wrongly in excess), toil (good if used to support a man's family, but evil if used for making a living from murder or robbery), and feminine beauty (good if used to please the husband, evil if misused to pursue the woman's passions). All these, while vulnerable to abuse, are most truly good divine "gifts" which should be used rightly.[84] Mining, in particular, hurts "no mortal man" and is useful to everyone, from physicians who rely on minerals for treatments, to artists, to those in commerce: "In a word, man could not do without the mining industry, nor did Divine Providence will that he should."[85]

Agricola was remarkably successful in persuading leading religious and political figures in Saxony—and then internationally—that there was not an inherent moral consonance between the orders of creation and divine will. Just ten years after its publication Italians and Spaniards had embraced Agricola's text and put its knowledge to work in locations like Potosí.[86] Similarly, Agricola's work also became influential in Britain where Michael Northcott traces the environmental ethical implications of nominalist shifts. Northcott points out that monks holding vast tracts of land in Britain's coal-rich Tyne valley had known of the presence of coal on their land for centuries, but the ancient alignment between *logos* and *voluntas*, the will of God and the physical order of the world, kept them from digging it up. Northcott explains, reflecting on a similar expansion of mining efforts in England, that once the inherent connection between the *logos* of God and the *logos* of the created world was severed, moral restraints against uncovering what God had covered were dissolved. With moral impediments removed, when Britain's forests began running thin, the monks no longer had qualms about mining their Tyne valley coal in earnest.[87] Thus began the British love affair with coal and the fossil economy.

Racial Displacements

Imaginaries of modern Man and extraction are fully imbricated. When Pope Julius II commissioned Michelangelo to design and construct his lavish tomb, the original plan featured what Michelangelo called "prisoners," referred to since the seventeenth century as Michelangelo's "slave sculptures."[88] The original plans for the tomb never came to fruition, so Michelangelo gifted these figures to friends and dignitaries and many now reside in the Louvre. Some of the figures are bound by leather ties, but most of them seem incomplete in that the human figure is still embedded in raw stone, bound merely by their incomplete, unformed, and undifferentiated geological existence. While the intended symbolism of these figures as part of Pope Julius' tomb is still debated,[89] the sculptures themselves have transcended their original placement and meaning, resonating with the Renaissance (from *rinascita*, "rebirth") imaginary emerging in Michelangelo's time of the courageous struggle of Man to break free of material fetters to rebirth/liberate the enlightened self.

While resonating with an emerging sense of a modern self, Michelangelo's influences are also ancient. Indeed, Michelangelo famously interpreted his role as sculptor in an Aristotelian sense of freeing an already existing form from its marble prison rather than of imposing or creating form. In his view, the role of the sculptor was to liberate by removing only what was unnecessary. The trope of an epic human struggle to free the spirit from matter is clearly layered with ancient Greek philosophical and Christian influences. But in modernity these ancient dynamics take on new valence and start to function in new ways—primarily as a point of racial distinction and justification for colonization, enslavement, and extraction.

Historical ties between extraction and human enslavement are readily apparent. The project of colonizing North America was effected only by the dual and intertwined projects of mineral extraction and enslavement. Recently, though, in *A Billion Black Anthropocenes or None*, Yusoff has demonstrated the entanglements of extraction and the construction of race as well. Geology, a science initiated by extractive aims, also, according to Yusoff, "made race a technology at its inception."[90] Resisting the narrative of a neutral science free of sociocultural impact and influence, Yusoff demonstrates that current debates about the origins of the Anthropocene consistently erase the imbrications of geology, the colonial project, and the construction of race. Founding figures of geology like Charles Lyell articulated race as a function of geological time and environmental formation. Upon a close reading of *The Principles of Geology*, Yusoff concludes that "Lyell's speculations on race are firmly underpinned by the language he has forged for geology, as he defines the problems of the races and their respective (as he understands them) positions in relation to time, in much the same way as his descriptions of geology define the stratification of rock formations and species in time."[91] Yusoff thus emphasizes that through the colonial project and the extractive aims of geology from its beginnings, race has not just been constructed with biology; it has been sculpted from stone as well.

Framing Yusoff's analysis of race, colonialism, slavery, and geologic time is the honing question, "How is geology an operation of power?"[92] This question allows Yusoff to analyze the seemingly neutral or objective science as power-laden. However, the question is curiously approached without addressing the theo-political operations of power, exemplified in the Doctrine of Discovery, which historically and conceptually functioned in the expressed logics motivating and justifying colonization, mineral extraction, and transatlantic slavery. Claims to colonial land possession, mineralogical rights, and the subjugation of humans as property were all made with explicitly theological justifications, made newly possible by the shifts we've identified in the ideal form of political and religious power. Such theo/logics are a crucial part of this "larger field of production and semiotics of extraction"[93] and call for a critical theological analysis that accounts for the kind of political, ecclesial, and colonial power that could envision the kind of authority and rule necessary for the initiation of colonial projects in the first place. In this vein, theologian Willie James Jennings provides key links in his analysis of the production of race as a function of theological displacement effected in the colonization of North America.

Though Jennings' work does not explicitly engage Yusoff's, his spatial account of the theological imaginary of race resonates with Yusoff's emphasis on the geological formation of race. In accounting for this racial imaginary, Jennings identifies a geographical "overturning of space" as a key characteristic of modernity:

> The loss [of place-based identities] indicates the destruction of fine webs that held together memory, language, and place to moral action and ethical judgement. It is a loss almost imperceptible except to the bodies of those for whom specific geography and animals continue to gesture to them deep links of identity. The loss is the overturning of space that *is* modernity.[94]

With remarkable insight, as we will see, Jennings articulates this "overturning of space" as a theological opening that also made possible modern race. For Jennings, "the story of race is also the story of place."[95]

Religion scholars have, for some time, noted a de-emphasis on the role of space tied to anti-Judaism in the Christian tradition. In his pathbreaking text on religion and place, J. Z. Smith's opening epigraph is taken from John Selden's *Table Talk* (1689) wherein the devaluation of space—and the key theological distancing from Judaism—is highlighted. Selden writes,

> The Jews had a peculiar way of consecrating things to God, which we have not. Under the law God, who was master of all, made choice of a temple to worship in, where he was more especially present: just as the master of the house, who owns all the house, makes choice of one chamber to lie in, which is called the master's chamber. But under the gospel there is no such thing.[96]

Smith thus highlighted the way that Christian identity has been constructed in terms of a Gospel understood as a transcendence of the limitations of Jewish identity rooted in law and the particularities of place.

While Smith, along with ecowomanist, ecofeminist, and religion and ecology scholars, has routinely highlighted a devaluation of materiality, earthly identity, or rootedness in place within Christianity, Jennings adds to this critique by brilliantly elucidating the loss of place as the opening of race-based identity. Jennings highlights a persistent Christian temptation to reject the doctrine of incarnation— God become Jewish flesh—in favor of a neoplatonic, docetic Christianity that transcends the particularities of Jewish flesh, materiality, and boundedness to a particular place. This persistent (even ancient) tendency took on new utility in the colonial era. As explorers, colonizers, and missionaries crossed boundaries with their universal message, organizing centers of identity shifted from place-based particularities to universal traits identified according to what was most familiar to Europeans—themselves.

Columbus and other colonizers used comparative terms to describe new peoples they encountered with the European self as organizing center. Like others at the time, Columbus theorized differences in skin tone, morality, and behavior as an extension of place and environment. Yet, this aesthetic, as Jennings notes, is both "of the land but not of the land, of the people but not of the people."[97] Such comparisons may have started with connections to the land, and blackness may have begun as a comparative—like "us" or not—but this aesthetic quickly slid into racial transcendentals, fully disconnected from particularities of place. Shared moral and intellectual characteristics were expected of people in Africa and North America who shared similar skin tones, just as shared superior moral and intellectual characteristics were expected in Asian populations based on the similarities in skin tone with Europeans. As a universal concept of humanity was forged, identity lost its organizing center in place, pushed out by the new organizing concept of race with whiteness as the high point of human development. Jennings emphasizes that such comparisons were dependent on a logic of universalization implied in Christian doctrines of creation and salvation that failed to adequately account for the particularity of God made flesh in time, space, and Jewish flesh, resulting in a scale of human existence with whiteness as the high point of human development.

We might say with Jennings, then, that when human identity ceases to be seen as a distillation, condensation, or extraction (in the earliest sense) of place, race becomes the organizing center of a newly displaced or extracted modern identity. Jennings predicts that unless we deal with this loss of emplaced identity, race will remain the organizing center of modern identity construction because any claim to have moved "beyond" race will merely repeat the logic from which race arose in the first place.[98]

From this perspective, the entanglement of race and environmental concerns can be fully registered. Addressing a current Christian audience, Jennings writes, "I want Christians to recognize the grotesque nature of a social performance of Christianity that imagines Christian identity floating above land, landscape, animals, place, and space, leaving such realities to the machinations of capitalistic calculations and the commodity chains of private property. Such Christian identity can only inevitably lodge itself in the materiality of racial existence."[99] Yusoff, too, emphasizes the way displacement erases a certain organizing structure of selfhood such that "voiding subjects was also about voiding a relation to earth that was embodied, organized, and intensified by those relations to place; taking place is also taking ways in which people realize themselves through the specific geologies of a land."[100] Independently, Jennings and Yusoff provide a way to think through even current environmental racism that is not mere happenstance, nor solely or primarily the result of economic factors, but a logical consequence of the entangled emergence of colonialism, modern extraction, and race.

Their work also helps to bring into sharper focus the particular role extraction, as a mode of displacement, played in the construction of race. Once a universalized humanism was framed as *imago dei* of a sovereign, extracted deity whose power manifests as unlimited *potentia*, then populations whose identities remained tied to and organized by their relation to the particularities of place became seen through the lens of lack. Especially in comparison with the apparent traversing capabilities of whiteness seemingly evidenced in technological navigation triumphs, localized identity emerged as a lack, an inability to extract, an insufficiency of transcendence over the particularities of place to a universalizable organizing structure. As I read it, this is the courageous struggle signified in Michelangelo's prisoner/slaves and articulated by his contemporary, Pico della Mirandola in his "Oration on the Dignity of Man":

> Neither heavenly nor earthly, neither mortal nor immortal have We made thee. Thou, like a judge appointed for being honorable art the molder and maker of thyself; thou mayest sculpt thyself into whatever shape thou dost prefer. Thou cants grow downward into the lower natures which are brutes. Thou canst grow upward from thy soul's reason into the higher natures which are divine.[101]

As Yusoff highlights, the birth of Man, the enlightenment subject, is "coterminous" with the birth of "his Others" which "codified whiteness with freedom and Blackness with objectification and slavery."[102] Similarly, Alexander Weheliye identifies a "dis-dentification" functioning, the identification of whiteness only in relation to blackness as its obverse and lack.[103] In the project of colonization/extraction, blackness is constructed as enslaved to the matter from which whiteness had courageously and triumphantly extracted itself. From this perspective, on account of this seeming inability to extract themselves for unlimited *potentia* from the chains of material relations, blackness emerges as having an innate or natural inclination for subjugation, for being bound—as in Michelangelo's slave sculptures—merely by ties to place, naturally enslaved and enslavable by an inability to resist sedimentation.

Exceptional Modern Man and Extraction

At least as far back as Hegel, the emergence of modernity has been narrated as the result of the triumph of exceptional males and their technoscientific discoveries allowing humanity to disentangle itself from the limitations of materiality.[104] In this story of modernity, through rational capacity and force of will Man has been able to free himself, emerging as exception to the limitations of matter. Challenging narratives of modernity guided by Man and his *potentia* expanding, exceptional technoscientific advances, Enrique Dussel has argued that the discovery of the Americas and their conquest was not a *result* of modernity, but its precondition—it formed a modern subjectivity rooted in domination and this collective experience created the mental pathways and imaginaries necessary to redefine thought and man in the modern mode. Taking exception to Jürgen Habermas' and others' triumphant narrative of modernity, Dussel emphasizes that the "experience not only of discovery, but especially of the conquest, is essential to the constitution of the modern ego, not only as a subjectivity, but as subjectivity that takes itself to be the center or end of history."[105] Building from Dussel's important reversal of triumphal stories of modernity guided by new concepts and ideals, this chapter has emphasized the ways that material practices of mineral extraction, human extraction, and colonization resonated with theological and political shifts of ideal power. Again, my argument has not been that theological ideals—either problematically or triumphantly—guided material extractive practices, but that extractivism has emerged as material-discursive or natureculture phenomena wherein ideals of extractive divine-cum-political power have resonated with extractive material practices, amplifying a modern subjectivity of exceptional humans. In Potosí, extracted slave laborers mined mineral wealth for a divinely sanctioned sovereign will and provided the material conditions that would dramatically expand the horizon of the possible for a certain group of humans. Rather than analyzing mineral extraction purely as a technoscientific endeavor, sites like Potosí demonstrate the importance of examining the multiple layers of material and ideal extraction functioning. Such human and mineralogical extractions resonate with divine exceptionality of the sovereign will and the modern idealization of political power as sovereign. Extracted from constitutive ties, will becomes characteristic of exceptionalism—the exception that would come to define and make way for multiple forms of exceptionalism: resource extraction, political sovereignty, colonization, slavery, race, and modern conquistador masculinity.

Where enslaved Native Americans and Africans were transshipped (Glissant) by force, conquistadors were displaced by choice. As frontier men their job was to "apply force at the colonial frontier."[106] As sociologist R. W. Connell describes in "The History of Masculinity," the "conquistador was a figure displaced from customary social relationships."[107] Their displacement from social binds was essential— it allowed them the moral freedom to apply force as intended. Their extraction from social and ethical bonds of an emplaced identity became a key part of their identity and role—it provided for their exceptionalism. From the sovereign's perspective, the unanticipated effect was that this same extraction from customary social contexts also often produced violent, intractable subjects difficult for the crown to control. Significantly, then, the conquistador or frontier man is not innately violent, self-reliant, fiercely independent, and intractable— these are symptoms of the freedom from limitation and the lack of connection or accountability granted to him by his own often self-chosen extraction. While clearly resonating with modern political ideals of unconditioned power as sovereignty, Connell argues that the conquistador was likely the first group to become defined as a masculine cultural type in the modern sense. As such, the masculine ideal emerges as a self-reliant, independent, enforcer of commercial and political power.[108]

More than a mere advent of a gender type, the conquistador is part of what Sylvia Wynter and Denise Silva have identified as the "refiguring of humanness" that emerges as modern race.[109] As Zakiyyah Iman Jackson so persuasively demonstrates, blackness was not the denial of humanity but its plasticization. Slavery was not an unnatural ordering of humans and beasts, but an experiment— an "engineering project" in the plasticization of human matter. Such a project required the sovereign will of exterior force. Slavery presumed "by will alone that the enslaved, in their humanity, could function as infinitely malleable lexical and biological matter at once sub/super/human."[110] "The black(ended)" she continues, "are, therefore, defined as plastic: impressionable, stretchable, and misshapen to the point that the mind might not survive . . . We are well beyond alienation, exploitation, subjection, domestication, and even animalization; we can only describe such transmogrification as a form of engineering."[111] Like the conquistador, the slave master's "superior" humanity rested on the arbitrary nature of his power to mold human and more-than-human matter to his will.

With Jennings we can see how whiteness comes to replace land—or human/inhuman co-constitutive identity more generally—as organizing center of identity. Yet, more than displacement, whiteness takes on divine characteristics of an exceptional ability to enact force, forming human matter at will. As Jackson emphasizes, slavery—and we might add mineral extraction as well—becomes "an occasion for the theater of sovereign power and manipulated matter—a plastic."[112] The racialized modern human emerges as a function of the ability to dually extract himself and impose form on plasticized matter—self and other—by force. Together these two—displacement and external exceptional force—pave the way for the modern extractive imaginary and the intertwined reimagination of human subjectivity.[113]

In this sense, in terms of a dualistic dis-dentification of race, extraction functions here as a fulcrum, a pivot point between people and civilizations either bound to material constraints or liberated from them to envision unlimited *potentia*—the plasticization of materiality. Whiteness becomes constructed as capable of freeing itself from material binds, liberated to enact force—on new frontiers as well as mineralogical formations. Blackness and Indigeneity, by contrast, lack the capacity to transcend materiality and thereby remain justifiably bound to labor in the extractive project of civilization-building.[114] In this sense, the definition of the human, of Man, now revolves around extraction just as much as divinity—what it means to be Man is to have the capacity for force, for extraction, and conversely the ability to enact force, create remarkable technologies, peoples, and civilizations becomes divine. Prefigured in the eucharistic table in Potosí, extraction and divinity remain chained together.

Blackness and whiteness turn on a material/discursive theologic of extraction: blackness associated with plasticized materiality; masculine whiteness with the divine ability to remove oneself from the bounds of materiality and impose form on moldable matter. Here, energy emerges once again as an organizing center for the definition of humanness.[115] Just as to activate or liberate energy one must go beyond the surface and bring to the light of day the inner potentiality of reality, so too, Man is that being which, like the divine exception, has been able to extricate himself from the bounds of the surface, extracting himself from the bounds of materialization to inform it. Issuing from a lack of transcendence, a lack of exceptionality, the "Black Man is material energy."[116] Black bodies become plasticized as energy machines, producing energy for export. The slaves' energy is not their own, but extractable, produced only for the process of exchange. Black energy remains animal energy, material energy, energy meant for dispossession, meant for extraction, not intellectual/rational energy that cannot be dispossessed as a mark of a person's self-possession and full humanity. This is the mark of divinity that makes whiteness exceptional—that it can free itself from constitutive material relations, transcend the bounds of the inert, the bound, the Black, the passive, the feminine and impose form with arbitrary force on matter. Whiteness becomes exceptional because it alone is capable of attaining the divine extracted qualities to rise above its boundedness, freed for the project of directing the transshipments and extractions necessary for civilization-building. In this sense, the racialized modern subject turns not just on displacement, but on the exceptionality of extraction as well.

To activate or liberate energy moderns must go beyond the surface and bring to the light of day the inner potentiality of reality. So too, modern Man is that being which has triumphed in the struggle immortalized by Michelangelo, extricating himself from the bounds of the surface, extracting himself from the fetters of feminized and blackened matter. Here racialized anthropologies emerge with and through soteriologies. Moderns talk of liberating energy, suggesting it is entrapped in matter, restricted from actualizing its true purpose and potential. Implicit too is the soteriological chain reaction suggested: liberating energy ultimately frees it for its true purpose of liberating exceptional humans from their entrapped, weighed-down, purely material existence for an existence that transcends the merely material or animalistic.

Inasmuch as divinity, and thus power for the *imago dei*, emerged through the late Middle Ages as exception to the orders of creation; inasmuch as modern subjectivity has emerged as a function of displacement as the triumph of the (white) human spirit from the morass of feminized, blackened, uncivilized matter; inasmuch as normative humanity becomes identified with the ability to impose form on plasticized matter; inasmuch as constitutive moments of modernity are rooted in the historical domination and colonization of the Americas through mineral, conquistador, and enslaved extractions; and inasmuch as the Enlightenment philosophical, scientific, and technological triumphs of the Cartesian-Newtonian modern man depend on this new colonizing subjectivity, "modern extraction" emerges as a tautology. Extraction has become the functioning paradigm of modernity. What it means to be modern is to extract—and extraction, in this sense, is unique to modernity.

Notes

1 Portions of this chapter have been published in Schwerin Rowe, "The Crux of Matter: Theology of the Cross and the Modern Extractive Imaginary," in *The Crux of Theology: Freedom, Justice, Peace*, ed. Allen Jorgenson and Kris Kvam (Lexington Books, 2022).
2 Eduardo Galeano, *The Open Veins of America: Five Centuries of the Pillage of a Continent*, trans. Cedric Belfrage (New York: Monthly Review Press, 1973).

3   See Introduction.
4   See Chapter 1, "Energy."
5   Martin Heidegger, "The Question Concerning Technology," in *The Question Concerning Technology and Other Essays*, trans. William Lovitt (New York: Garland Publishing, 1977), 3–35 (14).
6   Marder, *Energy Dreams*, 17.
7   Ibid., 16.
8   See also, Gisa Weszkalnys, "Geology, Potentiality, Speculation: On the Indeterminacy of First Oil," *Cultural Anthropology* 30 (2015): 611–39, on affects of hope, potentiality, and oil.
9   Carolyn Merchant, *The Death of Nature: Women, Ecology, and the Scientific Revolution* (New York: HarperCollins Publishers, 1980).
10 Tina Asmussen, "Spirited Metals and the Oeconomy of Resources in Early Modern European Mining," *Earth Sciences History* 39 (2020): 371–88.
11 Carolyn Merchant, "Mining the Earth's Womb," in *Philosophy of Technology, The Technology Condition: An Anthology*, ed. Robert C. Sharff and Val Dusek, 2nd ed. (Malden: Wiley Blackwell, 2014), 471–81; Merchant, "The Secrets of Nature: The Bacon Debates Revisited," *Journal of the History of Ideas* 69 (2008): 147–62; and Katharine Park, *Secrets of Women: Gender, Generation, and the Origins of Human Dissection* (New York: Zone Books, 2010).
12 Mbembe, *Critique of Black Reason*, 40.
13 Sylvia Wynter in David Scott, "The Re-Enchantment of Humanism: An Interview with Sylvia Wynter," *Small Axe* 8 (2000): 119–207 (185).
14 Yusoff, *A Billion Black Anthropocenes or None*, 16.
15 Connolly, *Christianity and Capitalism*.
16 See Barad, *Meeting the Universe Halfway*.
17 See, for example, Michael Coulson, *History of Mining: The Events, Technology and People Involved in the Industry that Forged the Modern World* (Hampshire: Harriman House Ltd., 2012).
18 See Benjamin Farrington, *The Philosophy of Francis Bacon: An Essay on Its Development from 1603 to 1609 with New Translations of Fundamental Texts* (Liverpool: Liverpool University Press, 1964).
19 See Coulson, *History of Mining*.
20 Sandro Mezzadra and Brett Neilson, "On the Multiple Frontiers of Extraction: Excavating Contemporary Capitalism," *Cultural Studies* 31 (2017): 185–204 (189).
21 Hubert Alain, "Control: The Extractive Ecology of Corn Monoculture," *Cultural Studies* 31 (2017): 232–52.
22 Mezzadra and Neilson describe this as a common definition—a position they differ from in the end. See also Imre Szeman, "On the Politics of Extraction," *Cultural Studies* 31 (2017): 440–7; Szeman and Jennifer Wenzel, "What Do We Talk about When We Talk about Extractivism?" *Textual Practice* 35 (2021): 505–23.
23 Alberto Acosta, "Extractivism and Neoextractivism: Two Sides of the Same Curse," in *Beyond Development: Alternate Visions from Latin America*, ed. M. Lang and D. Mokrani (Amsterdam: Transnational Institute and Rosa Luxemburg Foundation, 2013), 61–86 (62).
24 Facundo Martin, "Reimagining Extractivism: Insights from Spatial Theory," in *Contested Extractivism, Society and the State: Struggles over Mining and Land*, ed. Bettina Engles and Kristina Deitz (London: Palgrave Macmillan, 2017), 21–44 (24).

25 Mbembe, *Critique of Black Reason*, "Extraction was first and foremost the tearing or separation of human beings from their origins and birthplaces," 40. See also Desmond Coleman's emerging work on Blackness and extraction, "Ruminations on the Black/Hypostatic Body and the G(l)ory (of) Art," in *Alchemy and Blackness*, Dissertation, forthcoming, which highlights a premodern entanglement of Blackness as extraction.
26 Mezzandra and Neilson, "On the Multiple Frontiers of Extraction," 185.
27 See especially, Charles Taylor, *Modern Social Imaginaries* (Durham: Duke University, 2003); Carolyn Marvin on the electric imaginary (*When Old Technologies Were New*); Willie James Jennings on the Christian imaginary (*The Christian Imagination: Theology and the Origins of Race* (New Haven: Yale University Press, 2010)); Irene Klaver, "Accidental Wildness on a Detention Pond," *Antennae, The Journal of Nature in Visual Culture* 33 (2015): 45–58; Lawrence Buell, *The Environmental Imagination: Thoreau, Nature Writing, and the Formation of American Culture* (Cambridge, MA: Harvard University Press, 1995), and environmental imaginaries.
28 Naomi Klein, "Dancing the World into Being: A Conversation with Idle No More's Leanne Simpson," *Yes!* March 6, 2013. Available online: https://www.yesmagazine.org/social-justice/2013/03/06/dancing-the-world-into-being-a-conversation-with-idle-no-more-leanne-simpson (accessed September 2020).
29 Leanne Simpson, Quoted in Ibid.
30 Anthony Lo Bello, *Origins of Mathematical Words: A Comprehensive Dictionary of Latin, Greek, and Arabic Roots* (Baltimore: Johns Hopkins University Press, 2013). ProQuest Ebook Central. Available online: http://ebookcentral.proquest.com/lib/unt/detail.action?docID=3318723
31 "extraction, n.". *OED Online*. June 2021. Oxford University Press. Available online: https://www.oed.com/view/Entry/67087 (accessed August 17, 2021).
32 "extract, v.," *Webster's 1913 Dictionary*. Springfield: C & G Merriam Co, 1913. Available online: https://www.webster-dictionary.org/definition/extract
33 Tina Asmussen and Pamela Long, "Introduction: The Cultural and Material Worlds of Mining in Early Modern Europe," *Renaissance Studies* 34 (2019): 8–30 (23).
34 Usher, *Exterranean*.
35 "extraction, n.". *OED Online*.1477: Caxton tr. R. Le Fèvre *Hist. Jason* (1913) 121, "Ye be comen of so noble extraccion of rial lignage," Available online: http://www.oed.com/view/Entry/67087#eid4870886
36 "extract, v.," *Webster's Revised Unabridged Dictionary*: "a decoction, solution or infusion made by dissolving out from any substance that which gives it its essential and characteristic virtue; essence," Available online: http://www.finedictionary.com/extract.html.
37 Ibid.
38 1794, J. Morse, *American Geography*, 592: "The extraction of gold [from mines] is neither very laborious nor dangerous in Brazil." Only two uses of the term are listed earlier. Neither, however, is used regarding minerals. The first is from British law, 1530–1. The second is in Francis Bacon's 1626 *Sylva Syluarum*, "extraction," *OED Online*.
39 Within political theological discourse, the exceptionalism of a sovereign is the infamous, yet still constantly (often critically) referenced, contribution of Nazi jurist, Carl Schmitt. From Slavoz Zizek and Georgio Agamben to Kelly Brown Douglas and Catherine Keller, Schmitt's legacy is critically engaged—most consistently on account of the still current positive influence of Schmitt's critique of liberalism

among legal scholars and politicians. Schmitt coined the phrase "political theology" in his text *Politische Theologie* (1922), making the argument that "all significant concepts of the modern theory of the state are secularized theological concepts" (*Political Theology: Four Chapters on the Concept of Sovereignty*, trans. George Schwab (Cambridge, MA: MIT Press, 1985), 36), that modern political sovereignty in particular is a secularization of divine omnipotence. Herein Schmitt also introduced the concept of the state of exception, arguing that the "sovereign is he who decides on the exception" and argued that a sovereign is one who both makes and is exception to the law (5).

In her analysis of the emergence of modern sovereignty, Jean Bethke Elshtain points out that though Schmitt does correctly identify a long and authoritative tradition of the secularization of Western religious thought into political concepts, this is by no means his exclusive or even original insight (*Sovereignty: God, State, and Self* (New York: Basic Books, 2008), 32). On these grounds, the current chapter refuses to centralize the figure of Schmitt.

40 Catherine Keller, *Face of the Deep: A Theology of Becoming* (New York: Routledge, 2003). See, for example, 49.
41 Elshtain makes this insightful connection in *Sovereignty*.
42 Elshtain, *Sovereignty*, 35.
43 Jürgen Moltmann, "The Kingdom of Freedom," in *Trinity and the Kingdom: The Doctrine of God* (Minneapolis: Fortress Press, 1993), 191–222.
44 Keller, *Political Theology of the Earth*, 14.
45 See Chapter 1, "Energy."
46 Michael Gillespie, *The Theological Origins of Modernity* (Chicago: University of Chicago Press, 2008).
47 See Elshtain, *Sovereignty*; Gillespie, *The Theological Origins of Modernity*; Francis Oakley, *Omnipotence, Covenant and Order: An Excursion in the History of Ideas from Abelard to Leibniz* (Ithaca: Cornell University Press, 1984), as well as philosophical and theological encyclopedias.
48 Gregory of Nyssa, "Address on Religious Instruction," in *Christology of the Later Fathers*, ed. Edward R. Hardy (Philadelphia: Westminster Press, 1954), 268–326 (296 and 291, respectively).
49 Ibid., 291. "Why did he take a tedious, circuitous route, submit to a bodily nature, enter life through birth, pass through the various stages of development, and finally taste death, and so gain his end by the resurrection of his own body? Could he not have remained in his transcendent and divine glory, and saved man by a command, renouncing such circuitous routes?" (291).
50 Ibid., 296.
51 Ibid., Emphasis added.
52 Moltmann suggests Nyssa's doctrine of the Trinity as an alternative model of political power, "The Kingdom of Freedom," in *Trinity and the Kingdom*.
53 Nyssa, "Address on Religious Instruction," 301.
54 Elshtain, *Sovereignty*, 21.
55 See Ibid., 32.
56 Etienne Gilson, *The Christian Philosophy of St. Thomas Aquinas*, trans. L. K. Shook (New York: Random House, 1956), 116, citing Aquinas, *Summa Contra Gentiles*, Book 1, 84.
57 "God as Logos means that God is not only knowable by [God's] creatures but is . . . the apogee of reason. By definition, truth and reason cannot run contrary to the

truths of the Christian faith ... God is the bearer of order in all things" (Elshtain, *Sovereignty*, 17).
58 Oakley, *Omnipotence, Covenant and Order*.
59 Francis Oakley, *Politics and Eternity: Studies in the History of Medieval and Early-Modern Political Thought* (Leiden: Brill, 1999), 43–4.
60 Quoted in Oakley, *Omnipotence, Covenant and Order*, 43, citing Jerome, 43.
61 Elshtain, *Sovereignty*, 22.
62 Gillespie, *The Theological Origins of Modernity*, 21.
63 Northcott, *A Political Theology of Climate Change*, 40.
64 Thanks to Brock Perry for advising the second aspect of this link in personal correspondence.
65 Elshtain, *Sovereignty*, 36.
66 Marilyn McCord Adams has contested the characterization of Ockham and Scotus as making a radical departure from Thomism. On the nominalist impact of Ockham's thought, see Gillespie, *The Theological Origins of Modernity*.
67 Elsthain, *Sovereignty*, 38.
68 Ibid., 26. Emphasis in original.
69 Summary of Scotus in *Ordinatio* 1, 44, vol VI, 363–9 and *Opera Ominia*, vol 17, (Vatican 1966), 535–6 and 254–6 (fn 103), quoted in Elshtain, *Sovereignty*, 26.
70 Other scholars have diagnosed a problematic shift to modern power as well. Though taking dramatically different approaches and posing quite opposing antidotes, both Radical Orthodoxy (RO) scholars and Kathryn Tanner emphasize a problematic shift to univocity of being wherein God and creation are on the same hierarchy of being with divinity at the apex. In seeking to avoid the modern conflation of divine power with human power, Tanner in particular emphasizes the importance of maintaining a strict divide between God and creation, emphasizing they are not on the same plane of being, which serves to underscore the importance of apophatic claims about God's wholly otherness from created being. Citing examples as far back as Eusebius' writings on Constantine, she argues for this separation on the grounds that affirming the correlation of the orders of the world and the will of God can and has led to the conservative affirmation and divine justification of whatever social order is currently in place. Indeed, given Ockham's writings in the context of power disputes between popes and emperors, this concern seems to be motivating Ockham's theo-philosophy as well. My sense is that this is precisely where it is important to emphasize a shift not from logos-centrism to voluntas-centrism, but to indicate a shift away from the multiple divine, co-constituting characteristics (*logos* ordering mercy, mercy ordering power, etc.) to the extraction of one divine characteristic—*voluntas*—above the rest. The implied antidote to the problem then is neither a return to a divinely sanctioned natural (or sociopolitical) order, nor an affirmed radical divide between creation and creator, but an affirmation that divinity can be discerned only within the mutual conditioning of these characteristics. For further discussion on this, see Tanner, "The Modern Breakdown of Theological Discourse," *God and Creation in Christian Theology* (Minneapolis: Fortress, 2005), 120–62, and for Radical Orthodoxy, see John Milbank, Catherine Pickstock, and Graham Ward (eds), *Radical Orthodoxy: A New Theology* (New York: Routledge, 1999), especially, 232–4.
71 What became known as the Doctrine of Discovery was informed by three infamous papal bulls: *Dum Diversas* (1452), *Romanus Pontifex* (1454), and *Inter Cetera* (1493). With these texts, papal authority granted unprecedented rights of conquest, possession, and enslavement to European monarchs. The first two, *Dum Diversas*

and *Romanus Pontifex*, were issued in the context of heightened competition between Portugal and Castile as well as intensified conflict with Islam. In these two, Pope Nicolas V declared war against all non-Christians throughout the world, granted to King Alfonso V of Portugal the right to all lands south of Cape Bojador in Africa, and the right to all possessions ("moveable and immovable goods") and bodies ("reduce their persons to perpetual slavery") of all Saracens (Arab Muslims) and non-Christians. Some forty years later, following Christopher Columbus' "discovery" of America in 1492, Columbus returned to Castilian Spain and, with Ferdinand and Isabella, successfully elicited the authority of Pope Alexander VI to grant to Spain the same rights issued to Portugal. *Inter Cetera* then authorized the moral, spiritual, and political authority for Spain to claim the rights granted to Portugal for these new lands "one hundred leagues towards the west and south from any of the islands commonly known as the Azores and Cape Verde" (*Inter Cetera*). While the text came to my attention too late to influence this chapter, Orlando Betancor offers a remarkably insightful analysis of the ways the justifications for mining and colonization of South America (Potosí in particular) relied on a shared Aristotelian metaphysical instrumentalism in *The Matter of Empire: Metaphysics and Mining in Colonial Peru* (Pittsburgh: University of Pittsburgh Press, 2017).

72 Yusoff, *A Billion Black Anthropocenes or None*, 8.
73 See José de Acosta, *Historia*, IV: 7, cited in Jennings, *The Christian Imagination*, 93.
74 Yusoff, *A Billion Black Anthropocenes or None*, 49.
75 Ibid.
76 See Chapter 3, "Capital," for more on the influence of mining on the Reformation and important, seemingly purely theological ideals like grace as a "free gift."
77 Ruffner, "Agricola and Community," in *Religion, Science, and Worldview: Essays in Honor of Richard S. Westfall*, ed. Margaret Osler and Paul Farber (New York: Cambridge University Press, 1985), 297–324.
78 Barba's *The Art of Metals*, first given as a report of the productivity of Potosí mines to the Crown representative was published first in 1640. The text was reprinted several times and distributed widely after being translated into English, German, and French. Albaro Alonso Barba, *The Art of Metals*, trans. R. H. Edward (London: S. Mearne, 1669).
79 See Farrington, *The Philosophy of Francis Bacon*, 34. More recently, see Ernst Hamm, "Mining History: People, Knowledge, Power," *Earth Sciences History* 31 (2012): 321–6, who also cites a CBS broadcast Herbert Hoover gave in 1955, where he reports, "There is a record somewhere that an ironbound copy was chained to the pulpit in a church at San Luis Potosi in Peru" (n.p.).
80 Confirmed in Dym: "The folklore and anthropology of smelting and mining suggests that such work was dishonorable and associated with magic since ancient times" (Warren Alexander Dym, "Mineral Fumes and Mining Spirits: Popular Beliefs in the *Sarepta* of Johann Mathesius (1504–1565)," *Reformation and Renaissance Review* 8 (2006): 161–85 (165)). See also Carolyn Merchant, *The Death of Nature*, as well as Isabel Barton: "mining had carried a strong social stigma throughout antiquity, making it perhaps the most distasteful of all tradecrafts to scholars steeped in the classical tradition [. . .] multiple classical authorities testified to the inherent immorality of mining, as well as to its sordidness and inhuman nature [. . .] hostility toward mining seems to have persisted in the scholarly literature in Agricola's days," (Isabel Fay Barton, "Georgius Agricola's *De Re Metallica* in Early Modern Scholarship," *Earth Sciences History* 35 (2016): 265–82, section 4.1).

81 See Merchant, *The Death of Nature*.
82 Georgius Agricola, *De Re Metallica*, trans. Herbert Hoover and Lou Henry Hoover (New York: Dover, 1950), 6–7.
83 Ibid., 18.
84 Ibid., 19.
85 Ibid., 20.
86 Jean Bodin explained that "the Italians and Spaniards enlist the services of German and English mining engineers on account of their supernatural skill in locating metallic veins and opening them up," (*Methodus ad facile historiarum cognitionem*, 1566, cited in Farrington, *The Philosophy of Francis Bacon*, 34).
87 Northcott, *A Political Theology of Climate Change*, 53–5.
88 Charles Robertson, "Allegory and Ambiguity in Michelangelo's 'Slaves,'" in *The Slave in European Art: From Renaissance Trophy to Abolitionist Emblem*, ed. Elizabeth McGrath and Jean Michel Massing (London: The Warburg Institute, 2012), 39–62 (40).
89 Ibid.
90 Yusoff, *A Billion Black Anthropocenes or None*, 61.
91 Ibid., 74.
92 Ibid., 8.
93 Ibid., 16.
94 Jennings, *The Christian Imagination*, 58.
95 Ibid., 289. See also, Jennings' remarkable essay, "Binding Landscapes: Secularism, Race, and the Spatial Modern," in *Race and Secularism in America*, ed. Jonathon S. Kahn and Vincent W. Lloyd (New York: 2016), 207–38.
96 J. Z. Smith, *To Take Place: Toward Theory in Ritual* (Chicago: University of Chicago Press, 1987), xi.
97 Jennings, *The Christian Imagination*, 30.
98 Ibid., 63.
99 Ibid., 293.
100 Yusoff, *A Billion Black Anthropocenes or None*, 35.
101 Quoted in Sylvia Wynter, "Unsettling the Coloniality," 257–337 (260).
102 Yusoff, *A Billion Black Anthropocenes or None*, 55. Yusoff adds, "And this is precisely why Whiteness (as a formation of power) gets to 'choose' environmental conditions and black and brown are still the colors of environmental exhaustion and the exposures to excess" (55).
103 Alexander G. Weheliye, *Habeas Viscus: Racializing Assemblages, Biopolitics, and Black Feminist Theories of the Human* (Durham: Duke University Press, 2014), 27.
104 See Gillespie, *The Theological Origins of Modernity*, 10–11.
105 Enrique Dussel, *The Invention of the Americas: Eclipse of "the Other" and the Myth of Modernity* (New York: Continuum, 1995), 25.
106 R. W. Connell, *The Masculinity Studies Reader*, ed. Rachel Adams and David Savran (Malden: Blackwell, 2002), 245–61 (246).
107 Ibid.
108 Ibid.
109 Denise Silva, "Before *Man*: Sylvia Wynter's Rewriting of the Modern Episteme," in *Sylvia Wynter: On Being Human as Praxis*, ed. Katherine McKittrick (Durham: Duke University Press, 2015), 90–105. See also Delores Williams, "Sin, Nature and Black Women's Bodies," in *Ecofeminism and the Sacred*, ed. Carol Adams (New York: Continuum, 1994), 24–9 for an analysis of the ways white supremacy, domination,

and patriarchy functioned within colonial Christianity to justify the objectification of Black women.
110 Zakiyyah Iman Jackson, *Becoming Human: Matter and Meaning in an Antiblack World* (New York: New York University Press, 2020), 47.
111 Ibid., 71.
112 Ibid., 66.
113 Cheryl Harris has also demonstrated the legal connections between the exceptionality of whiteness as a precondition for rights of property ownership. Harris, "Whiteness as Property," 1707–91.
114 See also Mbembe, who describes "the Black Man as the prototype of a prehuman figure incapable of emancipating itself from its bestiality, of reproducing itself, or of raising itself up to the level of its god. Locked within sensation, the Black Man struggled to break the chains of biological necessity and for that reason was unable to take a truly human form and shape his own world. He therefore stood apart from the normal existence of the human race." (Mbembe, *Critique of Black Reason*, 17).
115 See Chapter 1.
116 Mbembe, *Critique of Black Reason*, 79. Some energy humanities scholars have found it tempting to draw connections between the institution of slavery and the techno-mechanical energy slave. The relation between human enslavement liberation through technological advancement is complex. As we will see in Chapter 4, it has been common—as far back as abolitionist arguments at the advent of fossil-fuel discovery—to portray fossil fuels as liberator of human muscular enslavement. Yet, petroculture scholar Bob worries about what such an equivalence can obscure when employed from current privileged perspectives. He notes how an equivalence between the energy of slaves and that of fossil fuels (even in his own previous work) helps "blind us to the persistence of the muscular economy that still dominates much of the globe, where bodies are used up in old ways and where class exploitation has only been intensified and economized through the application of carbon's power" (Bob Johnson, "Energy Slaves: Carbon Technologies, Climate Change, and the Stratified History of the Fossil Economy," *American Quarterly* 68 (2016): 955–79 (974)).

Chapter 3

CAPITAL[1]

From its beginnings capitalism has been rooted in human and mineralogical extraction.[2] This long existent reality has relatively recently gained wider public consciousness, in great part due to remarkable movements such as #NoDAPL, the 1619 Project, and the journalism of Naomi Klein.[3] In the environmental humanities, human geographer Andreas Malm has highlighted the imbrications of extraction and capitalism by identifying the emergence of a "fossil economy": a phenomenon whereby a certain economic system and form of energy become welded together. In *Fossil Capital* Malm has explicitly addressed the *climate conundrum* I outlined in the Introduction, of increased knowledge of the anthropogenic causes of climate change coinciding with continued increases in CO_2 emissions. From his perspective, the response to global warming cannot simply be a drive to produce more and better data because the "main driver of global warming" is not lack of knowledge, but an economic system of "self-sustaining growth predicated on the growing consumption of fossil fuels, and therefore generating a sustained growth in emissions of carbon dioxide."[4] Malm has also challenged the common reasoning that fossil fuels became dominant because they were the most economically and mechanically efficient way to provide for increased consumption. By contrast, he has persuasively demonstrated that industrialists in nineteenth-century England decided to shift from water or steam power to heat generated by coal even though the latter was neither economically nor mechanically more efficient. Rather than cost or mechanical efficiency, the deciding factor in the shift to fossil fuels, Malm argues, was an expanded power over labor; coal became preferable because it offered industrialists the possibility of avoiding the demands of workers for better conditions.

In making these shifts, Malm crucially shifts the narrative of the beginnings of global warming from a story tragically, unavoidably, and unintentionally driven by technology to a particular drive of a few to consolidate power and capital. Malm therefore concludes that the energy-driven climate crisis heightens the importance of a labor analysis since "that is the point of contact between humans and the rest of nature."[5] For Malm, this allows for the remarkable insight that the power dynamics of energy and human labor intersect in significant ways around fossil fuels, resulting in fossil capital as the engine of global climate change.

Capitalism has been abundantly analyzed—even in relation to religions, and Protestantism in particular.[6] The role and valuation of labor—the Benedictine ordering of time according to *ora et labora*, or the broadened Reformation emphasis on the vocational work of all Christians rather than a select cloistered few, for example—has been a key locus of attention in examining the imbrications of Protestantism and capitalism. Yet, such analyses have often not adequately accounted for the particularities of fossil capitalism outlined by Malm, or extractive capitalism more broadly. An energy gap in analyses of Protestantism and capitalism has recently been addressed by one of the most compelling feminist responses to petro-capitalism. In *The Birth of Energy*, political theorist and energy humanities scholar Cara Daggett undertakes a genealogy of modern energy, identifying the ongoing effects of a Western Christian valuation of work and productivism in fossil-fuel consumption.

Consistent with the methodologies of the environmental humanities, Daggett analyzes the humanistic and political epistemologies of energy and its historical modern development. In the vein of feminist engagements with science, Daggett challenges the idea of energy as an objective, universal, neutral science, examining its political logics. In considering energy as a "historical figuration" Daggett wants to explore "how energy became a traveling metaphor that reinforced the material and capitalist relations of empire in the period following the birth of thermodynamics."[7] In highlighting this connection, Daggett offers a fascinating and crucial energy-angle to well-trodden debates about the ideologies of capitalism.

Daggett's approach has significantly influenced this current project. Her emphasis on the ways Protestant theology and work concepts have infused modern energy is particularly insightful. From Daggett's perspective, the conundrum of persistently rising CO_2 emissions in spite of increased knowledge of their danger is due primarily to the Western ideology of work: "when energy and work are understood as historically intertwined in this way, it becomes clear that the reign of fossil fuels is not only about our addiction to fossil fuels and their exponential power. It is also about addiction to the ideology of work, as well as to a particular way of distributing, compensating, and valuing work."[8] Resonating with the history of work ideals outlined in Chapter 1, Daggett has highlighted the profound influence Scottish Presbyterian theologies of work had on some of the most influential scientists of modern energy. This religious framing of work, as well as the profound commercial implications of the sciences, contributed to the science's pervasive popular influence and appeal. It constructed what Daggett has called a functioning "geotheology" informing current energy practices, values, and subjectivities. The industrial West's continued commitment to fossil fuels, therefore, is both mechanistic and ideological, informed and infused with religious values and anxieties. Emphasizing that "the urgency with which we burn fuel is tied to the urgency with which we pursue productivity and hard work," Daggett has demonstrated that a Protestant work ethic has informed not just economic but also energy subjects.[9] As such, work—and the Protestant work ethic in particular—remains key to her analysis of fossil-fuel use.

Given the problematic pairing of work theologies and modern energy, Daggett emphasizes the importance of decoupling work from energy in pursuing a sustainable energy culture. In the "spirit of a new planet politics" she highlights resonances between feminist de-work movements and the de-carbon movement, aiming to form a political alliance that might counter what William Connolly has identified as an "evangelical-neoliberal resonance machine"[10] where aspects of evangelical belief and affect resonate with neoliberal ideals like continual growth. Daggett highlights the postwork feminist scholarship of Kathi Weeks which problematizes the way that capitalist societies value work, productivism, or progress, tying a person's access to basic human necessities—health care, food, adequate housing—to paid labor. Where work functions as gatekeeper for access to basic necessities, subjects are rendered "supremely functional for capitalist purposes."[11] De-work intersects with feminist concerns by highlighting the contradiction embedded in the current economic system of granting paid labor significant moral and practical weight while simultaneously obscuring the ways the system depends on un- or under-paid "pink collar" care-work most frequently done by women. Weeks and others therefore suggest implementing policies like universal health care and a universal basic income that would allow for a decoupling of work from human value and worth. Daggett argues that such aims would also decouple work and energy, providing an alternative political vision where a person's value in society and access to basic life necessities do not depend on their work and productivity. Particularly since work, like heat and *energeia*, has so long been associated with an exclusive masculine-rational desire for human fulfillment (see Chapter 1), the importance of the capitalist work-energy connection for an intersectional gender analysis should not be underestimated.

Daggett's de-work approach to the climate conundrum is also compelling for a critical petro-theology on account of its alignment with de-work theologies such as those articulated by Jeremy Posadas and Kathryn Tanner. In Chapter 1 we saw that Jeremy Posadas has been critical of the consistent Western Christian positive appraisal of work.[12] In response, Posadas has emphasized that in the Judeo-Christian biblical tradition, work is a post-Fall condition, but should not be seen as an end goal or purpose of human life. These would be better identified as "life-enhancing joy, self-transformation, and deep solidarity."[13] Along similar work-critical lines, Kathryn Tanner concedes that Protestantism has historically lent itself to the confirmation of a strong work ethic, but demonstrates that the theological tradition also holds potential for an anti-work ethos that addresses particularly pernicious aspects of twenty-first-century finance capitalism. For Tanner, debt is the key characteristic of finance capitalism. In this sense, she suggests that the grace of God as release from debt can be a powerful counter-story to the enslavements of finance capitalism. Tanner emphasizes the ways that "Christianity can re-envision, and thereby contest, the sort of subject that finance-dominated capitalism encourages for its own purposes of profit maximization" and thus asserts the importance of decoupling Christianity from finance capitalism.[14]

There are clearly key areas of consonance between the de-work movement and counter-capitalist iterations of Protestantism. Yet, my sense is that both de-work and counter-capitalist Protestant theologies tend to rely on a more basic problem of a work/gift dualism functioning in extractive capitalism. Defining gift and work in mutually exclusive terms has key theological roots and, indeed, seems reinforced in de-work rhetoric that emphasizes a person's value beyond their work capacities. In the modern West, on account of influential theological shifts, gift and work concepts have been constructed over and against and in dialectical relation to one another such that one implies the other. Work has come to signify effort, activity, and exertion—to the exclusion of receptivity, passivity, chance, or the free gift. Conversely, commonly accepted gift ideals have come to assume that a gift is nothing if it is not free, unreciprocated, exclusive of exchange, work, or merit. For example, as I was writing my previous book on gift theory, climate change, and religion around 2011, my word processor grammar checker continually highlighted the phrase "free gift" as a grammatical error: a "redundant expression." Apparently, in this modern grammar, articulated in twenty-first-century philosophical debates about the gift as well,[15] the gift is free or nothing. "Gift-exchange" is thereby rendered a contradiction in terms. These gift ideals have become pervasive and often their implicit gender dynamics and related theologics go unidentified and uncritically accepted. Where de-work theological and political approaches do not challenge an underlying gift/work dualism that has become endemic in Western extractive capitalism they inevitably do not go far enough.

Coming to recognize the ways a gift/work dualism functions in extractive capitalism requires a critical focus not just on labor but on gift ideals as they relate to work. In this chapter I will analyze gift ideals in extractive capitalism and theology. This approach still embraces key goals of de-work lenses: namely, Daggett's goal of decoupling work from energy and Tanner's goal of decoupling Christianity from the work/debt drive of finance capitalism. However, I also want to address what I see as a more basic problem underlying the work ethic. I will suggest here that while a work ethic remains at play, increasingly in extractive capitalism the traditional Protestant ethic-enforced link between work and reward is *disrupted* by the value of gift, grace, and chance. If one considers the ways petro-capitalist risk anticipated the wagering inherent to twenty-first-century finance capitalism, then it becomes important to see how grace/gift has been *engulfed* by the current spirit of extractive and finance capitalism. Though the free gift is identified in modernity as purified of economy and exchange—and enticingly aligned with de- or anti-work ethics—we find evidence that the free gift has been *internal* to extractive capitalism, disrupting a rational work ethic from the inside.

I will highlight this kind of disruption in three key contexts of extractive capitalism: in its early period in the context of Reformation-era Saxony mining, in the articulation of modern energy science, and in early petro-capitalist figures and narratives. Where the free gift is already interrupting work and consumption from the inside of extractive capitalist endeavors, an intervention purely focused on decoupling work and energy or Christianity and work leaves unaddressed the simultaneous problematic couplings of free gift and energy extraction. Informed by decolonial engagements with reciprocal-gift exchange, I will argue that a holistic reframing, shifting away from a modern gift/work binary is necessary. In short, the alternative to a gift/work binary is also the alternative to extraction: in reciprocity, value is not found in or under *things*, but only through local relations.

The Gift, Free of Work or Exchange

Functioning within many modern pro- or anti-work ethics is a particular view of value defined in relation to labor. This much has become evident in twentieth-century gift discourse. Modern Enlightenment era shifts in gift ideals that cultivated a gift/exchange dualism are entwined with modern moral theory and subjectivity—and thereby, as we will see, gender and racialization. Immanuel Kant argued that for an act to be truly moral, it must be done altruistically from duty rather than desire. Excluding self-interest, a moral act must be entirely other-regarding. As Troels Engberg-Pedersen argues, this Kantian shift "underlies the modern insistence on the complete gratuitousness of a gift."[16] Such gift ideals inform not only social interactions, but also ideals of human subjectivity. Modern articulations of ideal, fully formed subjectivity as altruistic or selfless, for example, have incorporated the value of the gift as ideally free, unreciprocal, unmerited, unpaid, and without expectation of a return. As a result, most modern articulations of the gift emphasize that the gift is free or it is nothing, that any sense of reciprocity or exchange erodes the gift as such. Such an exclusive definition means that gift-giving is dualistically opposed to exchange and seen as external to economy.[17]

Critical analysis of gift ideals has been part of Western discourse especially since social anthropologist Marcel Mauss developed gift theory as a criticism of modern utilitarianism and individualism. Mauss saw these as stemming from a Western modern idealization of the gift as ideally, if not exclusively, free.[18] Critical of the free gift, Mauss emphasized the important role reciprocal giving plays in society. Where the free gift expects no return, the reciprocal gift is given—as Mauss theorized it—as an extension of one's personhood, a way of affirming a bond of relation that forms the basic structure of society.[19] Importantly, from Mauss' perspective, what gets exchanged is not just the gift object, but relationship.[20] Given its importance in building social bonds, Mauss concluded that though the free gift, exclusive of exchange, has been idealized in modern Western societies, it is detrimental to social cohesion. It encompasses a subject/object dualism that idealizes isolated individualism, utilitarian relationships, and has paved the way for gifts once imbued with personhood to become commodified objects. As Mauss suggested and later critical gift theorists more explicitly argued, the free gift makes way for the necessary ingredients of capitalism: isolated individualism and the reduction of value to economic exchange.[21] While Mauss identified gift exchange as a "total social fact," encompassing exchanges not typically identified in modern cultures as purely "economic" but social and religious, theorists since Mauss have emphasized more-than-social exchanges, encompassing other-than-human ecological exchange as well.[22]

In gift discourse, though, the extent to which theories of gift-exchange depended on ethnographies of Indigenous practices is often not given sufficient critical attention. Crucial questions have been raised about the extensive Euro-American anthropological and ethnographic studies of "potlatch" and other gift-related Indigenous practices. Christopher Bracken, for example, has argued that these ethnographies played a key role in the settler colonial project and that much of the analysis amounts to projections of Euro-American settler colonial desires. He argued that potlatch, for example, was identified and described first only in legal documents aiming to outlaw it.[23] It will be crucial, then, to attend closely to perspectives of Indigenous scholars themselves in any engagement with gift practices or symbols.

Biologist and citizen of the Potawatomi Nation Robin Wall Kimmerer, for example, identifies gift practice as integral to an ethic and ontology of reciprocal exchange. "Gifts from the earth or from each other," she explains, "establish a particular relationship, an obligation of sorts to give, to receive, and to reciprocate."[24] The establishment of an ongoing relationship is what differentiates gift exchange from commoditization. With commodities, once payment is made no further obligations to the giver remain. Kimmerer articulates this as a key difference between the gift ideals of Western perspectives and those that uphold a gift economy: "In Western thinking, private land is understood to be a 'bundle of rights,' whereas in a gift economy property has a 'bundle of responsibilities' attached."[25] Rather than the emphasis on and idealization of the free gift in Euro-American societies, for Kimmerer, gift exchange entails a reciprocity that establishes relationship and calls for responsibility.

The basic difference between free-gift and reciprocal-gift ideals is furthermore exemplified by Kimmerer in recalling the derogatory denominator, "Indian giver," that settler-colonists of the North American frontier gave to Indigenous populations. When Euro-Americans encountered and exchanged with Native Americans they were confronted with fundamentally different expectations and symbolic systems for gift exchange. That Native Americans would seek a reciprocal return gift was met with incredulity, scorn, and the derogatory identifier "Indian giver." Such reciprocal-gift expectations were interpreted as selfish, uncivilized, and inferior to the purportedly more developed "free gift" given with no expectation of a return.[26]

Citing Laguna Pueblo poet and literary critic Paula Gunn Allen, María Lugones also emphasizes the entwinement of gift-exchange ideals, gender, and race in the project of colonization. In order to institute colonial capitalist practices, Western gender and race constructs were necessarily imposed on peoples and cultures that had not relied on binary, heterosexual, or hierarchical relations and identities. Gunn cites several enforced practices and concepts that were necessary for the imposition of colonization and capitalism. Summarizing Allen, Lugones writes that "among the features of the Indian society targeted for destruction were the two-sided complementary social structure; the understanding of gender; and the economic distribution that often followed the system of reciprocity."[27] Together, nonbinary gender and the reciprocal-gift-exchange economic structure were necessary to overcome in order to impose colonial capitalism.

Free Gift and Grace

The derogatory denominator "Indian giver," fabricated by predominantly Protestant pioneering colonizers, is particularly illuminating as it exemplifies the clash of religiously influenced gift-exchange ideals. Euro-American gift theorists since Mauss have emphasized that the concept of the free gift emerged in modernity as an extension of the influence of Protestant grace.[28] As a consequence, some current Protestant theologians explicitly articulate the distinctiveness of grace in its "free gift" character that excludes exchange and emerges as external or in opposition to economy.[29]

Key to the Reformation movement was a heightened awareness and rejection of "works righteousness," or any effort on the part of the human to make one's self worthy of divine approval or attain high spiritual standing.[30] The rejection of the spiritual merit of works was paired with a strong emphasis on divine omnipotence and grace alone as salvific. Where the Reformers emphasized salvation through God's grace alone to the exclusion of works, it was emphasized that God gives without merit and has no need of a return gift.

Though popularized by the Reformers, this free-gift ideal and accompanying doctrine of God emerged much earlier, articulated clearly by William of Ockham who emphasized in accordance with his understanding of divine sovereignty that God was "no one's debtor"—God did not grant anything because it was owed, but solely on account of God's free and gracious will.[31] Though Martin Luther rejected much of Ockham's nominalism, received to him via Gabriel Biel's formulations, it has been argued that the Protestant formulation of grace, commonly interpreted in German theological tradition as free gift exclusive of exchange, draws on a nominalist emphasis on the almighty and sovereign power of God.[32] This interpretation of grace assumes a God whose power is supremely evident in being able to call something what it is not—the power of God to be able to reckon a sinner, who remains a sinner, actually a saint. In this particular interpretation of Protestant grace we see a break with realism (a break associated with the *via moderna* as outlined in Chapter 2) such that God is able to make and remake realities at will—namely, to treat a sinner as a righteous saint—even if contrary to reason, justice, or nature. According to this set of concerns, humans should not aim to return a gift to God because doing so would suggest they had some kind of sway or influence with God. The God of the free gift thus emerges as necessarily omnipotent and sovereign, not owing creation anything, above any reciprocal return from creatures, and acting out of sheer will. From this perspective, grace is only grace in as much as it excludes work or exchange.

Earlier Christian articulations of gift and grace were not conceptualized in such starkly oppositional terms. In Augustine's thought, for example, gift was understood primarily in terms of communal exchange, idealized as the bond of relation. Gift, in fact, was his designator for the Holy Spirit, understood in his trinitarian thought as the bond of relation between the first and second persons (Father and Son) of the Trinity.[33] While some Reformers would eventually articulate grace in counter-realist terms, claiming that God's grace is characterized by God's power to designate a sinner, who remains a sinner, actually a saint, other Christian articulations of grace emphasized a real change worked in the human such that one became, through grace, actually more righteous. Though modern Protestant interpretations of Augustine emphasize his understanding of grace as "sovereign,"[34] Augustine did allow for "cooperative grace" where a Christian's will, once liberated by grace, could collaborate with God toward growth in holiness. Similarly accounting for multiple kinds of gift and a realist change effected by divine grace, Aquinas differentiated between actual grace (that "which is freely given") and habitual grace ("grace which makes pleasing" or a "created habit of grace within the human soul").[35]

Eventually, though, habitual grace succumbed to Ockham's razor—God's hyperbolic power rendered it an "unnecessary hypothesis." God was fully capable, Ockham argued, of accomplishing the redemptive work of grace directly, having no need for intermediaries like habitual grace. In habitual grace Ockham identified a limitation on divine power. His voluntarist approach emphasized that God determines the meritorious nature of an action by divine will, not on account of anything like reason, nature, or divinely assisted habit.

By the fifteenth century, in great part due to Ockham's influence, habitual grace was widely seen as discredited. In the most common—distinctively German—interpretation of Luther, grace does not function by effecting a real change of imbued righteousness in the person. Rather, God's grace is given *extra nos* (outside us) with no emphasis on human action or indwelling grace (*intra nos*). Any attempt at reciprocity with the Giver thus became an attempt at self-justification—an attempt to rely on one's own strength and efforts. Where a vertical reciprocal return would effectively nullify the divine gift, the only proper response to divine grace was horizontal: gratitude to God in the form of a turn toward one's neighbors. While it is not within human powers to reciprocate a gift to God, the proper response from humans was not to waste or horde them, but distribute those gifts more broadly in service to one's neighbors and for the betterment of the community.

Whether or not Luther, Calvin, and other initial Reformers intended to idealize the free gift in its pure form is a source of continued debate.[36] What is clear, though, is that the free gift, exclusive of exchange, became commonly idealized in modern societies, while gift-exchange became seen as not only theologically questionable but also conceptually incoherent, an irrational mark of lesser civilizations and religions. Its enduring, secularized, influence can be found, as mentioned earlier, in the modern ideals of altruistic subjectivity, charity or philanthropic endeavors, philosophical gift theory debates, and programmed into word-processing grammar checkers. What's more, the free gift lives on in often-contradictory gendered dynamics, idealizing self-sacrifice and self-giving without expectation of return idealized in motherhood and wifely duties while in its masculine form, sacralizing autonomy, self-possession, separative individualism, and self-sufficiency.[37] The free gift in its pure form depends on an active/passive dynamic, masculinizing divine action as unilateral giver, working on a passive, even inertly receptive feminized humanity. Though it seems to deny the power of work, its dualistic divisions elevate spiritual work to the exclusive sphere of divinity and idealize merely utilitarian dynamics in the secular sphere.

Free Gifts of Extraction

The purification of gift from exchange has impacted economic and ecological spheres as much as the theological. This becomes particularly evident when attending to extractive capitalism. Where grace is aligned with that which comes without labor—a free gift given without payment or effort—the ease with which certain extractive resources can be gained has rendered them more clearly and enticingly divinely given. Though the free gift has been idealized as free of economy and exchange in modernity, the examples to follow—mining and the Reformation, free gift concepts in energy science, and divine grace in petroleum extraction—will demonstrate the influential ways free gift concepts have come to function from within extractive capitalism.

Extraction and the Reformation[38]

Capitalism has emerged in congruence with colonization, slavery, and mineralogical extraction. Potosí silver, for example, proved indispensable for the emergence of global capitalism by providing the vast majority of silver needed for coins spread in increasingly globalized trade.[39] As the previous chapter emphasized, the techniques and technologies employed to make Potosí so unprecedentedly successful depended on the insights of Georgius Agricola's *De Re Metallica*, written in the context of the Reformation-era Saxony mining boom. Though significant scholarship has focused on both the Reformation and the Saxony mining boom, these foci have most frequently been divided between religious disciplines like theology and church history and mining/technology histories. The influences of mining culture, desires, and affects have rarely been taken seriously as an influence on the Reformation. Conversely, Reformation-era theological, social, and cultural shifts have rarely been studied for their influence on mining culture.[40]

The year before Luther reportedly nailed his 95 Theses to the door of the Wittenberg Church, a silver mining boom began in Saxony. Joachimsthal became a center of Reformation activities as well as a particular locus for the silver boom. After a promising prospecting report, the small town was flooded with hopeful miners, first from surrounding towns, but then from as far away as the Hard Mountains, Switzerland, and Salzburg.[41] The region became profoundly significant for Germany and its princes. Mining historian Warren Alexander Dym, for example, emphasizes that "between 1545 and 1560 well over half of Germany's average yearly silver production came from the Ore Mountains, and sovereigns earned up to three-fourths of their total income from the mines."[42]

Agricola lived and worked in this context. While employed as town physician for Joachimsthal and Chemnitz in the mid-1500s Agricola visited mines at every chance, observing and learning their technologies and techniques. Most of the knowledge contained in *De Re Metallica*, he reports, came from firsthand observation in this context.

Agricola was also fully emersed in local intellectual spheres. As a lifelong Roman Catholic, it is not surprising that Erasmus of Rotterdam was a personal friend. But as town physician and then mayor of Protestant Chemnitz, it must have been important to have Protestant allies as well. His friendly relations with Phillip Melanchthon and other Reformation leaders were well known, and some Reformers took a particular interest in his mining research. Among them, Saalfield Lutheran pastor Christoph Entzelt (Christophorus Encelius, 1517–86) enticed Melanchthon to write the preface to Entzelt's own *De Re Metallica* inspired by Agricola's work. Similarly, Joachimsthal Lutheran pastor Johann Mathesius credited his theological and practical interest in mining to personal interactions with Agricola.[43]

Before becoming a pastor Mathesius taught at the Latin school in Joachimsthal. There he "witnessed the most rapid period of development in the mining activity there."[44] After a successful investment in a mining venture, attained by following Agricola's advice, Mathesius suddenly had a financial surplus. He took the opportunity to leave his post at the Latin school and move to Wittenberg. There he continued his theological training, came to be part of Luther's inner circle of friends and confidants, and presented a mining treatise to Luther and the Reformers (*Quaestio de rebus metalicis* (1540)). After being ordained by Luther himself, he was sent back to Joachimsthal in 1545 to serve as pastor to the miners.

The Christianization of mining was a long-term process predating the Reformation. Already by this time, for example, the naming of a mine was ritualized as a kind of baptism.[45] For both Mathesius and Agricola in particular, mining was portrayed as sacred because mineral generation was seen as providentially guided while the miner's role was portrayed as a partnership with divine agency. In Mathesius' work, we begin to see the extent to which the context of modern mining and the message of the Reformation in particular were entwined. Dym describes Mathesius' *Sarepta* as the "culmination of [his] life-long *fusion of mining and the spiritual life*."[46] In sermons addressed to the miners and collected into his published volume *Sarepta oder Bergpostille*, he consistently framed the Protestant message in terms of mining knowledge and metaphors, providing a solid theological sense for the life of a miner as a glorified and religious calling.[47] He portrayed biblical figures such as Adam and Job as early miners, God as the great metallurgist, and the pure gospel as refined silver.[48]

Specific to the Reformation, though, Mathesius portrayed mining and the Protestant event as wholly intertwined with God's providential aims for the world. Mathesius believed in the organic development of minerals: like plants and animals, they were theorized to develop from one form to their fully perfected form over time with the application of heat. Just as did Aristotle, Mathesius expressed this process—never gender neutral—as a process of perfection, moving from undifferentiated viscous clay to perfected silver or gold. He framed the process in terms of the Genesis creation story:

> In the beginnings, God created the heavens and the earth. This included the veins, cracks and layers of rock through which metal grows. God a great metallurgist and alchemist, continues to oversee the organic processes of the subterranean world. He creates a primordial substance out of water and earth, and He separates this into sulfur and mercury, as the male and female seed in the generation of mineral ore. This in turn combine under the influence of the sun, stars, and an earthly heat, which nurtures the mixtures as in the womb of a mother. The undifferentiated metallic product seethes upward through the cavities of the earth, losing impurities and exhuming vapors, coagulating slowly into distinctive mineral veins, as it passes from base to more noble forms.[49]

Adding a Pauline twist to Aristotle, Mathesius affirmed the spiritual implications of this material perfection by suggesting that mineralogical perfection was akin to the perfection of the human soul through love as St. Paul emphasizes in his letter to the Corinthians.[50]

Where minerals were believed to develop organically it was not uncommon for miners who had abandoned an unsuccessful mine to return and, upon finding significant mineral holdings, conclude that they had not been fully grown when they were there before, but now had reached "a state of perfection or fruition in the form of silver-bearing ore or gold."[51] Since minerals were constantly in a process of perfection, timing was key. Mathesius confirmed that finding a mineral too early, before it was properly perfected, was a common concern.[52] Consequently, miners and their pastors, like Johan Gottfried Rhese, prayed that they would not arrive at the minerals too early, before they were fully formed: "Let us come neither too early nor too late, but rather at the right time, when ore has reached its full power."[53] Miners and their pastors viewed this process of mineral development as fully guided by divine providence. Norris has explained that Mathesius' "profoundly providential attitude" provided mining a "positive perspective" by "glorifying minerals as evidence of God's generosity."[54] In this framework, minerals were taken as divine gifts, while mining was understood as a sacred calling inasmuch as the miners were able to become participants in a divine plan for mineralogical and societal perfection.

Mining and God's Gift Just as Mathesius let mining experience and philosophy shape his interpretation of St. Paul and the Genesis creation narrative, so too his understanding of mining influenced his interpretation of the Reformation and the Gospel message in human time. Just as undeveloped minerals sat in the earth, being perfected by time and heat and thus needed to be discovered only after they had been perfected, so also, he argued, the Gospel message had been proclaimed and then, after the time of the apostles, lay in wait, being perfected until mined by the Reformers and brought again to the light of day. For Mathesius, the correspondence of the perfection of minerals evidenced in the Saxony mining boom and the perfection of the Gospel message in the Reformation was not happenstance; their simultaneity revealed a providential plan. Both the mining boom and the Protestant movement *together* served as evidence to Mathesius that he was living in a time when God's influence was strongest, when the divine plan was finally coming to fruition. As Dym suggests, for Mathesius, "the Reformation inaugurated a second period of divine influence, which was most evident in Saxon mining, an arena for numerous arts and inventions."[55] God's providential guidance over the world was evident in the correspondence of the full development of modern mining and the full development of the Gospel in the Reformation message. Clearly, for Mathesius evidence of the significance of the Reformation was not just to be found in the souls of the faithful or in ecclesial, political, social, and economic shifts. The historical gravitas of the Protestant Reformation was also written in minerals and inscribed in the sedimented layers of earth.

Where Mathesius' understanding of the relation between mining and divine providence merged Christian expectations for the fulfillment of God's plan for creation with ancient Aristotelian associations of heat and perfection, these conclusions assumed an underlying theology of divine gift. Again, timing was key. If minerals could easily be discovered over- or under-ripened, their discovery at just the right time emerged more as divine gift than chance, hard work, or correct knowledge. The fact that such enormous quantities of them were being found at Mathesius' time served as further evidence of God's gracious gifts to humanity and shepherding care of the movement that had rediscovered God's burried Gospel message in its most pure form.

Even though Agricola, as a Roman Catholic, would not have subscribed to Mathesius' sense of providential timing around the Reformation, there was a theology of divine gift at work in his mining philosophy as well. Early on, around 1530, he had become a major investor in the endeavor of a Joachimsthal "poor miner." That poor miner eventually became so successful that Agricola and his family were able to mainly live off this investment for the rest of their lives. Indeed, Agricola credited the successful investment with allowing him the time and resources to continue writing and publishing on mining. In *De Veteribus Novis Metallis*, published prior to *De Re Metallica*, Agricola praises the goodness of God for giving such gifts of wealth from this mine. Fittingly, the name given to the mine—as was the custom, in a ritual likened to a baptism—was *Gottesgabe*, God's gift.[56]

Interestingly, therefore, with Agricola, even more than Mathesius, we see a distinct alignment between the *success of extraction* and an *absence of work* as *evidence of divine gift*. In Agricola's opening argument of *De Re Metallica* for the honorability and morality of mining he argued that mining was not ignoble, but rather a laudable, moral profession since great wealth can result quickly without resorting to immoral methods such as stealing or deception: "For that art, the pursuit of which is unquestionably not impious, nor offensive, nor mean, we may esteem honourable. That this is the nature of the mining profession, inasmuch as it promotes wealth by good and honest methods, we shall show presently."[57] Continuing, he added that quick wealth serves as evidence of the morality and pious nature of the mining vocation: "the miner is able to accumulate great riches in a short time, without using any violence, fraud, or malice."[58] More than associating mining with morality, here he placed a distinctive emphasis on the success of mining as divine gift—evidenced by the ease of little labor or effort. A sure mark of divine approval, for Agricola, was not just the success of mining in the form of wealth, nor that it could be done without recourse to immorality, but that it can be done with *ease*: "[W]ho . . . will hate the man who gains wealth as it were from heaven?"[59] "Certainly," he continued, "though it is but one of ten important and excellent methods of acquiring wealth in an honorable way, a careful and diligent man can attain this result in *no easier* way than by mining."[60] In this stunningly early articulation of prosperity gospel from a Roman Catholic surrounded by Protestants in the midst of the Reformation upheaval, wealth—particularly wealth that comes with little work—becomes a sure sign of divine blessing. From these early moments of capitalism where a Protestant work ethic linking effort and divine blessing will eventually be affirmed, a seed of disruption between any pure alliance between labor and divine providence is also planted in extractive capitalism.

Since the modern valuation of the free gift to the exclusion of economy or exchange is widely attributed to theological shifts in the doctrine of grace during the Protestant Reformation, theologically, one would expect Mathesius' more ancient Stoic and Aristotelian providential and developmentalist views of a Roman Catholic. Conversely, one would expect Agricola's association of divine providence with a divine gift to the exclusion of human works of a Protestant. This curious reversal requires further investigation as it seems to suggest that influences on doctrinal shifts during this time were broader than the theologies that divided Protestants and Catholics—that theological shifts in gift concepts and ideals might have been inspired by resonance with their environmental/economic contexts and not just by theological debates. Recall how fleeting the chances of finding minerals must have seemed—one needed to not just dig in the right places, but also arrive precisely on time to discover the fully perfected minerals. While some miners could work hard for years and never strike it rich, others with a comparatively minimal effort and not nearly the same work investment, could gain considerable wealth in a short amount of time. Word of such experiences could easily have unhinged a providential logic aligning work and reward, interrupting it with an ideal of divine will seemingly arbitrarily granting grace apart from any exchange of work investment. If this was not the case yet in sixteenth-century German mining, as we will see, it certainly became the case in nineteenth-century American mineral and energy extraction.

Energy's Gift Economy

In the nineteenth-century-Euro-American context, the gift, exclusive of exchange, took on new and unprecedented resonance with the emergence of modern energy science. While theological and philosophical debates about the gift have consistently acknowledged the way gift ideals travel between religious and economic spheres, these debates have, by and large, not incorporated energy. Economist Philip Mirowski has already made clear the imbrications of economic ideals in energy science—and conversely the influence of energy science on economic policy. Considering the value both sciences place on neutrality and hard objectivity, he notes that when it comes to energy the "history of physics and the history of economics are so intimately connected that it might be considered scandalous."[61] The infusion of economics into energy science is especially evident in the case of William Thomson (Lord Kelvin).[62] At times throughout his career, historians Crosbie Smith and M. Norton Wise explain, Thomson was criticized by his peers for allowing commercial pursuits to "contaminate" his science. By contrast, in *Energy and Empire*, the duo suggests that it wasn't just that Thomson let commercial interests at times influence his science, but that his entire project focused on promoting a modern science of energy was from the start fully immersed in commercial, industrial, and imperial pursuits. In short, the scientific, commercial, industrial, and imperial concerns were not incidental, but "essential to one another."[63]

In addition to the imbrications of economic and energy science during this time, and particularly in the context of Scottish Presbyterianism, a distinctly Protestant emphasis on the free gift became incorporated into the economies of nature employed by some of the leading scientists of the thermodynamic revolution. Incorporating the free gift into nature-energy economies had a particularly potent effect on perceptions around energy extraction. With the influence of the free gift paired with the threat of waste in modern energy, we see a shift from a more passive *sanctification* of extraction characteristic of Agricola's and Mathesius' writings to a moral and cosmological *imperative* to extract emerging in modern energy science.

Energy and the Free Gift Recall that for Edinburgh Scottish Evangelical Presbyterian energy scientists the first law of thermodynamics was seen as scientific verification that creation owed its genesis and sustenance to an omnipotent and omnipresent divine force, while the second law seemed to also confirm that this good creation was fallen and so subject to universal corruption—the kind that required divine redemption.[64] According to Smith, as interpreted by these evangelical energy scientists, the new energy principles "fitted perfectly a Presbyterian economy of nature."[65]

This Presbyterian economy of nature fully reflected the economy of the free gift. Just as the Protestant doctrine of grace emphasized a clear distinction between God's active agency and human receptivity, so too, energy was interpreted by Thomson and others as a sovereign divine gift such that no return gift could be possible or proper. Since humans could only receive from the divine and not reciprocate, "they can only draw upon those divinely filled storehouses of nature." Smith continues, summarizing the Scottish evangelical Chalmers, "Man was in no position to enter into a gift-exchange with the Almighty, still less to enter into some form of trading relationship akin to that of the sale of indulgences."[66] Tait and Rankine also articulate these views, while Maxwell, who started out as Thomson's lab assistant, puts it succinctly in terms of a divine gift economy. Though his theological influences were more Anglican than Thomson's evangelicalism, his conclusions about energy share the same theological framing. In a letter to his wife, Maxwell emphasizes the "free gift" nature of God's grace according to the Gospel, contrasted with "certain Judaic Practices" and the worldly exchange economies of "labour and wages."[67] While the world worked according to such exchanges, God granted free gifts such as light, air, water, and energy. Since God has given such gifts,

> so we ought to use the world and our bodies as means toward the knowledge of him, and stretch always as far as our state will permit toward Him . . . the fruit of the spirit comes when, like good trees we stretch our best affects upwards till we see the sun, and breathe the air and drink the rain, and receive all free gifts.[68]

Since a gift of a sovereign divine cannot be reciprocated, the only proper response to a divine gift—as in grace, so with energy—is its proper, responsible use in service of humanity.[69]

Yet, clearly the gift of energy was not just given and then lying in wait. According to the second law of thermodynamics, it was slipping away at every moment. Entropy injected a clear sense of urgency into creation's evident need for redemption: each and every day, with every passing moment, heat, energy, and life itself were being lost to waste. As Cara Daggett explains, building on the work of Smith, entropy was interpreted as indicating that "the energy of the Earth, and perhaps the solar system and even the wider cosmos, was running down, and this meant that time was running down too."[70] Such news of impending heat death contributed to "eschatological anxiety."[71] With energy being lost to waste at every moment, evangelical energy scientists felt a strong moral compulsion to develop ways to improve the efficiency of machines and industries. The stakes were not only on the scale of national economies or civilizations. Since all creation was subject to entropy, its force, cosmic in scope, was felt locally at the level of inefficient machines. Energy needed to be grasped and put to work before it dissipated.

More than an option or opportunity, in Protestant thought, humans had an *obligation* to accept the divine gift and not let it go to waste. As in the frequently referenced Parable of the Talents, gracious gifts of God were not to be hoarded, left buried in the earth.[72] As Smith suggests, summarizing Chalmers, "to refuse divine gifts is to remain a lost and fallen soul, condemned to sin, idleness, and poverty."[73]

Where leaving a gift unaccepted was a sin, so was an attempt to return the divine gift. Any attempt to return a divine gift sank the human further into the sin of self-aggrandizement and pride. The only proper response was to not let it go to waste and thus use it for the betterment of humanity rather than attempting a return gift. This dual dynamic—the imperative to (1) accept the gift and to (2) not return it but put it to use for the service of humanity led to a dynamic Smith and Wise refer to as an "ethos of work and waste." In terms of energy this resulted in a "moral imperative to milk the most out of whatever energy they could by maximizing work and minimizing waste."[74] If energy was a divine gift with redemptive potential that was quickly slipping away, the only theologically and morally responsible thing to do was use it to hold heat death at bay. The only way to do that was to put it to work as efficiently as possible. Consequently, from the perspective of these evangelical energy scientists, humans had "a duty to employ engines for the benefit of mankind.... Failure properly to direct and harness those gifts of energy was therefore only a waste, and in that sense a sin of 'dissipation.'"[75] To let it slip away would mean humans would have failed to respond properly with gratitude and good sense to God's gracious gifts. Indeed, with energy as with salvation, "once the gift of grace had been accepted, man had a moral duty to direct, and not waste, the natural gifts."[76]

From this perspective we can note key continuities and important differences from the framework of minerals as gift constructed by Agricola and Mathesius. For Agricola, Mathesius, and the Scottish energy scientists, the concept of free gift is associated with aspects of the created world like minerals or energy. For each, a divinely driven purpose brings some element of timeliness to their discovery and extraction. However, with the case of modern energy science, the timing had a stronger sense of urgency. Unlike the organic interpretation of minerals which were in a constant state of growth, decay, and regrowth, the gift of energy was framed within the—now seemingly scientifically verified—sense that post-Fall humans and all creation existed in a state of corruption, tending toward heat death with energy being lost to waste every minute.

This moral imperative to preserve God's gift of energy from going unused—being "wasted"—is a key turning point in the ethos of modern extraction. While Agricola affirmed that gifts are intended by God to be put to work, there was not a corresponding sense of waste. Agricola and Mathesius' sanctification of extraction as human participation in God's unfolding providential plans for creation introduced a positive reinforcement for mineral extraction, but there was not yet a sense of impending punishment if one did not extract. For the later Scottish energy scientists, not using God's gift emerged as the equivalent of rejecting it. The concern about waste, about not properly using limited human freedom to employ God's gifts in service of fending off an apocalyptic heat death, added a new imperative to extraction. For Agricola and Mathesius, mineral extraction was painted merely as a divinely blessed opportunity that may be taken up. By contrast, the geotheology of work and waste added a sense that energy was not only a gift to be used but it was a sin if it was *not* used.

As Cara Daggett emphasizes, the moral and theological weight given to the ethos of work and waste became integrated into the modern science of energy and subsequently infused the Euro-American desire for, and use of, fossil fuels. Yet, while Daggett focuses on delinking the work ethic from energy concepts, the dynamics of the free gift are also clearly functioning in the early ways modern energy science was conceptualized and, as we will see, continue to infuse the ethics of oil-extraction endeavors.

Evangelicalism and the Divine Gift of Oil

From Titusville, Pennsylvania, in 1859, to Texas' 1901 Spindletop gusher, to California's late-nineteenth-century oil rush, narratives of oil discovery consistently communicated the providential timing of oil. In the United States' early oil narratives, we see a continuation of the language and Protestant natural economy of free gift, applied not just to energy but now, also to oil. Protestant Pastor to the Titusville region, Rev. S. J. Eaton clearly theologized oil, seeing in it providential timing not only for divine redemption, but also for divine omnipotence. With the layman and evangelical initiator of the fundamentalist movement Lyman Stewart, we find evidence of oil extraction being infused with the free gift of divine grace, thus profoundly disrupting a Protestant work ethic as it is traditionally analyzed. For these Protestant oil prophets, petroleum emerged as another Reformation moment—this time in US American capitalism rather than the Roman Catholic Church. Led onward by Reformation zeal reminiscent of Luther's steadfast vision, oil here effected a purification of capitalism from works righteousness to reveal full divine dependence.

Omnipotence and Oil As seeds planted at the first moments of creation, Mathesius' minerals came to full fruition at their divinely appointed time with a corresponding Gospel message. Such was also the case with oil for Presbyterian pastor, Rev. S. J. Eaton of Venango County. Eaton had served a long career in this area encompassing Titusville, PA. In 1866, a mere seven years after the first discovery of oil in his county, he published a book, *Petroleum*, wherein he recorded a history of his county and reflected on the changes oil had brought. *Petroleum* narrated this history as a story of divine revelation, a momentous occasion in the history of creation similar to the theological weight of the Reformation.

Eaton began by articulating oil in the scope of a creation narrative, writing,

> Before man was created, the great store-house in the earth's bosom was filled with its minerals, and as the centuries rolled by, in their slow and solemn march, these treasures were gradually brought to light. Not at once did the earth disclose her mighty resources; but just as man needed them, and as they should tend to his own best interests, and the glory of the great Giver.[77]

Once again we see a Stoic-influenced Christian logic functioning in this extraction theology: God plants seeds (*logoi, seminales*) of resources within the earth to meet human needs and just as they are needed they are providentially brought to full fruition, revealed to humanity to meet their needs and to demonstrate the beneficence of God.[78] Eaton is explicit about the timing in Pennsylvania:

> it was no mere accidental circumstance that this vegetable deposit was changed to coal and oil, nor was it a merely fortuitous event that in these last years these stores of wealth were brought to light. It was the time appointmed in the eternal counsels for their appearance. It was the fulfillment of the word of life, that earth should supply abundantly the wants of all the creatures moving upon its surface.[79]

For Venango County and, indeed, the entire United States, oil had been sitting, lying in wait since the beginnings of creation, coming to light only at the ordained time to redeem human need.

Eaton paints a desperate, even hopeless, portrait of his county before oil: "The iron business had ceased," the arrival of the steamship and railroad proved disappointments, the lumber industry "that nurtured and strengthened all the northern portion of the county began to decline."[80] In short, "hope was just about ready to die out in the hearts of the people," when they faced the "great frost of June 5, 1859" effecting "ruin and desolation" for the entire county.[81] Venango County was not the only place suffering: indeed, the entire nation, headed toward Civil War, seemed to be crying out for deliverance.

Shaped by Eaton's pen, oil's discovery in the midst of such widespread and urgent need resulted in a new Reformation moment, a time guided by providence when something new was being disclosed. Echoing Mathesius, once again the message revealed is simultaneous with the material resource unveiled. Indeed, the two were fully intertwined: the message is performed in the material, the material communicates the message. In Venango county, something new was struggling to emerge, a new "grand idea struggling into the light."[82] Oilmen like Colonel Edwin Drake emerged as providentially guided Reformation men—not unlike Luther they were single-mindedly possessed by truth, persevering to bring it forth even in the face of skepticism and scorn. According to Eaton,

> there was a new era just on the threshold, and the whole rested with one earnest, resolute heart. There was the pressure of the one great thought, that by some mysterious power had got possession of the man's heart, urging him forward, and likewise on the other hand there was the dread of failure, the fear of ridicule—the shadow that falls so heavily upon men's hearts from time to time, when in pursuit of some uncertain object. . . . It reminds us of grand old Martin Luther at the Diet of Worms, crying out, "Here I stand. I cannot do otherwise. God help me. Amen!" So all grand ideas are wrought out, and all grand purposes carried forward under the mysterious guidance of a power, that seems invincible in its operations.[83]

It wasn't just the courage, self-assurance, independent-mindedness, faith, and boldness of men that made the discovery of oil in Titusville a new Reformation moment. For both—Reformation era and petro-Reformers—the thing that possessed them, urging them forward, was grace. In spite of the courageous and tenacious role played by these singular humans, the gift of oil was not due to human efforts, labor, or wisdom:

> Neither human foresight, nor strong muscle, nor golden coins, nor the perfection of machinery can claim the credit of this vast wealth. Wisdom and power placed it in the rock, and neither man's reason, nor wisdom, nor cunning could reach it until the appointed time had arrived. If it is given freely, with little labor, the grounds of gratitude are all the stronger that should influence the hearts of the recipients of this rich bounty.[84]

Here oil emerged as divinely given: a sovereign gift, exclusive of exchange, void of human wisdom and works—"freely given, with little labor." Just as with nineteenth-century energy, oil here worked according to a Protestant economy: rejecting a return gift, the only proper human response was acceptance, gratitude, worship toward God, and a "liberal spirit" of generosity with the gift they are merely stewards of.[85]

Where God is sovereign, lacking nothing and needing no reciprocal exchange from creation, divine omnipotence is secured. Yet, in spite of the rigorously defended Protestant divide between creator and creaturely agencies, divine omnipotence does bleed into oil in Eaton's theology. Toward the end of the text, Eaton reflected on questions—already emerging *seven years* in—regarding the limits of oil: Are we extracting too much, too fast? Will it last forever? Eaton forthrightly replied: we can't know for certain about the limits of oil, but we can draw conclusions from "the structure of the rocks in our own region and the general operations of Providence."[86] Eaton called on the wisdom of science, rocks, and divinity together. Based on this wisdom the calculation is sure, the reply resolute: "There is no limit, surely, to Omnipotence. And if we take the mode of his operation, as we see it carried forward on the earth's surface, as a criterion by which to judge, we shall be strengthened in the belief that the same course of production and supply is carried out in the regions below."[87] The answer to the question of the limits of oil was the same as the answer to the limits of God: the gift of oil will sustain as long as God sustains. Since God's power, evident in the world above the ground was unbounded, so oil's supply under the earth is "exhaustless."[88]

For Eaton, oil served as witness, preaching in the style of the Reformers, proclaiming its "grand idea struggling into light" to all the world. "A new lesson has been taught the world," Eaton wrote, "that God's treasures are inexhaustible, and that his hand can never be shortened."[89] Eaton had "no doubt" "that the supply of petroleum will be kept up while there is need of artificial light to carry on the operations of life."[90] Eaton clearly proclaimed: to trust in God's gracious providence is to trust in unlimited oil. While humans have need of oil, God's beneficence and omnipotence will ensure their needs are fulfilled.

In this new Luther-style "grand idea" of God's inexhaustible treasures proclaimed uniquely and distinctly by oil, beliefs in divine providence, omnipotence, and unlimited oil resonate with one another. As Eaton articulated it, unlimited oil and divine power become so inextricably linked that to question one is to question the other—to lose faith in oil implies loss of faith in God; questioning the limits of oil entails questioning the limits of divine power. He writes, "The great Benefactor would teach us that however strained we may be, he is never confined, that his resources are unlimited, that for every emergency in our history there is provision made, and that our time of need is but the beginning of his overflowing bounty."[91] Apparently, oil, like grace, is nothing if not excessive. While we humans are "often disposed to distrust Providence" there is no ground to question whether God can or will supply for human need. Consequently, one can place the same kind of trust in the unlimited supply of oil—"to go upon any other supposition would be to suppose that the course of nature, and the operations of Providence would be changed, and God's wisdom and power cease to be adequate to the supply of the wants of his creatures."[92] In Eaton's petro-theology, late medieval, masculinist, voluntarist ideals of unchecked and unlimited power overflow from divinity into oil. The theological mechanism lubricating this transfer was grace, conceptualized as a free, unilateral, unworked-for gift.

Oil, Grace, and Work This sense of oil as unmerited gift, even to the point of effecting a disruption in what was, by the nineteenth century, a well-established Protestant work ethic, emerged as a key theme for Eaton's fellow Pennsylvanian, Lyman Stewart. In many ways Eaton's theological approach to oil was shared by Stewart. Yet, influenced by dispensational premillennialism, Stewart took the portrayal of oil as divine gift one step further, allowing oil to infuse his capitalist spirit with a new, purifying embrace of the free gift.[93] The uncertainties of oil extraction broadly enhanced the sense of the necessity of chance and risk in extractive capitalism, effectively disrupting the logical and moral link between work and consumption that the Protestant work ethic advanced.

Lyman Stewart grew up in Pennsylvania, observing firsthand, as Eaton did, the profound changes that oil brought to his home context. He and his family members made several attempts to tap oil, finding some limited success. Whatever success he could find in Pennsylvania, though, brought him within the sphere of Rockefeller's refinery monopoly. Consequently, he eventually left Pennsylvania for California to move out from under Rockefeller's thumb. This was an extremely risky move. Experts and popular opinion at the time agreed that no significant oil would be found west of the Mississippi. Driven by a Reformer's singular vision, though, Stewart was not swayed and soon he and his California Union Oil company had more oil on their hands than they could sell. Ever the entrepreneur, Stewart refused to settle for the existing market and set to work creating new desires for oil: he played an instrumental role in creating and promoting oil-based asphalt and the petro-burning locomotive.[94]

Raised in a strong and conservative Presbyterianism, Stewart attended the 1894 Niagara Bible Conference where he came under the influence of dispensational premillennialism. As religion scholar B. M. Pietsch notes, "Stewart was immediately entranced by the idea of hidden truth."[95] Suddenly biblical interpretation found a profound resonance with Stewart's geological pursuits. Dispensationalism gave Stewart the framework to see that there were hidden treasures in the Bible as well as in the earth—and, since they were placed there by God for the good of humanity, God gave keys for uncovering both. Though the methodologies of reading a geological landscape and reading a biblical text in hopes of uncovering hidden truths and treasures were different, as Pietsch explains, "seeking hidden oil" and "hidden truth" "created the same emotional experience."[96] There is no evidence Stewart was aware of or had read about early Protestant mining and the extractive theologics of Reformers like Mathesius. He didn't need to. The basic conceptual framework that allowed for resonance of affect between uncovering hidden signs of the Bible and of the earth remained the same: the narrative of God's providential and sustaining care for creation through resource development corresponded to the revelation of the Gospel and thus both were received as unmerited gift.

With the Scottish energy scientists, Stewart shared a sense of urgency behind the call to make good use of divine gifts and not let them go to waste. Within the scope of a dispensationalist fixation on providential timing, both Stewart's biblical interpretation and his oil excavation encouraged a sense that there was no time to tarry. Living in the end times when unsaved souls were at stake required immediate action—as did the competitive oil market. For Stewart, the two—saving souls and extracting oil—served one another on a practical level as well as the symbolic. Lyman consistently framed oil extraction as a divinely given tool for the spread of the Gospel and that is mainly how Lyman spent his oil profits. In response to Rockefeller's postmillennial style of Protestantism which inspired the Standard Oil magnate to found the University of Chicago and their divinity program, Stewart founded the Bible Institute of Los Angeles, now BIOLA University, to combat what he saw as the secularizing threats of Rockefeller's more liberal version of Protestantism.[97] Yet, Stewart's most broadly influential contribution was to initiate and fund the pamphlet series *The Fundamentals,* credited with inspiring the now worldwide fundamentalist movement.

While the example of Agricola and Mathesius makes evident that other resources and industries beside oil have historically been associated with Godly blessing, the particularities of oil made it especially disruptive for a traditional Protestant work ethic.[98] In the Victorian era, capitalism had been infused with an ethos of rationalism and restraint. Coal extraction functioned well within this ethos: its slow methodical extraction required a stable march of time over the long haul. Like railroads, coal respected social hierarchies in that it required expensive machinery, and thus deep sources of capital and a stream of replaceable workers.[99]

According to Marx and Weber, wealth resulted from an exploitation and excess of human labor (Marx) as well as a restrained rationalism and asceticism (Weber). Gold, though a mining endeavor like coal, was more disruptive of established class hierarchies and a work ethic. The US gold rush, predating the oil rush by just a couple of decades, disrupted class divisions, a work ethic, and rationality. As environmental historian Paul Sabin reports, "The gold rush threatened to disrupt the social order by rewarding the lucky rather than the hardworking, and by propelling lower-class miners into wealth and power."[100] Discoveries were unpredictable and the small amount of capital needed upfront to start panning or mining meant the opportunity to try one's luck was less limited by social class and wealth. A relative newcomer who had invested only a small amount of capital, time, and labor might be just as likely to strike gold as someone who had already invested years of time and labor.

Early oil shared many of gold's characteristics. Like gold, early oil was unpredictable, with low upfront costs. Rather than confirming a strong work ethic, it profoundly disrupted it: just as with gold, someone could strike it rich on the first try with very little effort or investment while the unlucky could work and wait for years and never strike it rich. But as Pietsch and Sabin emphasize, in the context of divinely blessed industries and even in comparison to gold, oil stood out.[101] While striking it rich on gold could be associated more with chance than hard work or a long-term commitment, as with coal, theories of where to look for it and how to extract it were already well established. Oil was a relative newcomer with no established tradition for how to discover it. In this sense, oil was still much of a mystery and elicited stronger correlations with luck—or divine grace. With no established traditions to aid in its discovery, as we will see in the next chapter, many oilmen turned to religion and spirituality to aid their discoveries.

Oil's sheer abundance was also a distinguishing factor. With gold one might be lucky enough to find a large nugget or creek bed riddled with small nuggets, but one's ability to contain the gold discovered was never overwhelmed. By contrast, as Pietsch explains, "once struck, oil would often geyser from the earth, leading to the problem of not how to extract it but how to contain it."[102] Such overflowing, overwhelming wealth that could defy worldly expectation clearly resonated with the excesses of omnipotent divine grace. These unique factors then—oil's unpredictability, immediacy, super abundance, and mysterious nature—resonated to an unprecedented extent with a sense of divine blessing and agency at play.

These characteristics of oil directly impacted what several scholars have called the re-enchantment of capitalism, disrupting its rationality and methodical ascetic investment logics.[103] Pietsch emphasizes that Stewart's mode of "oil wildcatting defied the traditional Protestant-capitalist alliance that linked hard work and thrifty living to material success."[104] The rationalism of significant capital and labor investment over a long period of time resulting in wealth was simply not compatible with oil extraction. With the hidden riches of oil, one needed to take risks, move quickly, expect the unexpected, and spend extravagant wealth from an oil boom before it disappeared in a bust cycle. Rather than hard work and knowledge, early oil discovery required luck, or divine blessing.

From the perspective of many evangelical Protestants like Stewart, always theologically wary of according value to works, oil offered to do for nineteenth-century capitalism what the Reformers had done for a medieval Christianity become overly dependent on exchange logic: oil made way for a theological purification of economic exchange once again. With oil, divine action was not seen as mediated through any human exchange or hierarchy of human authority, but was granted immediately to the human apart from their labor or worthiness. Just as Ockham had rendered habitual grace unnecessary in the face of divine omnipotence, so also oil's uncontained power rendered habit, effort, labor, or work toward divinely sanctioned blessing superfluous. While the Protestant ethic had sanctified labor with the promise of worldly wealth as a sign of divine approbation, "for many early oil wildcatters," by contrast, wealth did not come from hard work, but "straight from God."[105] With oil, the rationalism of the Protestant work ethic was replaced once again with sovereign divine agency—merit and work once again displaced by grace.

Gratia et labora

Medieval Benedictine monks lived their lives ordered by *ora et labora*, their daily rhythms of work seen as ways to enhance their prayer life—and conversely, contemplation enhancing work. In a modern, post-Reformation context, extractive petro-capitalism orders life according to a dualistic and contradictory rhythm of *gratia et labora*. Whether one is on the underside of global capitalism, disenfranchised from its modes of production, or among those still ostensibly benefiting from global capitalism but shifting companies (let alone careers) several times in a lifetime, or on the powerful side of capitalism where control is gained not by seizing the means of material production, but by garnering wealth through risk, chance, and speculation, the rational connection between work and reward upheld by a work ethos is both reinforced and profoundly disrupted in twenty-first-century capitalism. Though defined in modernity as mutually exclusive with exchange or work, the logic of the free gift has been historically incorporated into the logic and desires of extractive capitalist exchange. Every moment of life in extractive petro-capitalism is ordered and infused with either the drive to fulfill one's meaning and value through work, or embrace an ethos of freedom from work through the free gifts of extractive- and petro-capitalism. These drives are admittedly contradictory, ironic, and irrational, but as Weber noted already a century ago, this has been the experience of capitalism nearly from its beginnings.

While capitalism emerged as a central feature of the "disenchantment" of the world, extractive capitalism's reliance on divine providence, power, and grace has rendered it profoundly enchanted. Just as Jason Storm (see Introduction) has sought to demonstrate that Europe and the United States have not been exceptions to the "primitive" or "uncivilized" tendency toward enchantment, similarly this history of divine gift entangled with extractive capitalism demonstrates a sense of enchanted capitalism at the heart of the "disenchanted" world. Others, too, have noted the enchantments of petro even into the twenty-first century: Anna Tsing has analyzed the ways that current geological analyses of oil are framed as a kind of conjuring,[106] and Gisa Weszkalnys has focused on the ways that geological analyses of the potential for oil even in the twenty-first century still rely heavily on speculation and fantasy. Weszkalnys writes, "since its inception, petroleum exploration has combined the bold assessments of oilmen with the speculative fantasies of urban financiers and the hypothetical inferences of a new breed of geoscientists in what an oil executive of the time called 'the gamble of drilling for oil.'"[107] Framing extractive capitalism within a modern secularizing work/grace dichotomy as I have done here demonstrates that Stewart's enchanted capitalism disruptions rely on a theology of divine omnipotence and providential guidance of the Gospel message and corresponding gifts of creation that were articulated as far back as the Reformation era Saxony mining boom. For Agricola and Mathesius, Thomson and the Scottish energy scientists, Eaton and Stewart, energy extractive activities so central to capitalist endeavors depend not only on a purely rational work ethic, but on their enchanted free-gift-exclusive-of-work disruptions as well.

In the end, it isn't that analyzing capitalism through the locus of work is misplaced. Daggett's proposed decoupling of energy from work and Tanner's proposed decoupling of Christianity from the new work ethic of finance capitalism offer key insights and suggest crucial strategic alliances that should be pursued. Postwork feminist and theological critiques of work remain deeply relevant, but do not adequately account for the profound ironies and contradictions of simultaneously heightened emphases on work and the free gift emphasized particularly in *extractive* capitalism. In Tanner's analysis of Protestantism and twentieth-century finance capitalism, for example, the theologian emphasizes that while still "hard work is made the reason for success," "yet the profit-generating mechanisms of finance-dominated capitalism give little reason to valorize hard work."[108] Tanner here acknowledges the ways finance capitalism profoundly disrupts the very identity-forming power of production that remains her locus of constructive theological work.

When it comes to energy extractive capitalism a de-work response will remain insufficient and incomplete. The dualistic definitions of free gift/anti-work keep holding them together. As Derridean deconstruction has demonstrated, any dualistically defined term only excludes its opposite by referencing it. As long as gift is defined in terms that exclude work, effort, or exchange, it will continue to inadvertently underscore work. As long as a critical locus of work does not also recognize the ways the free gift continues to interrupt the centrality of work in extractive capitalism, the free gift and its economy will go unchallenged.

From the perspective of extractive capitalism, attending to the ways the free gift has already been interrupting the link between work and consumption, countering the evangelical-neoliberal resonance machine will require more than an alliance with the postwork movement. It also requires the disruption of free gift ideals that continue to energize extractive capitalism. Here we might seek a more intersectional-feminist alliance with a post-carbon movement that has already demonstrated its symbolic and political significance: protests like #NoDAPL, the NDN Collective, and Idle No More linking Indigenous rights with a post-carbon future.

Energy, Reciprocity, Responsibility

That work and gift have been defined in oppositional terms in extractive capitalism reflects an underlying problem with basic assumptions about reality that are rooted in settler colonialism. Defining work and gift exclusively makes sense only in a world of isolated individuals and substances—in a world where surface-level changes are undergirded by something solid, stable, and unchanging that is more real/true/divine than the surface. Such divisions between work and gift make no sense in a world of reciprocal relations where what is can only be (alive, real, sacred, valued) in relation. Extraction and modern energy are comprehensible only in a worldview where value, life, energy, and sacredness are found inherently in, above, or under *things*.

This is a problem that relatedly shows up in environmental ethics debates about intrinsic versus instrumental values. Indigenous philosopher and citizen of the Cherokee Nation, Brian Burkhart, analyzes the false division between intrinsic and instrumental value in Western environmental philosophy and ethics.[109] He demonstrates that the basic division between the two is based on the premise, deeply rooted from Plato and Aristotle through modern Western thought, that things have static, inherent, and isolated qualities.[110] Where this is the case, one is left with either value inherently found *in* something (intrinsic, a given—as it were, apart from work) or value made out of the *use* of something (instrumental, according to work). From the perspective of Burhkart's trickster methodology, the choice is a false one. Value and sacrality are not found in or under things, but emerge only in local relationship.[111]

This is the trap modernity, influenced by a Protestant rejection of use or work value within the bounds of a Western substance ontology, falls into. In wanting to contest use or work value, the other option in a substance ontology is to emphasize intrinsic (inherent, freely given) value. From this perspective, the problem in both isn't prioritizing use- or intrinsic-value: it is the basic ontology that makes the choice between them necessary in the first place. The alternative therefore is not to emphasize one over the other, but to shift the basic terms of the debate—and basic assumptions about reality, value, being, and life.

The alternative to the work/gift binary is also the alternative to extraction. As Michi Saagiig Nishnaabeg scholar and Idle No More leader Leanne Betasamosake Simpson writes, "the alternative to extractivism is deep reciprocity. It's respect, it's relationship, it's responsibility, and it's local."[112] From the perspective of a relational reality, value is neither found in things nor according to their work/use. The de-work approach tends toward the humanistic view that value is found in, under, within something or someone apart from work. What it misses is the opportunity to emphasize that value understood as *reciprocal*-gift relation is not something to be uncovered or discovered. It is only ever between, only ever reciprocally expressed. In a relational ontology where value, life, energy, and sacredness are found in relations, extracting—taking some*thing* out of constitutive relations—is unthinkable; value is not to be uncovered, tapped into, or revealed, it emerges only in relation. In such a relational ontology, the free gift that commodifies emerges as incomprehensible, and work loses its power to define identity or give value.

What neither capitalism nor a work/gift dualism can abide is a reciprocal relational ontology. As Lugones and Allen have emphasized, together, nonbinary gender relations, forms and ideals of exchange, and models of human relations to the sacred all shared a basic value of reciprocity and together became untenable for the march of settler colonial-cum-capitalist progress. A feminist de-work alliance with decarbonization movements therefore is on track, but doesn't go far enough. It stays within the gift/labor, work/anti-work dualism and doesn't adequately make the case for the kinds of alliances that could be possible between feminist critiques of extractive energy capitalism and Indigenous scholars/activists calling for a radical reimagining of all relations—gendered and other-than-human.

Grace need not be defined in opposition to work, activity, or effort. Grace can also be an expression of gratitude for the multitude of creaturely and sacred gifts that hold us up and, like gravity, bind us to the earth. Return gifts in the form of responsibility entail rather than exclude grace. Rather than the free gift exclusive of exchange, grace can be experienced at the nexus of a multitude of divine and creaturely gifts. While these gifts may defy economic reductionism in that they are un-purchased, they are not anti-exchange because they are embedded in multiple systems of dependence and reciprocity.[113]

From this perspective we might also start to glimpse an alternative energy that resists extraction—not a free-gift substance buried under the surface, waiting to be "discovered" to do its work, but as constituted through reciprocal exchange that emerges only in local relations. Decoupling work from energy remains incomprehensible from Western modern perspectives that define energy by the ability to do work. As long as a substance ontology undergirding isolated individualism remains, energy will continue to be unthinkable without work. Energy must be remapped, away from not just work, but also substance metaphysics and the isolated individualism characteristic of Western thought as far back as Parmenides. From a perspective of reality constituted only through local relations, though, this alternative energy is not held within, but something that emerges between—in relation.

Notes

1. Portions of this chapter have been published in Rowe, "The Crux of Matter."
2. Early-modern mining historian Tina Asmussen points out that "Notable mining historians such as Johann Kohler and Adolf Laube discovered the 'germs of capitalism' (Kohler 1955) in the Saxon mining industry (Laube 1974)" (Asmussen, "Spirited Metals," 374).
3. #NoDAPL is the hashtag associated with the movements protesting the Dakota Access Pipeline from the Bakken oil fields of North Dakota.
4. Malm, *Fossil Capital*, 11.
5. Ibid., 19.
6. Some recent examples include Tanner, *Christianity and the New Spirit of Capitalism*; Devin Singh, *Divine Currency: The Theological Power of Money in the West* (Stanford: Stanford University Press, 2018); and from an economics perspective, Benjamin M. Friedman, *Religion and the Rise of Capitalism* (New York: Knopf, 2021). These are highly insightful projects on the intersection of religion and capitalism, but they do not address the extractive aspects of capitalism historically or currently functioning.
7. Daggett, *The Birth of Energy*, 133.
8. Ibid., 100.
9. Ibid., 206.
10. See Daggett, "Conclusion: A Post-Work Energy Politics," in *The Birth of Energy*, 187–206, referencing Connolly, "The Evangelical-Capitalist Resonance Machine," 869–86.
11. Kathi Weeks, *The Problem with Work: Feminism, Marxism, Antiwork Politics, and Postwork Imaginaries* (Durham: Duke University Press, 2011), 12.
12. Posadas, "The Refusal of Work," 330–61.
13. Ibid., 356.
14. Tanner, *Christianity and the New Spirit of Capitalism*, 101.
15. This logic is also highlighted and analyzed also in Derrida's *Given Time* where the philosopher laments that in emphasizing gift exchange, Marcel Mauss wrote about everything *but* the gift (Jacques Derrida, *Given Time: Counterfeit Money*, trans. Peggy Kamuf (Chicago: University of Chicago, 1992)).

16 Troels Engberg-Pedersen, "Gift-Giving and Friendship: Seneca and Paul in Romans 1–8 on the Logic of God's Χάρις and Its Human Response," *The Harvard Theological Review* 101 (2008): 15–44 (16).
17 While some feminists have been critical of the dynamics of reciprocal giving implied in the free gift and others have emphasized that the free gift or exchange does not encompass all possible social and economic relations, at times the free gift is valorized by feminist voices and theological perspectives. Robin James and Genevieve Vaughn, for example, lift up the free gift as resistant to exchange and an alternative to economies of growth and accumulation which men usually control and are often characterized by competition. See Robin James' definition of feminist care as free gift—as resistance to neoliberal economics (*Resilience and Melancholy: Pop Music, Feminism, Neoliberalism* (Winchester: Zero Books, 2015), 174).
18 See Mary Douglas' foreword to Marcel Mauss, *The Gift: The Form and Reason for Exchange in Archaic Societies*, trans. W. D. Halls (New York: W. W. Norton, 1990). While Mauss emphasized the gift as binding for society, Claude Levi-Strauss took up Marcel Mauss' gift theory, but emphasized that the key phenomenon binding society together was not the gift in particular, but exchange.
19 Mauss, *The Gift*, 46.
20 "What they exchange is not solely property and wealth, movable and immovable goods, and things economically useful. In particular such exchanges are acts of politeness: banquets, rituals, military service, women, children, dances, festivals, and fairs, in which economic transaction is only one element, and in which the passing of wealth is only one feature of a much more general and enduring contract" (Ibid., 5). Milbank summarizes: "gift-giving is a mode (the mode, in fact) of social being" (John Milbank, *Being Reconciled: Ontology and Pardon* (New York: Routledge, 2003), 156).
21 For examples of gift theory applied to debates about capitalism and Protestantism, see John Milbank, "Can a Gift Be Given?: Prolegomena to a Future Trinitarian Metaphysic," *Modern Theology* 11 (1995): 119–61; Marion Grau, *Of Divine Economy: Refinancing Redemption* (London: T&T Clark, 2004); and Kathryn Tanner, *Economy of Grace: Christian Theologies and Social Justice* (Minneapolis: Augsburg Fortress, 2005).
22 See, for example, Anne Primavesi, *Gaia's Gift: Earth, Ourselves and God after Copernicus* (New York: Routledge, 2004); Mark Manolopoulos, *If Creation is a Gift* (New York: State University of NY Press, 2009); and Schwerin Rowe, *Toward a Better Worldliness*.
23 Christopher Bracken, *The Potlatch Papers: A Colonial Case History* (Chicago: University of Chicago Press, 1997).
24 Robin Wall Kimmerer, *Braiding Sweetgrass: Indigenous Wisdom, Scientific Knowledge, and the Teachings of Plants* (Minneapolis: Milkweed Editions, 2013), 25.
25 Ibid., 28.
26 Ibid., 27–8.
27 Lugones, "Heterosexualism and the Colonial/Modern Gender System," 186–209 (199), citing Paula Gunn Allen, *The Sacred Hoop: Recovering the Feminine in American Indian Traditions*, 18.
28 See John Milbank: "modern purism about the gift which renders it unilateral is in part the child of one theological strand in thinking about agape which has sought to be over-rigorous in a self-defeating fashion," ("Can a Gift Be Given?" 132). Milbank here refers to Protestant Anders Nygren's *Eros and Agape* which associates

Christian love with agape as self-giving, self-sacrificing, not expecting reciprocation, contrasted with eros which is characterized by desire and seeking reciprocity and exchange. See also, Catherine Keller and Stephen Moore, "Derridapocalypse," in *Derrida and Religion: Other Testaments*, ed. Yvonne Sherwood and Kevin Hart (New York: Routledge, 2005), 189–208.

29 Tanner argues in *Economy of Grace* that grace offers a "radical alternative to the present [capitalist] system" (x). Though Tanner resists "free grace," she emphasizes the crucial importance of grace—particularly as articulated in the Protestant tradition as a gift unconditioned, unmerited, and exclusive of exchange—as an important counter to work value granted capitalist subjects. Berndt Hamm, on the other hand, argues that the uniqueness of Protestant grace is fundamentally defined by its status as free gift exclusive of exchange, "Martin Luther's Revolutionary Theology of Pure Gift without Reciprocation," trans. Timothy J. Wengert, *Lutheran Quarterly* 29 (2015): 125–61.

30 Martin Luther, "Sermon on Two Kinds of Righteousness (1519)," in *The Annotated Luther, Vol. 2: Word and Faith*, ed. Kirsi Stjerna, trans. Else Marie Wiberg Pedersen (Minneapolis: Fortress Press, 2015), 9–24.

31 Gillespie, *The Theological Origins of Modernity*, 22.

32 For more on the influence of nominalism on the Reformers, see Gillespie, "Luther and the Storm of Faith," in *The Theological Origins of Modernity*; Heiko Oberman, *Luther: Man Between God and the Devil* (New Haven: Yale University Press, 1989); and Steven Ozment, *The Age of Reform, 1250–1550: An Intellectual and Religious History of Late Medieval and Reformation Europe* (New Haven: Yale University Press, 1980).

The reading of Luther's grace as free gift exclusive of exchange, it should be noted, is characteristic of predominant *German* interpretations of Luther. This interpretation has been contested most persuasively by the *Finnish Interpretation* of Luther which reads Luther as encompassing a realist/ontological aspect of divine presence in grace as well as an idealization of reciprocal rather than free gift. For more on the debate of whether Luther's grace is accurately characterized by a separative, free gift or a gift exchange that also incorporates the presence of Christ, resulting in an ontological union between Christ and the sinner, see Bo Kristian Holm, "The Gift in Martin Luther's Theology," *Oxford Research Encyclopedia of Religion*, March 29, 2017. Available online: https://oxfordre.com/religion/view/10.1093/acrefore/9780199340378.001.0001/acrefore-9780199340378-e-356 (accessed August 25, 2021). See also Simo Peura's essay, "Christ as Favor and Gift: The Challenge of Luther's Understanding of Justification," and other essays in Carl E. Braaten and Robert W. Jenson, *Union with Christ: The New Finnish Interpretation of Luther* (Grand Rapids: Eerdmans, 1998) that argue against the "free gift" interpretation of grace.

Similar reinterpretations of Calvin's concept of gift, traditionally also interpreted as unreciprocal and "free," have also been suggested. See, for example, J. Todd Billings, "John Milbank's Theology of the 'Gift' and Calvin's Theology of Grace: A Critical Comparison," *Modern Theology* 21 (2005): 87–105.

33 See *De Trinitate*, especially Book V.

34 Jaroslav Pelikan, *The Christian Tradition: A History of Development of Doctrine, Book 1: The Emergence of the Catholic Tradition (100–600)* (Chicago: University of Chicago Press, 1971), 294.

35 Alister McGrath, *Christian Theology: An Introduction*, 6th ed (New York: John Wiley and Sons, 2016), 335.

36 See note 27 above.
37 Though the main focus of this chapter will be on work/free-gift dynamics in extractive capitalism, it should be noted that extensive scholarship on women and the gift has been produced. Morny Joy's edited collection, *Women and the Gift*, in particular, both critically analyzes the ways women and femininity have been portrayed or overlooked in gift discourses. See Morny Joy (ed.), *Women and the Gift: Beyond the Given and All-Giving* (Indianapolis: Indiana University Press, 2013) for more on this theme of women as "the given" and as self-denying, "all giving" (6).
38 See also portions of this chapter published in Rowe, "The Crux of the Matter."
39 Anthropologist Jack Weatherford and Ignacio Gonzalez Casanovas, experts on Potosí, emphasize the crucial importance of Potosí silver in providing the foundation for the new globalized capitalist economy: exchangeable coins. Weatherford suggests that Potosí supplied as much as 80 percent of the global silver for coinage. See Weatherford, *Indian Givers: How the Indians of the Americas Transformed the World* (New York: Three Rivers Press, 1988) and Casanovas, in Patrick Greenfield's "Story of Cities #6: How Silver Turned Potosí into 'the First City of Capitalism.'" Available online: https://www.theguardian.com/cities/2016/mar/21/story-of-cities-6-potosi-bolivia-peru-inca-first-city-capitalism (accessed June 21, 2021).
40 Notable exceptions that this chapter will rely on include the work of Tina Asmussen, John A. Norris, and Warren Dym.
41 John A. Norris, "The Providence of Mineral Generation in the Sermons of Johann Mathesius (1504–1565)," in *Geology and Religion: A History of Harmony and Hostility*, ed. M. Kölbl-Ebert (London: The Geological Society, 2009), 37–40 (37).
42 Dym, "Mineral Fumes and Mining Spirits," 163.
43 Christoph Entzelt, *De Re Metallica*, trans. Nellie E. Lutz and Lloyd M. Swan (Canton: Ohio Ferro-Alloys Corporation, 1943), first published, 1557.
44 Norris, "The Providence of Mineral Generation," 37–8.
45 Dym, "Mineral Fumes and Mining Spirits," 166.
46 Ibid., 168.
47 Norris, "The Providence of Mineral Generation," 38.
48 Dym, "Mineral Fumes and Mining Spirits," 168.
49 Mathesius, *Sarepta*, 108, cited in Dym, "Mineral Fumes and Mining Spirits," 180.
50 Mathesius *Sarepta*, xxxvii, xxx, cited in Norris, "The Providence of Mineral Generation," 39.
51 Dym, "Mineral Fumes and Mining Spirits," 180, citing Mathesius, *Sarepta*, 108: "So raises the common occurrence among our miners that when they strike at bismuth, they say they came too early; by which they mean that if the ore had only sat longer in the mountain fire, it would have become silver."
52 Ibid., 180, citing *Sarepta*, 139.
53 Ibid., 181, citing Rhese, 367.
54 Norris, "The Providence of Mineral Generation," 38.
55 Dym, "Mineral Fumes and Mining Spirits," 175.
56 "We, as a shareholder, through the goodness of God, have enjoyed the proceeds of this 'God's Gift' since the very time when the mine began first to bestow such riches" (quoted in *De Re Metallica* (Hoover translation), Book I, footnote 9, 74 from Agricola's *De Veteribus Novis Metallis*).
57 Agricola, *De Re Metallica*, 20.

58 Ibid.
59 Ibid., 22.
60 Ibid., 24. Emphasis added.
61 Mirowski, *More Heat than Light*, 3.
62 See Chapter 2 for an introduction on Thomson.
63 Crosbie Smith and M. Norton Wise, *Energy and Empire: A Biographical Study of Lord Kelvin* (Cambridge: Cambridge University Press, 1989), xx.
64 See Chapter 1 for a fuller exposition of this summary.
65 Smith, *The Science of Energy*, 120.
66 Ibid., 21.
67 Cited in Ibid., 217–18.
68 Maxwell, cited in Ibid.
69 Summarized in Ibid., 101.
70 Daggett, *The Birth of Energy*, 71.
71 Ibid., 56.
72 Matthew 25.
73 Smith, *The Science of Energy*, 22.
74 Daggett, *The Birth of Energy*, 70.
75 Smith, *The Science of Energy*, 101.
76 Ibid., 309.
77 S. J. M. Eaton, *Petroleum: A History of the Oil Region of Venango County, Pennsylvania* (Philadelphia: J. P. Skelly, 1866), 60.
78 "It has always been a feature of the economy of Providence, that the stores of his bounty are brought to light just as they are needed. The minerals of earth have lain hid in its bosom until absolutely needed" (Ibid., 43).
79 Ibid., 251–2.
80 Ibid., 35.
81 Ibid.
82 Ibid., 69–70.
83 Ibid., 69–79.
84 Ibid., 294.
85 Ibid., 294–5.
86 Ibid., 258.
87 Ibid., 264.
88 Ibid., 42.
89 Ibid., 61.
90 Ibid., 268.
91 Eaton, *Petroleum*, 62.
92 Ibid., 268.
93 Dispensationalism was popularized in the US context at Niagara Bible Conferences. Dispensationalism draws on a long Christian tradition of belief in salvation history and "end times." It depends on a biblical literalism that interprets scripture as outlining God's action in the world in distinct dispensations, or time periods in salvation history. Where postmillennialists interpreted Revelation 20 to indicate that Christ would return after a millennial Golden Age where Christ's rule would be established on earth, premillennialists held that the "rapture" of the faithful would precede Christ's return. The rapture would be followed by the rise of the anti-Christ who would eventually be destroyed with Satan by Christ on his return. Only after this return would Christ establish the millennial kingdom.

94 B. M. Pietsch, "Lyman Stewart and Early Fundamentalism," *Church History* 82 (2013): 617–46 (623). Toward the end of his career in 1923 he reflected on his successful efforts to expand the market for oil, writing "in '83 we had to scratch our heads to think of a market for our oil when we did get it; we didn't have the oil-burning locomotive, steamship, stationary engine, the automobile, truck or tractor" (cited in Ibid., 624).
95 Ibid., 625. See note 89. Dispensationalism depends on a biblical literalism lauded as plainly accessible to anyone. Yet, it also relies on numerology and symbolism that evokes a sense of hidden truth just waiting for the right lens to correctly understand its meaning for the current context.
96 Ibid., 626.
97 Dochuk, *Anointed with Oil*. In contrast to premillennialism, postmillennialism held that Christ would return *after* Christ's kingdom of millennial rule was in place. For Christians like Rockefeller, this expectation evoked a more optimistic sense of history often characteristic of liberalism. Influenced by Christianity, the expectation was that if Christ would return only after his kingdom of justice and mercy had been established on earth, then necessarily the broad strokes of history continually progressed toward this aim.
98 In Dochuk's *Anointed with Oil* the historian admits, "To be sure, coal, cotton, and rubber had long evoked their own narratives of deific favor" (82). *Consuming Religion* author Kathryn Lofton and others have analyzed the tendency to attribute godly blessing to various resources and industries in the US. They define these "industrial religions" as "a discourse that attributes superhuman power to raw materials and the mechanical technologies employed to convert those materials into consumer goods" (Callahan Jr., Lofton, and Seales, "Allegories of Progress") 1–39 (1). Yet, as we will see, even among industrial religions, there were several aspects of oil that made it uniquely suited to being characterized as divine gift, disrupting rather than undergirding a Protestant work ethic.
99 See Paul Sabin who outlines these various industries, emphasizing the unique aspects of oil. Sabin, though, does not emphasize the evident resonance between oil and religion. Paul Sabin, "'A Dive into Nature's Great *Grab-bag*': Nature, Gender and Capitalism in the Early Pennsylvania Oil Industry," *Pennsylvania History* 66 (1999): 472–505.
100 Ibid., 489.
101 Sabin, "A Dive into Nature's Great *Grab-bag*,"; Pietsch, "Lyman Stewart," 621+.
102 Pietsch, "Lyman Stewart," 621.
103 See Jean Comaroff and John L. Comaroff, "Millennial Capitalism: First Thoughts on a Second Coming," *Public Culture* 12 (2000): 291–343, who focus especially on "millennial capitalism" and "occult capitalism."
104 Ibid., 621.
105 Ibid., 622.
106 Anna Tsing, "Prosperity," in *Friction: An Ethnography of Global Connection* (Princeton: Princeton University Press, 2005), 21–80.
107 Weszkalnys, "Geology, Potentiality, Speculation," 617.
108 Tanner, *Christianity and the New Spirit of Capitalism*, 196. Similarly, Tanner writes, "those making the most money in finance-dominated capitalism may be working all the time with incredible intensity, but commonly there is only an incidental connection between that effort and those profits. For example, a financial trader may spend all his time glued to a computer screen, looking for that perfect

arbitrage opportunity, but a billion dollars can be made in a nanosecond at the touch of a button, following a signal from a computer program beyond the trader's comprehension. Nothing could be easier—or more profitable" (Ibid.).
109 Brian Burkhart, "Everything is Sacred: Iktomi Lessons in Ethics without Value and Value without Anthropocentrism," in *Indigenizing Philosophy Through the Land: A Trickster Methodology for Decolonizing Environmental Ethics and Indigenous Futures* (East Lansing: Michigan State University Press, 2019), 177–222.
110 Ibid., 293.
111 See Ibid., "The Naturalness of Morality in Locality: Relationships, Reciprocity, and Respect," 271–306.
112 Leanne Simpson, *As We Have Always Done: Indigenous Freedom Through Radical Resistance* (Minneapolis: University of Minnesota Press, 2017), 75.
113 Schwerin Rowe, *Toward a Better Worldliness.*

Chapter 4

OIL

I tell you, if these were silent, the stones would cry out

—Luke 19:40

Considering that modernity is supposed to be inherently disenchanted, the material world made dead and inert, rocks have had a surprising amount to say in the turn toward extractive energy modernity. As Jennings and Yusoff have emphasized, modern racialization has consistently been managed in relation to geologic time and often extracted from geographic space. At what is generally identified as the turn to modern mining in Saxony, for Lutheran pastor Johannes Mathesius, the rocks themselves gave witness to the redemptive aims and Gospel message of God. Nearly 300 years later in the United States, as Presbyterian pastor S. J. Eaton witnessed the remarkable transformation the world's first oil strike brought to his community, Eaton marveled at the "testimony of the rocks."[1] Similarly, when the "prophet of Spindletop," Patillo Higgins, heard of the first Texas oil strike, an event that justified his antics and solidified his prophetic status, he made specific reference to the Gospel of Luke, proclaiming that the "rocks [had] broke their silence."[2]

By contrast, where modern mechanisms have resonated with ancient Western conceptions of matter as passive or merely receptive, feminized and racialized creatures have consistently been portrayed as closer to, or having a more innate, intimate, or natural connection to, nature and materiality. In response, ecowomanist, ecofeminist, new materialist, Black vitalist, postcolonial, and ecotheological voices have commonly, but variously, sought to reanimate, re-enchant, or re-emphasize the active agencies of matter.[3] Donna V. Jones, for example, highlights the ways Black vitalist and decolonial thinkers employed vitalisms to construct affirmative African and Caribbean identities and worldviews. Considering their ability to both create and resist racial hierarchies, Jones emphasizes that today questions of vitalisms lie at the heart of colonial and postcolonial tensions.[4] Among ecofeminist perspectives, Carolyn Merchant has famously analyzed the modern rendering of nature as inert within the scope of colonial capitalist patriarchal orders in *The Death of Nature* while Val Plumwood has promoted animism as resistant to Western colonial, patriarchal dualisms in *Feminism and the Mastery of Nature*. Such analyses have influenced more recent attempts to reanimate matter in new or feminist materialisms. Feminist materialists such as Stacy Alaimo and Susan Hekman, feminist vitalists like Jane Bennett, and queer materialists like Karen Barad not only critically analyze a consistent Western tendency to articulate a sense of matter as inert and lacking innate agency or activity, they also propose important constructive, nondualist conceptions of mind and matter.[5]

Among new materialists, the environmental implications of challenging dead, feminized, and racialized matter are often explicit. Jane Bennett asserts that the vitality of matter counters "the image of dead or thoroughly instrumentalized matter . . . [which] feeds human hubris and our earth-destroying fantasies of conquest and consumption."[6] Similarly, in Frost and Coole's influential edited volume on new materialisms, the authors draw important connections between coming to terms with the environmental consequences of modern modes of thought like reductionistic materialisms and nature/culture dualisms and the ways that climate change itself fundamentally disrupts these modern modes.[7]

An interest in the environmental implications of conceptions of matter is something scholars of religion and ecology share as well. Religion scholars have long identified disenchantment, desacralization or de-animation of nature as a key turning point in modernity that has had disastrous spiritual and environmental implications. At least since Lynn White Jr.'s infamous essay on the Western Christian dominion tradition and the ecological crisis, it has been common to associate negative environmental impacts with the monotheistic eradication of animisms.[8] In response, influential Christian ecotheologians from Jürgen Moltmann to Alister McGrath and, more recently, Mark Wallace with his proposal for a *Christianimism*, have sought ways within the tradition to reaffirm a sense of animation or divine presence with and in the other-than-human world.[9] The often explicitly articulated aim is to inspire more profound attachments to the world and thus a more resilient environmental ethic among the Christian faithful.

Despite a shared concern over environmental implications of dead matter materialisms, alliances between religious eco-enchantments, new materialisms, and anti-racist decolonial vitalisms are not always smooth. Where traditional vitalisms and some theologies seem to suggest matter as inert but capable of being infused by an animating S/spirit, new materialist perspectives (including various religiously engaged new materialisms) insist on the animacy and agency of *matter itself*—its ability to self-organize, initiate change, impact and thwart human decision-making processes, its resistance to being reduced to dead matter and predictable, controllable, fully knowable actions.[10] New materialists often resist the sense of matter as dead, inert, or lacking agency as well as the view of matter as animated by something like *logos* or S/spirit since these would only reinforce a view of matter as dead and inert, animated by something external. New materialisms also seek to disrupt views of human exceptionalism tied to an exclusive association of agency with consciousness—and thus, certain humans as the sole bearers of divinely appointed rationality, consciousness, and agency.

The insights and contributions of theorists critical of constructions of matter as passive, inert, or feminized are diverse and, in many cases, they make crucial interventions into traditional Western philosophies and religions. Yet, they commonly have inadequately accounted for the complexities of the modern Western relationship with enchantment.[11] Such complexities become especially evident in Western Christians' early encounters with the particular materiality of oil. Early US American responses to oil suggest that between oil and modernity, enchanted animation is, indeed, *precisely* the issue, though whether curse or cure might depend on a host of other factors. Applying the lens of Jason Storm's "myth of disenchantment," we begin to see how electricity and oil proved particularly appealing to religiously inclined modern Western folk—often on account of the ways these forms of matter seemed to empirically and materially *resist* modern reductive and mechanistic materialisms.

These cautions are often more relevant for religious re-enchantments, but critical energy concerns about the idealization of activity over passivity in new materialisms apply broadly. Analyzing rationalities and theologies of Western energy concepts as we have done in Chapter 1 highlights the importance not just of calling into question the alignment of matter with a racialized feminine passivity, but of simultaneously contesting a Western preoccupation with liveliness, animation, vim, vigor, and vitality as well. Jones, for example, emphasizes that rather than challenging associations of blackness with the inert, European vitalisms often facilitated and reinforced racial hierarchies while Black vitalisms of the Négritude failed to challenge racial essentialism.[12] Reflecting specifically on feminist materialisms, Claire Colebrook worries about "the ways in which the current politics of life intensifies, rather than overcomes humanism."[13] She identifies this amplification of life as "intensely theological, insofar as the central image is that of a life that generously gives and creates in order to yield an image of itself."[14] Finally, regarding the materiality of petroleum in particular, Gisa Weszkalnys discerns a "vibrant concern with the potentiality of matter [lying] at the heart of petroleum production"[15] in her ethnographies of oil-extraction sites.

Given the ways animacy, vibrancy, activity, and activation have been racialized, masculinized, theologized, and are internal to petroleum imaginaries, I see the need for a more life-critical new materialism that would place a stronger emphasis on analyzing the delineations of life and death, liveliness and inertness, activity and passivity. Without this, I fear even new materialisms risk uncritically continuing gendered and racialized patterns of affirming activity over passivity; miss important ways energy policies, practices, technologies, and resources have been profoundly infused with the masculine theo-logics of life, liveliness, and vigor; and, generally, overlook the fact that aims to animate and re-enchant matter have not always led to environmentally friendly results. In this chapter I want to highlight the ways oil proved enticing for religious folk precisely for its seeming ability to resist reductive materialisms, material/spiritual dualisms, and animate/inanimate divides. In particular, I will demonstrate the ways these appealing resonances of oil and Christianity informed oil redemption narratives that still reverberate in more secularized forms today. Together, these issues point to a key problem in the Christian West with the ways life and death, liveliness and inertness have been framed.

Embarrassment of Oil

In the Introduction, I suggested that part of the reason oil and religion have not been analyzed closely together is that their conjunction may, in Amitav Ghosh's words, intensify a sense of oil as a "matter of embarrassment verging on the unspeakable."[16] The unspeakability of oil remains closely entwined with the unthinkability of climate change. As one of India's most influential current novelists, Ghosh has reflected on the problem that while he may be personally profoundly concerned with and occupied by climate change, he cannot write it into his novels. This is the case, at least, to the extent that the modern novel has been constructed as a mode of fiction constrained by modern limits on the probable: "Probability and the modern novel are in fact twins, born at about the same time, among the same people, under a shared star . . ."[17] Echoing Max Weber, Ghosh explains how the modern novel helped convey a new "rationalization" of life through the banishment of enchantment, unpredictability, and the animation of the other-than-human world. By contrast, Ghosh reflects on the uncanny sense of being hunted rather than hunter in surprise attacks of Bengal tigers in the Sundarbans, provoking him to query: "'Commonplace'? 'Moderate'? How did Nature ever come to be associated with words like these?"[18] In the case of climate change, then, its unthinkability emerges as more than a measure of unprecedented conditions or appalling consequences. For Ghosh, climate change materializes as unthinkable because modernity has explicitly excluded its characteristics and symptoms from its definition of thought. In the rationalization of the world, spread with efficiency by the accounting logic made so desirable by a Protestant work ethic and its imposition of the "regularity of bourgeois life," both the other-than-human and its unpredictable animation are excluded from the world of the probable. Ghosh concludes that as a result of these exclusions, climate change strikes moderns not just as unexpected or unbelievable, but as *unthinkable*.

While climate change does confront one with agencies and animacies beyond the consciousness of the human world—what Jane Bennett refers to as the "force of things"[19]—this is not the first time modern Westerns have had to face such inscrutability. While oil introduced the very conditions of the kind of unthinkability Ghosh addresses, its first "discoveries" ironically elicited similar reactions for surprisingly similar reasons.

Reporters returning from the Titusville oil boom in the 1860s consistently expressed disbelief, shock, or an inability to comprehend or communicate what they had witnessed: "'astonished beyond measure'" at this "'mystery of the age,'"[20] they had "'no language at our command by which to convey to the minds of our readers any adequate idea of the agitated state at the time we saw it'."[21] They referred, in part, to the behavior of other humans in response to oil and this new race for wealth, but petroleum also disrupted something deeper than social norms and cultural expectations. More than social acts, observers were particularly shocked by the *behavior of oil*—its unpredictability, intractability, and defiance of basic laws of nature like gravity.

Paul Sabin has researched early oil narratives extensively and found that entrepreneurs in particular were "surprised and confused when oil refused to bend to their will."[22] Sabin's analysis of primary sources led him to conclude that during the late nineteenth century, oil disrupted US Americans' basic worldviews and expectations for nature. Reflecting on the remarkable stories about oil and its characteristics, one reporter wrote, "One is almost constrained from his intuitive notion of the natural world to suspect such a story is a whopper, and that the man who talks in this manner of oil flowing up, has been drinking poor whisky."[23] Less "intuitive" than Cartesian-Newtonian, this mechanistic, law ordered, and predictable world had, by the later part of the nineteenth century, become so pervasive that it could easily be confused with good, old-fashioned, objective "common sense." Oil, with its mysterious defiance of Newton's law of gravity and uncanny disruption of Cartesian conclusions about a lack of mind and agency in the other-than-human world, introduced profound questions for the mindset of a rational and controllable nature.[24]

The obstinance of oil, starting and stopping at will and thus causing "considerable consternation among investors and observers alike"[25] was one thing, but its animacy evoked a frenzy among witnesses. Oil wells would often make rumbling, digestive noises: "During the upheaving of the gas, it seems as if the very bowels of the earth were being all torn out and their sides must soon collapse."[26] The commotion of an oil discovery would attract massive crowds, overwhelming small towns with an influx of investors and gawkers. In an attempt to impress these onlookers, oilmen would summon oil to "perform." As with a lion and its trainer, teasing and testing the edge between controlled and uncontrolled, oilmen provoked their wells, getting them "stirred up" to "perform" for first time viewers.[27] Sabin concludes that "During the 1860s petroleum seemed to reawaken a perception of the earth as animate and mysterious Nature."[28] More than human control of nature, oil disrupted even the deeply "intuitive" sense that nonhuman matter is dead and inert.

Temperamental Crude and her Ingenious Oilmen

One of the most striking reactions to the unthinkable animation of oil is the reemergence of feminine metaphors for nature. While Merchant has emphasized how feminine imagery and metaphors for nature receded as the material world became rationalized in the modern mechanistic view,[29] by the 1860s, the inability of rational science to fully explain or predict oil had the effect of sparking a reemergence of gendered metaphors for nature. Specifically, Sabin finds evidence that oil "assumed the characteristics of a productive and temperamental female best managed by ingenious oil men."[30] Poetry, songs, and journalistic reports employed imagery of oil as a nursing or birthing mother.[31] John J. McLaurin, author of an influential early account of oil discovery in America discussed further later, reflects this trend:

> After sixty centuries the game of "hide-and-seek" between Mother Earth and her children has terminated in favor of the latter. They have pierced nature's internal laboratories, tapping the huge oil-tanks wherein the products of her

quiet chemistry had accumulated "in bond," and up came the unctuous fluid in volumes ample to fill all the lamps the universe could manufacture and to grease every axle on this revolving planet![32]

As the mysteriousness of oil elicited images of unruly females, masculine language of control, domination, and imposition of order became heightened as well. Oil wells were often portrayed, in Sabin's words, as "unpredictable intemperate women whom the male worker could not fully understand but still hoped to master."[33] Mystified by oil's unthinkability and uncontrollability, nineteenth-century Americans fell back on gendered metaphors for nature and matter, while its ineffability evoked new religious and spiritual interpretation.

Divining Oil

While Sabin insightfully emphasizes the gendered implications of oil's unthinkability, he does not adequately account for similar seismic shifts in spiritual and religious spheres. In the face of the inability of Cartesian-Newtonian knowledge systems to account for the animation of oil or accurately predict where to find it, people turned not just to feminine metaphors, but also to spiritualism and religion. As Storm emphasizes, ever since religion and science became construed as operating in separate and opposing spheres, convergences of religion or magic and science have gained appeal in certain spheres precisely for their ability to resist such modern dualisms of spirit/matter, mind/body entailed in mechanism. Most of what are today identified as esoteric movements arose precisely around these aims. Consequently, rather than finding religion or magic retreating from the march of modern science and technology, we are more likely to find "séance and science" in the same room, religion and science "piggybacking" on one another.[34]

Gendered and religious responses to oil were informed by previous energy sciences and technologies: electricity, magnetism, and thermodynamics. Recall that for some evangelical energy scientists like William Thomson, energy sciences and technologies gained appeal in part because they seemed to offer empirical verification for the fact that the material world was neither dead nor self-sufficient. There was something animating, enlivening, and enchanting the natural world that needed to be attended to—and could be put to good use for human betterment.

The enchantments of modern energy science were also anticipated by earlier views of electricity and magnetism. Seventeenth-, eighteenth-, and nineteenth-century material-discursive constructions of electricity and magnetism were profoundly gendered and divinized on account of influences from medieval alchemy. Conversely, the influence of electricity and magnetism on religion was so strong that the main metaphors for divinity in the West shifted from the transcendent sun to the remarkable immanent powers of electricity and magnetism.[35] Where Romantics resisted the reduction of matter to mechanism by emphasizing aesthetics, wonder, the arts, and the incalculable mysteries of the natural world, Spiritualists like Andrew Jackson Davis resisted the same by insisting on the transcendent significance of machines and technology. Electricity in particular was interpreted as a subtle form of matter capable of bridging spiritual–material divides and moving society to a higher plane of existence.[36]

While electricity has been divinized and associated with masculine vitality, scholars have also noted the consistent curious presence of Native Americans in nineteenth-century séance parlors and narratives of electricity.[37] Religion scholars have theorized this strange pairing in nineteenth-century Spiritualism since Werner Sollors took note of this "palpable fascination with the modern machine and the spirit of the Indian, in a manner that spiritualized them both" in a 1983 essay.[38] More recently, Darryl Caterine has persuasively demonstrated that the pairing of the modern machine and "Indian spirits" reflects Davis' Spiritualist Harmonial alchemical cosmology. Where Davis' Harmonial cosmos devolved from a primordial Sensorium into increasingly diffuse forms of matter, he emphasized that "progression" through technological and social reform could reverse the pattern, working to return creation to its original spirit/matter unity. Nature, romantically characterized, played a key role in the process. Caterine explains that

> Spiritualists saw the transformation of the American "wilderness" into the mechanized grid of modernity as a cosmic process of alchemical refinement, wherein the raw stuff of nature became rarefied into a finer, or more purified, form of matter. The end products of this metamorphosis were electrical machines—whose value lay not in their utilitarian applications, but in making electricity known to humanity as the *anima mundi* of the universe.[39]

Consequently, Harmonialism did not support a modern technology/nature, mind/body, spirit/matter dualism. According to this cosmology, a continuous relationship exists between spirit and matter such that the other-than-human world, too, was merely a more diffuse form of matter that could be refined into technology as a higher form of spirit/matter.

Seen as extensions of "Nature," Native American spirits were portrayed as wise and admirable guides for a return to communion between spirit and matter. However, according to Davis' Spiritualism, Indigenous guidance toward unity of spirit and matter inevitably led to their erasure. On account of Harmonialism's alchemical view of the cosmos, "progression" required that Nature—and Indigenous Americans with it—be subsumed into higher forms of techno-alchemical refinement. Davis explicitly articulates this as a universalized-Anglo-centric cosmic process. In a particularly revealing passage, Davis portrays race relations in terms of consumption—diverse peoples are literally ingested, metabolized, by universal Caucasian technoscience.

> When a man sits down to a table and partakes of beef, he does not become beef, but beef becomes him. That is true of the Caucasian world. The Negro, the Malayan, the Indian and the Mongolian are walking and working together—as none of them could walk and work singly . . . [Caucasians] go anywhere on the face of the planet, shake hands with the people, and affiliate with them all as

brother associates with brother. The Negro cannot do this; the Malay cannot do it; no Indian can do it; only the Caucasian goes all over the world and makes it contribute its riches to his science.[40]

Harmonialism's nondualistic vitalism clearly creates rather than dispels racial hierarchies. Here, cosmic progression is driven by Anglo-technoscience, "redeeming" races through its universalizing capacities as it subsumes them.

Firsthand accounts of early oil discoveries in the US demonstrate that like electricity and magnetism before, it too was seen as a form of matter that could bridge spiritual/material divides. Even before the combustion engine and its widespread industrial use, the curious materiality of oil, like electricity, gained appeal for spiritual reasons. In her research of nineteenth-century Spiritualism and oil, Rochelle Raineri Zuck highlights a kind of "practical spiritualism" that saw its interests as wholly entwined with those of oil. Enticed by the spiritual potential not just of electricity but also of oil, this movement "took mediums and spirits out of the parlour and into the oil fields" becoming "deeply involved in marketing the oil industry to the American people."[41] Such "practical spiritualism" was often personified in local figures whose advice on where to look for oil was widely sought.

One famous figure was Abraham James who, in 1867, near Pleasantville, Pennsylvania, became "suddenly possessed by the 'spirit guide,'" fell unconscious, and woke to (accurately) announce that oil could be extracted from that very spot. His success sparked a flood of oil prophets. James' "spirit guides," so instrumental in locating oil, were consistently Native American figures: "Mountain Bear," supposedly a Seneca chief, and Lalah, a "beautiful Indian maiden."[42] James was profoundly influenced by Davis' electrical Harmonialism which he now applied to oil. He even inscribed his indebtedness to this Spiritualism by Christening his first well "Harmonial 1." James' work with oil, like that of Davis' with electricity, was seen as revealing the inherent interconnection of spirit and matter by communicating with the spirit world to receive guidance on how to locate oil as subtle matter capable, like electricity, of transforming society and raising it to a higher state.

James' work was also portrayed as resisting reductive scientific materialism by bridging a religion/science dualism and demonstrating that religion, too, could produce practical, empirically verifiable results. James' biographer, J. M. Peebles, himself a Spiritualist, explicitly framed James' life and accomplishments as evidence that "religion and science are a unit."[43] More broadly, Zuck reports that "[s]piritualist and nonspiritualist publications rehearsed James's biography in order to establish his credibility as a medium and challenge the notion that religion was diametrically opposed to science and industry."[44] James' work, like that of other practical Spiritualists, also seemed to demonstrate that the sciences did not have a corner on practical application. Spiritualists increasingly turned to the oil industry not just because of its "lucrative financial opportunities" but also because of its "potential to demonstrate the 'practical' applications of Spiritualism."[45] Zuck reports, for example, that a group of Christian Spiritualists created the Chicago Rock Oil Company not just for material gains, but also because they "hoped that oil itself could function as a kind of medium and persuade nonbelievers that Spiritualism could make practical contributions to modern life."[46] Such connections appeased modern empirical desires for practical applicability and concrete verifiability, realms and aspirations modern religion generally had to concede to the sphere of science. Here oil emerged as a unique form of matter that, like Spiritualist mediums, could aid communication between worlds and demonstrate the fallacy of religion/science, spirit/matter divides.

Though some Christians remained skeptical of the excesses of Spiritualism, more conservative dispensationalist premillennial Christians similarly found the practical application of religion for oil-extraction enticing. As noted in the previous chapter with regard to Lyman Stewart, resonance between oil discovery and Christian dispensationalism, associated with end-time apocalypticism and prediction-style biblical prophecy, was particularly compelling.[47] In addition to Stewart, Darren Dochuk emphasizes the importance of religious motivations for the oil endeavors of the Pew family (devout Presbyterians and founders of Sun Oil), Patillo Higgins, and many others.[48] Texas Baptist Patillo Higgins famously employed prayer and biblical interpretation to predict the location of the first major oil gusher west of Pennsylvania. Texas' Spindletop gusher produced more oil than had been previously imaginable, defying common belief that there was no major oil to be found in the West, and is thus credited with ushering in the modern petroleum industry. For his ability to exegete land and scripture together, Higgins was honored with the moniker the "prophet of Spindletop."[49] So even for Christians who might have been skeptical of Spiritualism, the mysterious materiality of oil still proved appealing because it could demonstrate the fundamental inadequacy of reductive and dualistic materialisms; it could empirically demonstrate that there was more to the surface than could be seen. In the case of early oil exploration and extraction, then, a spiritually infused sense of wonder and expectancy informed a sense of mysterious treasures buried under the surface of what others mistook for dead, lifeless, limited, or deficient nature.[50]

Redemptive Oil

Like energy sciences and technologies before it, oil had the ability to seemingly disrupt or bridge modern dualisms between religion and science, spirit and matter. Oil's facility as a medium—a practical Spiritualism and industrial religion, demonstrating practical and empirically verifiable transformations of society—has rendered it remarkably resonant with Christian redemption narratives. In addition to the broader divinization of oil by Christian Spiritualists and millenarians, it has also been more explicitly animated as a Christ-like redemptive figure and granted salvific agency.

These Christ-like figurations have been informed by the long history of confluence between Christian narratives of redemption and Western science and technology. Historian David F. Noble has examined these histories and the now secularized impact of them on science and technology aims in current Western culture. Through the early Middle Ages of Latin Christianity, the Augustinian tradition had aligned technology and the mechanical arts solely with the fallen nature of humanity. As such, it could make material contributions, but had no spiritual efficacy. Noble notes a key shift in the Western Middle Ages with Irish theologian John Scottus Eriugena (c. 800–c. 877 CE) who departed from this particular Augustinian conclusion, asserting, instead, that the liberal and mechanical arts can have transcendent, spiritual effects for fallen humanity as well. Emphasizing that knowledge of the arts was innate in humanity, something given by God from the moment of creation, Eriugena asserted that in the Fall humans lost this knowledge, obscured by sin.[51] In its post-Fall state, humanity was a dim reflection of what it had been created to be. Yet, the arts, Eriugena asserted, remained "man's links with the Divine" and "their cultivation a means to salvation."[52] By progressing in technological or mechanical arts, humans could regain their lost perfection, fulfilling their human nature as given by God.

While Eriugena was the first to assert the usefulness of arts for humans not just in their fallen state but also for the redemptive fulfillment of their humanity by reclaiming their image-likeness of God, he was certainly not the last. Hugh of St. Victor, a twelfth-century French theologian, like Eriugena, "linked the mechanical as well as the liberal arts directly to salvation and the restoration of fallen man."[53] Hugh was an Augustinian and so identified technology with fallen human nature, but unlike Augustine he emphasized that these arts may serve as a way that humans could recover their lost perfection and fulfill their humanity as the image of God. In his *Didascalicon* he writes, "This, then, is what the arts are concerned with, this is what they intend, namely, to restore within us the divine likeness."[54] Others followed Eriugena and Hugh of St. Victor so that by the time of the emergence of modern science there was already a long line of interpreters influenced by the ancient Christian theme of redemption, interpreting the recovery of a pre-Fall human image of God not only in terms of spirituality, but by the mechanical arts as well.

In particular, Francis Bacon was influenced by this tradition and asserted that the goal of modern science was to help humans reclaim a God-given aspect of their humanity that was lost in the Fall. In *Novum Organum* Bacon retells the Christian Fall and Redemption story in terms of modern science: what humans lost in the Fall was not just innocence, but also domination of nature: "For man by the fall, lost at once his state of innocence, and his dominion over creation, both of which can be partially recovered even in this life, the first by religion and faith, the second by the arts and sciences."[55] Here science emerges as an agent of redemption, retriever of a lost, divinely given state of humanity. The "sons of science," as he articulates in *Masculine Birth of Time,* emerged as a "blessed race of Heroes or Supermen" who have, with the implementation of the redemptive tools of modern science, "overcome the immeasurable helplessness and poverty of the human race."[56] With science as redemptive figure, the sons of science arrived on the world stage as heroes and supermen, uniquely fulfilling their humanity and aiding the restoration of humanity, more broadly.

The contextual history of oil discovery in the US also aided its ability to emerge as redemptive. The first oil wells aligned with social division leading up to the Civil

War (1861–5), and many expressed hopes that petroleum would prove salvific for the country, providing a way out of or beyond war. Darren Dochuk, for example, emphasizes that from the start "petroleum registered as a mystical fount that might ease America out of bloodshed and into a new age of peace and prosperity. Oil was to be a healing balm for the body politic."[57] Oil was seen as a divinely bestowed blessing to replace cotton and thus maintain economic stability, but as it became clear that oil could be used as a fuel for machines, it was furthermore framed as an agent of God's redemptive freedom, saving enslaved bodies from the bondage of physical labor.[58] As such, oil seemed to emerge as divine endorsement for the cause of the North—a sentiment later expanded as evidence of divine sanctification of the United States in general. Oil thus seemed to confirm earlier Puritan "city on a hill" or "redeemer nation"[59] notions of a divinely ordained role for the United States, affirming the "practical mind of the American people," leading toward technological advancement as well as "the blessing of Providence on American economic expansion."[60]

Hurrah for Jesus! Hurrah for Petroleum!

Lubricated by the alignment Bacon encouraged between modern science and the redemptive Christ figure, this same slide between petroleum and Christ can be seen in John J. McLaurin's 1896 *Sketches in Crude Oil*. The text, McLaurin explains, was intended to give a busy, occupied public "a glimpse of the grandest industry of the ages and of the men chiefly responsible for its origin and growth."[61] McLaurin aimed to preserve early stories of oil, saving them from being lost from memory entirely. With twenty English editions published between 1896 and 2007, McLaurin's text has been influential and its impact significant.[62] In Walter Rundell Jr.'s "Centennial Bibliography" of key works on the history of petroleum in the United States, the historian reports that McLaurin's text has been "widely cited as an accurate source of information on the early days in the Oil Region."[63] However, what seems to have passed under the radar of commentators, either dismissed as archaic or so unconsciously assumed and pervasive in the industry that it has seemed unremarkable, are the frequent biblical references and key religious framing of petroleum. One might even read McLaurin's as no mere history text, but a work of redemption theology.

The consistent slippage between petroleum and redemption in the first three chapters—"The Star in the East," "Glimmer in the West," and "Nearing the Dawn"—is crucial for McLaurin's framing of oil and its historic significance. True to form for a traditional theology of redemption, McLaurin starts with the first moments of creation: "mineralogists think [petroleum] was quietly distilling 'underneath the ground' when the majestic fiat went forth: 'Let there be light!'"[64] And there was light—illuminating, transformative, redemptive light. Anxious to demonstrate that petroleum is not a "mushroom upstart," but a "veritable antique," McLaurin emphasizes that petroleum was known of and prized by ancient people—from Asia, to Africa and Europe, but especially by biblical authors.[65] This first "Star in the East" chapter unfolds, then, as a compilation of ancient eastern references with special emphasis on the Hebrew Bible, from Genesis and Deuteronomy, to Micah and Job. Confirming the priority of biblical wisdom, even on the subject of petroleum, the author concludes, "Evidently the Old-Testament writers, whose wise heads geology had not muddled, knew a good deal about the petroleum situation in their day."[66] In the narrative of petroleum's genesis, McLaurin makes clear that wisdom about oil is rooted in the Bible while, more subtly at first, encouraging slippage between the technoscientific narrative of oil and the redemptive Christ figure.

Beginning with this compilation of ancient references to petroleum in the global East, the ostensible "star in the East," traditionally associated with Christ, is here clearly petroleum. The reference to Christ would have been apparent in the text's contemporary context. In 1890, just six years before the publication of his text, lyricist George Cooper and musician Amanda Kennedy wrote a Christmas carol, "Star of the East," that would be wildly successful and widely popular in the United States. A verse in particular eases a slide between star and savior: "Smiles of a Savior are mirror'd in Thee! Glimpses of Heav'n in thy light we see! Guide us still onward to that blessed shore, After earth's toil is o'er!"[67] McLaurin is depending on such cultural associations, and his original audience would not have been mistaken in reading McLaurin as framing oil as a Christ figure.

Though the reference to oil as the Eastern Star is subtle (and could suggest that oil, like the star of the Magi, remains something that *points to* Christ), McLaurin is just getting started. The slide between petroleum, modern science, and redemption gradually becomes more explicit, aided by the fact that for McLaurin, oil and Christ function in the same way.

Chapter 1 builds in a crescendo to the triumphant, global proclamation of the Eastern Star. But before McLaurin shifts from the "Eastern Star" to the "glimmer" of petroleum in the West, he inserts a brief intermezzo. His "A Petroleum Idyl [sic]" serves as a climax, simultaneously linking Christ and petroleum while bridging East and West. This intermission in the form of an idyllic scene is worth quoting in its entirety:

> A ragged street-Arab, taken to Sunday-school by a kind teacher, heard for the first time the story of Christ's boundless love and sufferings. Big tears coursed down his grimy cheeks, until he could no longer restrain his feelings. Springing upon the seat, the excited urchin threw his tattered cap to the ceiling and screamed "Hurrah for Jesus!" It was an honest, sincere, reverent tribute, which the Recording Angel must have been delighted to note. In like manner, considering its wondrous past, its glowing present and its prospective future, men, women and children everywhere, while profoundly grateful to the Divine Benefactor for the transcendent gift, may fittingly join in a universal "Hurrah for Petroleum!"[68]

Again, McLaurin's affirmation of a slide between oil and Christ turns on their similar effects: "in like manner." Here science and oil are no longer witnesses to Christ, no longer pointing to Christ, but because they effect redemption they emerge as Christ figures.

"The demon of darkness has been exorcized from the gloomy caverns of old to make room for the modern angel of light. Science, the rare alchemist which converts the tear of unpaid labor into a steam-giant that turns with tireless arm the countless wheels of toil, lays bare the deepest recesses of the past to bring forth treasures for the present."[69]

Oil and Christ produce the same material and affective transformations—and both are driven by missionary zeal to spread their Gospel light around the globe.

Chapter 2's "glimmer" extends the celestial illumination to the West and then the entire globe. "In like manner," the aims of oil and Christ are bound in global redemption:

> Alike in the tropics and the zones, beneath cloudless Italian skies and the bleak Russian firmament, amid the flowery vales of Cashmere and the snow-crowned heights of the Caucasus, by the banks of the turbid Ganges and the shores of the limpid Danube, this priceless boon has ever contributed to the comfort and convenience of mankind. The Star in the East was crowding into line as the full orb of day.[70]

In McLaurin's petro-theology, petroleum functions by the same logic relied on for colonizing the "new" world. As Sylvia Wynter argues, to legitimate the stealing of land Columbus relied on the logic that the whole earth needed redemption.[71]

Chapter 3, "Nearing the Dawn," focuses on the "full development"[72] of the "great petroleum boom!"[73] beginning in the United States, symbolized as the dawning of the morning sun which readers would clearly align with the anticipation of redemption, resurrection, and the apocalyptic new age when Christ will return in full glory. Just as with the proclamation of the Gospel, begun in the East with full intention of global redemption, so too, "With John Wesley [petroleum] may exultingly exclaim: 'The whole earth is my parish.'"[74] With finality, Christ and oil slide into one another and converge. Oil is no mere tool for the spread of the Gospel. Here oil becomes animated and enlivened, acting as agent of redemption; its arch of salvation history is Christ's, its message and acts of redemption are Christ's. Together, the Gospel of Christ and oil are proclaimed from McLaurin's pulpit.

Petro-theologies of Redemption

While religious authors like Eaton and McLaurin encouraged the enchantment of oil through the lens of Christian theology, eventually the shock of oil wore off: its discovery methods became rationalized, its unpredictable animations regulated, and its ontological and socioeconomic disruptions quelled.[75] With the shift to regularity, the magic of oil became mundane, the unthought background feature of the modern American lifestyle. As the mechanized Cartesian-Newtonian narrative of the regularity and controllability of life regained ground, continued associations between oil and redemption into the twentieth century were helped along by the US American oil industry.

By the 1920s—in the wake of the Standard Oil trust-busting drama, oil labor disputes in the 1910s, and the Teapot Dome scandal[76]—Americans had grown disenchanted with the oil industry. Even though Americans, as evidenced by the increase of car ownership and use, were more addicted to petroleum than ever, oil was now seen more as a necessary expense than a means to transcendence.[77] This, at least, was how oil executives assessed their situation in the early twentieth century. In response, leaders of the American Petroleum Industry (API)—run by the Pew family whose ties with Evangelical Presbyterianism were widely and openly acknowledged—sought the advice of America's most famous adman at the time, Bruce Barton.[78] Barton was the son of a successful Congregational minister. His religion and advertisement strategies informed one another so that he "knew the powerful hold visions of the holy could have over people," and so he sought ways to connect desires for commercial products with those of transcendence.[79] Conversely, his employment shaped his perception of Christianity. In 1924 he wrote a book called *The Man Nobody Knows*, portraying Jesus as the "world's greatest business executive."[80] Consistent with the masculinizing aims of Muscular Christianity, which was also broadly influential at the beginning of the twentieth century in the United States, he sought to portray Christ as a "man's man," someone who mentored "his disciples and followers with a conquering spirit," transforming him from the overly-feminized Jesus he grew up with.[81] The success of the book led to a national book tour which caught the eye of API leader Edgar Pew.

Barton was invited to speak to an API gathering in 1928 where he suggested an ad campaign aimed to change US American perceptions of oil. He told the executives, "there is a magnificent place for imagination in your business." Where previous generations had found inspiration in the exploration and discovery of oil, Barton suggested a shift in strategy: they must excite the American public imagination "on the other side of the pump." In other words, they must focus on all that can be done with this "juice of the fountain of eternal youth." Instead of being a resented, necessary expense, pumping petro—like drilling for it—should evoke the miraculous and carry associations of "health," "comfort," and "success." Barton and the API therefore helped re-excite American imaginations after the novelty of oil discovery had become mundane, regularized, and disenchanted by focusing on the miraculous things one could do with oil "on the other side of the pump."[82]

Thanks to the efforts of the API, Americans were re-enchanted with oil. The miraculous and even soteriological power of oil still emerges in overtly religious or secularized framing in the twenty-first century. A recent BP ad, for example, simply states: "beyond darkness there is light."[83] The simplicity of the narrative depends on deep historical, cultural associations. It assumes its audience can—and readily will—connect the dots and fill in the gaps between the symbol of light and petroleum, clearly relying on resonance between energy, Platonic enlightenment, and Christian creation-salvation narratives. The ad assumes its audience will equate oil not just with the techno-mechanical ability to produce light, but also with an ability to bring redemptive light into a culture that would otherwise remain in a fallen state of darkness.

Petro-colonial Salvation Narratives Petroculture scholar Sheena Wilson highlights the gender dynamics at play in a recent Canadian "Ethical Oil" ad campaign. Clearly, a redemption narrative is also functioning. Wilson explains that the "Ethical Oil" campaign aimed to sway Canadian public opinion toward support for Canada's oil through a series of billboards suggesting that extracting and relying on petro from Canadian oil sands was the most ethical option for Canadians. Each billboard was split between contrasting images: a Canadian "ethical oil" example on one side contrasted with an Arabian or African "unethical" oil image on the other. The campaign especially thematized the "salvation" of foreign or native women by Canadian oil. One image, for example, portrays burka-clad women, identified with the tag line: "Conflict Oil Countries: Women Stoned to Death."[84] Its contrasting image featured a graduating female identified as the woman who would be mayor of the largest urban center in the tar sands region. Her images bear the tag line: "Canada's Oil Sands: Woman Elected Mayor."[85]

Just as this billboard erases histories of Western sexism and colonialism consistently aligned with high-energy consumption/production culture, so does another ad bearing an image of an Indigenous Canadian woman in a hard hat and oil rig suit. Her tag line, reading "Canada's Oil Sands: Aboriginals Employed," is contrasted with an image of armed men marching through a desert past a human skull.[86] This image bears the caption: "Sudan's Oil Fields: Indigenous People Killed."[87] These campaigns promote a particular view of women, Indigenous people, and two-thirds-world populations as vulnerable and in need of salvation by Western industrial-mechanical means. This racialized technoscientific salvation narrative is prefigured in early oil narratives like those of Abraham James that narrate oil discovery as dependent on Native American spiritual insight. As portrayed in the twenty-first-century "ethical oil" campaign, then, it is clear that Anglo-scientific supermen are still "saving" other races by subsuming them into the universalized petro-technoscience project.

Where fossil fuels are framed as a redemptive force, bringing society into greater prosperity, wealth, and liberation from constraints of manual labor, countries with excess oil are, in the words of former Department of Energy Secretary Rick Perry, "blessed" to be able to "provide fossil fuel globally," especially to those needing "better quality of life or better opportunities"—namely, countries with low consumption and production rates.[88] Bacon's supermen of science and technology are still busy saving the world.

Petro Parley

Oil has long emerged as exceptional matter capable of bestowing exceptionality. Petro-theologies like those of McLaurin build off modern religious enchantments with electricity and energy. But even from ancient times, oil has conferred blessedness, purification, and consecration. The Judeo-Christian tradition retains a long history of ritual anointing to confer blessedness, a special calling, or sacred role. Jewish messianisms upheld a High Priest or King as the anointed one. In this vein, Jesus of Nazareth was given the title Christ, the anointed, and his followers, early Christians, dubbed the "oily ones."[89] Greco-Roman culture, too, associated the olive and its oils with divinity and immortality. Crowns of olive branches were donned by rulers, given to triumphant athletes, and placed on the bodies of the dead as signs of immortality.[90]

In addition to its ancient divinizing capacities, even resonance articulated between masculinity and the textures of oil is not recent. Aristotle theorized this connection explicitly. In his *On the Generation of Animals*, Aristotle argued that oil shares not just symbolism with semen, but material properties and basic composition as well (GA 2.2 735b10). He undoubtedly referred to olive oil, but it was the sebaceous qualities he relied on. Unlike most liquids, Aristotle suggested, oil and semen resist solidification in heating or cooling. Most liquids change form, becoming dry or hardened with heating or cooling. These, he concluded, are composed of water and earth. But oil and semen resist change, retain their form, and thus are not composed of water and earth, but of water and that changeless, semi-divine element, residue of ether—*pneuma*.

Gad Freudenthal has suggested it was likely these qualities of oil, its "persistence, stability, and permanence," its "indestructible moisture," that influenced its symbolic dimensions.[91] In other words, oil likely gained its place in religious rituals because it could perform what it symbolized: its facility as a cleanser gave it symbolic purchase in cleansing rituals; the olive and its oil's resistance to decay and ability to aid preservation led to symbols of health, stability, longevity, and immortality. Oil's religious symbolism has been reinforced by its performance. Since ancient times oil has seemingly earned its place as signifier of the stasis of divinity and rational masculinity on account of its peculiar materiality.

Perhaps fossil fuel oil has been subject to divinization in modernity for reasons similar to the ancient. It didn't just irrationally or baselessly signify divine qualities and characteristics of preservation, transformation, energy, power, illumination, and liberation. At least for those who could most benefit from its extraction, its empirically verifiable uses and applications seemed to perform divine activities as well. Like ancient oil, petro seemed to hold redemption within it because it transformed, seemed to contain enlightenment because it illumined, and seemed imbued with freedom because it appeared to liberate. Even more than oilve oil, petroleum has successfully conveyed sanctification and exceptionalism where its presence miraculously transformed landscapes, resurrected dead or dying economies, and liberated certain muscles from wearing work. While such historical alliances and associations of oil with divinity and masculinity do not entirely account for a modern petro-obsession, they do highlight the curious materiality of oil as something that proved enticing to religious and spiritual folk precisely because it of its ability to resist modern reductive materialisms.

Oil emerges as a fascinating and important point of new materialist engagement. Yet, the oil narratives and redemptive petro-theologies outlined here (and in Chapter 5) suggest the need for a more critical approach to life and liveliness as well as the deadness of matter. In particular, the petrocultural dependencies on the "vibrant concern with the potentiality of matter"[92] have been highlighted by energy humanities scholar Stephanie LeMenager in her influential text, *Living Oil*. In a modern petroculture, she argues, "Liveness, as in seeming to be alive, now relies heavily upon oil."[93] Such alliances between petro and vitality, vibrancy, potentiality, and liveliness highlight a key problem: How does one proceed if, with feminist materialists, ecotheologians, animists, or postcolonialists, one sees the eco-social justice significance of challenging the Cartesian-Newtonian, mechanist view of the material world as dead, and yet also wants to challenge the petro-infused obsession with liveliness, energy, and vigor? In other words, how do we both challenge a view of the other-than-human world as disenchanted, and yet emphasize that in some sense oil has remained altogether too enchanted?

Mel Y. Chen's approach to the problem of matter rendered dead while resisting theo-masculinized forms of liveliness seems particularly insightful when applied to oil. Rather than "reinvest[ing] certain materialities *with* life," Chen suggests "remap[ping] live and dead zones away from those very terms leveraging animacy toward a consideration of affect and its queered and raced formations."[94] Chen insists we move away from a binary consideration of death and life and embrace a continuum of animacies—attending to evoked responses, that which animates, rather than innate or inherent characteristics of liveness and deadness. Here animacy emerges not as an inherent stable quality or category, but as phenomena that emerge in responsiveness when bodies meet.

Similarly, Brian Burkhart emphasizes the importance of localizing characterizations of life or animacy, framing them always within the relationship of kinship. From this perspective, rocks and trees around me are "alive in this relation,"[95] yet nothing is innately alive or dead. Burkhart explains that this perspective, informed by his experience in Cherokee and other North American Indigenous communities, of life "not as a property of things but as something that exists in the relationship between things . . . runs directly against some of the most standard Western philosophical assumptions."[96] In particular, it resists the common Western association of life, sacrality or divinity, and masculine human fulfillment with stability, stasis, and self-sufficiency. By focusing on relations rather than on innate properties, oil itself is neither rendered dead, nor granted a property of life, nor the agency of redemption. The example Burkhart gives is of tobacco and the question of whether it has the property of being natural or artificial:

> Naturalness . . . is based on kinship; it is a relation, not a property of something. Tobacco is not natural, but it is how I act toward this relation, with respect toward our kinship, that makes my relations natural or unnatural. When I act unnaturally toward tobacco (when I do not treat it with respect), it is rather harmful to me, but it is not the harmfulness that makes the action bad. I am acting disrespectfully and so behaving badly.[97]

Like Chen, Burkhart here emphasizes the importance of attending more closely to the space between, to that which animates rather than inherent characteristics of dead or liveness, good or bad, natural or unnatural. Oil, then, might not be inherently good or bad, redemptive or demonic, enlivened or dead, but in need of proper respect, relation, and communication.

As Chen's approach to animacy highlights, an ontological divide between life and death is policed with key gender, race, dis/ability political implications. They remind us that the boundary between life and death is often reinforced by associations between uncleanliness, disgust, and the un-living. Chen describes the project of *Animacies* as considering "how matter that is considered insensate, immobile, deathly, or otherwise 'wrong' animates cultured life in important ways."[98] From this perspective, even Western environmentally oriented portrayals of oil as "wrong" often affectively draw on associations of oil with death, blackness, and immorality to evoke disgust. Images of oil-soaked birds and humans frolicking in oil gushers—important as they may have been for mobilizing public outcry that led to stronger regulations of offshore drilling—have often evoked disgust by drawing on a gut-level association with oil as dirty, ugly, and inherently immoral.[99] From Chen's perspective, a persistent association of the materiality of oil (oil corporations are another matter) with immorality, disgust, and crudeness animates pro-environmental agencies by reiterating an alignment of immorality with inertness of feminized death and blackness.

Avoiding rendering oil dead or alive, good or evil, it might be creatively engaged as queer matter, a kind of trickster figure teasing Western binaries and toying with the entrenched desire to identify innate, stable properties. While oil since ancient times has been granted properties of longevity, stasis, permeance, masculine vim, vigor, and life, there are other characteristics of oil that have not been closely attended to, other materialities that disrupt the alignment of life with "petromasculinity."[100] A Western association of stasis and permanence with divinity and masculinity has obscured from view oil's evident slipperiness, its ambiguity, inconstancy and trickster-like materializations, taking on the shape of (and often seeping out of) whatever contains or constrains it. From this angle, LeMenager emphasizes the ways the materiality of oil itself deconstructs a binary between life and death: "oil challenges liveness from . . . [an] ontological perspective, as a substance that was, once, live matter and that acts with a force suggestive of a form of life."[101] As former lives, capturing the sun's energy in the form of carbon, oil defies any easy association with the triumph of life. Rather than solidifying boundaries between dead and alive, animate and inanimate, agent and passive receiver, closely and critically attending to the materiality of oil troubles any clean dualism.

From this perspective, we might be able to better and more critically account for and divest from the ways oil, North American culture, anti-blackness, misogyny, and Western Christianity have resonated with and amplified one another. Tim Morton's queer ecology also offers insights for rethinking oil and liveliness. Morton has emphasized an important shift in queer ecologies away from static and dualistic materialities to envision "liquid life"—a "concatenation of interrelations that blur and confound boundaries at practically any level: between species, between living and nonliving, between organism and environment."[102] In this flow, Whitney Bauman has similarly argued that a queering of ecology reveals that in the liquidity of bodies "we are deeply intertwined with the bio-historical evolutionary flows of other species and organisms: plant, animal, and mineral."[103] As such, living beings do not exist on an individualized linear path from birth to death, but always persist "in the thick of things" embedded in a web of life/death of microorganisms living inside ecosystem bodies and bodies living in wider systems of reciprocal exchange of nutrients, energy, and elements. In this thickness, liquid lives are sustained in deaths and deaths are interrupted with life.

Bauman furthermore suggests thinking queer ecology alongside dualism-disrupting figures like tricksters, magicians, shamans, and radical faeries which often function to "blur the boundaries between right and wrong, life and death, male and female, humans and animals, human and the divine."[104] More than just disrupting rigorously defended binaries, though, attending to the queer, liquid, trickster-like de/animations and dis/enchantments of oil focuses attention on the interface of oil and religion to better account for what is getting animated, for whom, and toward which ends.

From the perspective of religion and oil in North America, then, the imperative role of religiously engaged feminist new materialisms is not necessarily to resurrect a dead world, but to attend more critically to its enchantments and disenchantments, the ways it becomes gendered and racialized, profaned and sanctified by whose logic and toward what aims. As Donna Haraway suggests, "Perhaps the world resists being reduced to mere resource because it is—not mother/mater/mutter—but coyote, a figure of the always problematic, always potent tie between meaning and bodies."[105] Haraway continues, "Perhaps our hopes for accountability, for politics, for ecofeminism, turn on revisioning the world as coding trickster with whom we must learn to converse."[106] Where religiously engaged new materialisms can resist the reduction of materiality to dead, inert matter *as well as* the resurrection of dead matter to unrestrained liveliness, they will better be able to attend to animacies that emerge when bodies encounter one another.

Critical Petro-theologies

From this perspective, oil might again become *thinkable* in all its queer ontological slippages, the ways it remains an "always potent tie between meaning and bodies." Yet in rendering it thinkable, one should not suppose a pure disenchantment is called for. Indeed, being able to better *think* oil should also render it more *conversable* as oil becomes recognized as nature/culture entanglements of matter and discourse.

In the end, a critical petro-theology cannot demand pure demythologization if it is to avoid the trappings of mechanized materialisms. After all, in some instances, particular expressions of sacred relation have infused oil and, in turn, animated remarkably persistent resistance to extractive petro-capitalism. The Latin American, Andean U'wa enchantments of oil, for example, express very different cosmologies and materialize with dramatically different results. From the U'wa perspective, oil is the lifeblood of sacred Mother Earth and thereby should be reverenced and not exploited or instrumentalized. This particular sacralized relation to oil has inspired acts of civil disobedience against the Columbian government and two transnational oil companies, Shell and OXY, both with strong support from US politicians and investors. Though the struggle continues, the U'wa have successfully thwarted efforts to extract oil from nearby and on their territories for over two decades.[107]

In concluding a text devoted to debunking myths and myths about myths, Jason Storm affirms that attempts to eradicate myth-making endeavors are often just as fraught as the myths themselves.[108] Both mythologizing and demythologizing, when taken to extremes, are distorting—and ultimately fold into one another. He acknowledges that while "it might seem that [he has] become a partisan of disenchantment," actually his point is the reverse: "we can never fully escape myth." In conclusion he advocates a kind of demythologization that simultaneously recognizes that "we merely exchange one tale for another, albeit hopefully, a better one."[109] Such pursuits are not without perils and pitfalls. They never have been. This is not because of an inherent danger in enchantment or mythmaking, but because matter and meaning have always been inextricable. And given the persistent modern Western academic overemphasis on critique, analysis, tearing down, or looking behind that has been so importantly called out by Indigenous, postcolonial, and deconstructive voices, continued pursuit of meaning in material relations is an important risk to take.[110] My sense is that increased awareness of the problematic nature of both extremes of enchantment and disenchantment can call for even closer critical attention to our many and various animations and enchantments—greater awareness and even scrutiny of the kinds of materialities they form, the types of bodies they incarnate, who or what they excite, the varieties of patterns and habits they vivify.

In the face of seemingly inevitable climactic doomsday scenarios it becomes all the more important to be able to work toward creative constructions and reimaginations of alternative energy futures. When exchanging one narrative or figuration for a (hopefully) better one, one might note a sense of immanent bodily transcendence[111] in the creative and co-constructive acts of theopoeisis or remythologization, and thereby recognize that mythology and sacrality do not necessarily entail the closure of thought. They might piggyback on one another—even toward alternative energies.

Notes

1 Eaton, *Petroleum*, 252.
2 Quoted in Dochuk, *Anointed with Oil*, 5–6.
3 Like the environmental humanities, new materialism is interdisciplinary, transcending, in particular, an entrenched disciplinary gap between the sciences and humanities. Early and influential voices include Karen Barad, Rosi Braidotti, Manuel DeLanda, Elizabeth Grosz, Vicki Kirby, and Jane Bennett. More recently Zakiyyah Iman Jackson has emphasized the importance of and expanded upon Sylvia Wynter's theory of sociogeny as key for new materialisms in the wake of associations

between Blackness, animality and inert materiality. Though, as I will explain in what follows, new materialists contest mechanistic and reductionistic accounts of matter in conversation with the life and physical sciences, theorists are also often critical of an overemphasis on language and textuality in gender and philosophical constructivisms.

4   Donna V. Jones, *The Racial Discourses of Life Philosophy: Negritude, Vitalism, and Modernity* (New York: Columbia University Press, 2012).
5   Stacy Alaimo and Susan Hekman (eds), *Material Feminisms* (Bloomington: Indiana University Press, 2008); Karen Barad, *Meeting the Universe Halfway* and *"Nature's Queer Performativity"*; and Jane Bennett, *Vibrant Matter: A Political Ecology of Things* (Durham: Duke University Press, 2010).
6   Bennett, *Vibrant Matter*, ix.
7   Diana Coole and Samantha Frost, *New Materialisms: Ontology, Agency, and Politics* (Durham: Duke University Press, 2010), 16.
8   White, "The Historical Roots of Our Ecologic Crisis," 1205.
9   Jürgen Moltmann, *God in Creation: A New Theology of Creation and the Spirit of God* (Minneapolis: Fortress Press, 1993); Alister McGrath, *The Re-Enchantment of Nature: Science, Religion and the Human Sense of Wonder* (London: Hodder & Stoughton, 2003); and Mark I. Wallace, *When God Was a Bird: Christianity, Animism, and the Re-Enchantment of the World* (New York: Fordham University Press, 2019).
10 See Bennett's clarification that "what I am calling impersonal affect or material vibrancy is not a spiritual supplement or 'life force' added to the matter said to house it," xiii. On religious engaged new materialism that often thinks along the lines of Bennett's desire to think the vibrancy of materiality itself and not a spirit within it, see Karen Bray, Heather Eaton, and Whitney Bauman (eds), *Immanent Religiosities, New Materialisms, and Planetary Thinking* (New York: Fordham University Press, forthcoming).
11 Josephson Storm, *The Myth of Disenchantment*.
12 Jones, *The Racial Discourses of Life Philosophy*. See also, Mbembe, who writes that during the first half of the twentieth century, "The figure of Africa as a reservoir of mysteries corresponded with a certain desire within Western discourse . . . for a celebration both joyous and savage, without limits or guilt, in search of a vitalism that had no awareness of evil" (*Critique of Black Reason*, 41).
13 Claire Colebrook, "On Not Becoming Man," 75.
14 Ibid.
15 Weszkalnys, "Geology, Potentiality, and Speculation," 612.
16 Ghosh, "Petrofiction," 29.
17 Ghosh, *The Great Derangement*, 16.
18 Ibid., 21
19 Bennett, *Vibrant Matter*, 1.
20 Paul Sabin, "'A Dive into Nature's Great *Grab-bag*'," 57.
21 Ibid., 477, quoting *Crawford Journal*, September 4, 1860.
22 Ibid., 475.
23 Quoted in Ibid., 477.
24 Sabin suggests, "it forced onlookers to confront what they did not know or control in the natural world" (Ibid., 490).
25 Ibid., 475.
26 Ibid., 481, citing *Crawford Journal*, September 4, 1860.

27 Ibid., 483, citing *The Warren Mail*, August 18, 1860.
28 Ibid., 473.
29 Merchant, *The Death of Nature*.
30 Sabin, "'A Dive into Nature's Great *Grab-bag*'," 473.
31 Ibid., 481.
32 John J. McLaurin, *Sketches in Crude Oil: Some Accidents and Incidents of the Petroleum Development in All Parts of the Globe*, 2nd ed. (Harrisburg: Published by the Author, 1898), 33.
33 Sabin, "'A Dive into Nature's Great *Grab-bag*'," 479.
34 Josephson Storm, *The Myth of Disenchantment*, 3.
35 Benz, *The Theology of Electricity*.
36 See Chapter 1 for details of this summary.
37 Caterine ("The Haunted Grid") emphasizes Native American spirits in Spiritualist narratives of electricity. Zuck ("The Wizard of Oil") notes the presence of Native American spirits in oil "discovery" narratives.
38 Quoted in Caterine, "The Haunted Grid," 372.
39 Ibid., 373.
40 Ibid., 386.
41 Zuck, "The Wizard of Oil," 36.
42 Ibid., 34.
43 Cited in Zuck, "The Wizard of Oil," 23.
44 Ibid., 26.
45 Ibid., 21.
46 Ibid., 27.
47 See Chapter 3.
48 Dochuk, *Anointed with Oil*.
49 Higgins was by no means alone in the practice of intertwining geology and biblical exegesis. Several other leading religious figures, particularly in the South, took up this dual vocation of pastor-geologist. See Dochuk, *Anointed by Oil*.
50 Relevant also here is Brett Grainger's recent recovery of nineteenth-century US evangelical embrace of nature not as disenchanted but as fully infused with divinity (*Church in the Wild*). Grainger hopes, in the end, that this history suggests the possibility again of an evangelical embrace of environmentally friendly ethics. He does not recognize, though, the ways such nature Spiritualities, a love of nature, a sense of wonder at divine presence immanent in nature also evidently influenced and inspired early oil-extraction endeavors.
51 David F. Noble, *The Religion of Technology: The Divinity of Man and the Spirit of Invention* (New York: Alfred A. Knopf, 1997), 17.
52 Ibid.
53 Ibid., 19, Hugh of St. Victor, quoted in Ovitt, *Restoration*, 120.
54 Ibid., 20, See also, Hugh of St. Victor, *Didascalicon* (c. 1127).
55 Francis Bacon, *Novum Organum*, ed. Joseph Devey (New York: P. F. Collier & Son, 1902), Bk II, Aph 52, 290.
56 Francis Bacon, "Masculine Birth of Time," in *The Philosophy of Francis Bacon: An Essay on Its Development from 1603 to 1609 with New Translations of Fundamental Texts*, ed. Benjamin Farrington (Liverpool: Liverpool University Press, 1964), 72.
57 Dochuk, *Anointed with Oil*, 9.
58 See, for example, Andrew Nikiforuk, *The Energy of Slaves* (Vancouver: Greystone Books, 2012). Such arguments are still referenced in a current context, especially

among evangelical Christians. See, for example, J. D. King's argument in "Climate Change and Evangelicals: Thou Shalt Not Fear Fossil Fuels," *The Christian Post*, January 26, 2015. Available online: https://www.christianpost.com/news/climate-change-and-evangelicals-thou-shalt-not-fear-fossil-fuels.html (accessed June 2021). See Chapter 2, fn 110 for a further critique of these arguments.
59 Ernest Lee Tuveson, *Redeemer Nation: The Idea of America's Millennial Role* (Chicago: University of Chicago, 1968).
60 Sabin, "'A Dive into Nature's Great *Grab-bag*'," 475.
61 McLaurin, *Sketches in Crude Oil*, 9.
62 Available online: https://www.worldcat.org/wcidentities/lccn-n91084857 (accessed February 2018).
63 Walter Rundell Jr., "Centennial Bibliography: Annotated Selections of the History of the Petroleum Industry in the United States," *The Business History Review* 33 (1959): 429–47 (439).
64 McLaurin, *Sketches in Crude Oil*, 61.
65 Ibid.
66 Ibid., 38–9.
67 "Star of the East," 1890 (lyricist George Cooper, music by Amanda Kennedy; see William E. Studwell, *The Christmas Carol Reader*, 90).
68 McLaurin, *Sketches in Crude Oil*, 73.
69 Ibid., 33.
70 Ibid., 60–1.
71 Sylvia Wynter, "1492: A New World View," in *Race, Discourse, and the Origin of the Americas: A New World View*, ed. Vera Lawrence Hyatt and Rex Nettleford (Washington: Smithsonian Institution, 1995), 5–57 (26).
72 Ibid., 102.
73 Ibid., 104.
74 Ibid., 46.
75 This was, in great part, thanks to Rockefeller's Standardization of oil production, informed as it was by his assumption of the orderliness, predictability, and accountability of the Protestant work ethic.
76 The oil industry received a series of blows to its public relations in the early twentieth century—these three in particular. Standard Oil was declared a monopoly and broken up into thirty-four different companies. Though the decision was made by the Supreme Court, public awareness of the problem had been raised primarily by Ida Tarbell's nineteen-part investigative journalism series in *McClure's* magazine. Work hazards and low pay led to unionization among laborers. Some very public strikes were met with violence that swayed public support for the laborers. Public sentiment that oil had gained too much economic and political power was confirmed when it was revealed that members of President Harding's administration had accepted bribes from oil companies in exchange for cheap and noncompetitive land leases in Teapot Dome, WY, and other CA locations where the United States held petroleum reserves. Before Watergate, this was considered the height of US government scandals.
77 See Dochuk, *Anointed with Oil*, 210–11 on increase of cars and their usage in the US during this time period.
78 Dochuk describes the API as "a clearinghouse for industry concerns, a command post for application of industry-wide standards, and a lobby through which oil representatives could impress their wishes upon Washington and the public" (*Anointed with Oil*, 218–19).

79 Ibid., 222.
80 Quoted in Dochuck, *Anointed with Oil*, 223.
81 See Ibid., 222. On Muscular Christianity, see Putney, *Muscular Christianity*. For a more recent rendition and analysis of muscular Christianity in twenty-first-century US American politics, see Kristin Kobes Du Mez, *Jesus and John Wayne: How White Evangelicals Corrupted a Faith and Fractured a Nation* (New York: Liveright Publishing, 2021).
82 Barton, quoted in Dochuk, *Anointed with Oil*, 223.
83 Cited in Wilson, "Gendering Oil," 255.
84 Ibid., 250.
85 Ibid., 251.
86 Ibid., 252.
87 Ibid.
88 Miranda Green, "Rick Perry: US 'Blessed' to Provide Fossil Fuels to the World," *The Hill*, January 24, 2018. Available online: https://thehill.com/policy/energy-environment/370585-rick-perry-us-blessed-to-provide-fossil-fuels-to-the-world (accessed February 2019).
89 Grau, "From Refiner's Fire to Refinery Fires," 166. See also, Grau, "Petro-eschatology."
90 Freudenthal, *Aristotle's Theory of Material Substance*, 179.
91 Ibid., 178.
92 Weszkalnys, "Geology, Potentiality, and Speculation," 612.
93 LeMenager, *Living Oil*, 6.
94 Mel Y. Chen, *Animacies: Biopolitics, Racial Mattering, and Queer Affects* (Durham: Duke University Press, 2012), 13.
95 Burkhart, *Indigenizing Philosophy Through the Land*, 297.
96 Ibid., 195.
97 Ibid., 297.
98 Chen, *Animacies*, 2.
99 This could apply even to aspects of LeMenager's work. As a resident of Santa Barbara who has studied the oil spill of 1969, one might sympathize with LeMenager's oil aesthetic: her book's cover image of a jubilant human positively dripping with crude seems aimed to evoke disgust, and she repeatedly asks and responds to the question throughout the text, "why is oil so bad?" (See, for example, *Living Oil*, 68, 70, 80, 92, 101).
100 Daggett, "Petro-masculinity."
101 LeMenager, *Living Oil*, 6.
102 Timothy Morton, "Queer Ecology," *PMLA* 125 (2010): 273–82 (275). Cited also in Whitney Bauman, "Queer Values for a Queer Climate: Developing a Versatile Planetary Ethic," in *Meaningful Flesh: Reflections on Religion and Nature for a Queer Planet*, ed. Whitney Bauman (Santa Barbara, CA; Earth, Milky Way: Punctum Books, 2018), 103–24 (115).
103 Ibid., 117.
104 Ibid.
105 Donna Haraway, "Situated Knowledges: The Science Question in Feminism and the Privilege of Partial Perspective," *Feminist Studies* 14 (1988): 575–99 (569).
106 Ibid.
107 Margarita Serje, "ONGs, Indios y Petróleo: El Caso U'wa a Través de los Mapas del Territorio en Disputa," *Bulletin de l'Institut Français d'études Andines* 32 (2003).

Available online: http://journals.openedition.org/bifea/6398; DOI: https://doi.org/10.4000/bifea.6398. See also Ángela Uribe Botero, *Petróleo Economía y Cultura el Caso U'wa* (Bogotá, Columbia: Editorial Universidad del Rosario, 2005). Many thanks to my colleague Miguel Gualdrón Ramírez for alerting me to this case and suggesting these resources.

108 See Introduction for overview of Storm's work and its importance for the framing of this project.
109 Josephson Storm, *The Myth of Disenchantment*, 316.
110 See, for example, Robin Wall Kimmerer, "Skywoman Falling," in *Braiding Sweetgrass*, 3–10; Walter D. Mignolo and Catherine E. Walsh, "Introduction," in *On Decoloniality: Concepts, Analytics, Praxis* (Durham: Duke University Press, 2018), 1–14; and Burkhart, *Indigenizing Philosophy Through the Land*, xxvi.
111 See Myra Rivera's postcolonial, Levinasian reinterpretation of the "touch of transcendence" as transcendence between bodies on a horizontal plane in *The Touch of Transcendence: A Postcolonial Theology of God* (Louisville: Westminster John Knox Press, 2007).

Chapter 5

ALTERNATIVE ENERGIES

I came so that you might have life and have it abundantly

—John 10:10

The Gospel of John's Jesus declares he has come to give life and give it abundantly (NRSV). Another influential translation communicates Jesus' message as giving life fully, "to the full" (NIV). Concurrently, an Enbridge Energy campaign plainly states, "E=life itself." As the Petrocultures Research Group emphasizes, this ad constructs a reality where "our social and personal lives . . . are only possible with the energy that Enbridge provides. . . . Enbridge uses these expertly crafted images to tell us that happy and fulfilling lives depend on them."[1] According to Enbridge, today energy *is* petroleum and life remains unimaginable if not impossible outside a petroculture. What kind of theology is implicitly enacted when life is divinely given in abundance while its definition "relies heavily upon oil"? What happens to the Gospel message of life abundant when life means energy and energy means oil?

Resurrecting the Carbon Cycle

It could, for instance, take the form of the redemption petro-theology offered by E. Calvin Beisner, founder of the Cornwall Alliance for the Stewardship of Creation, a major promoter of climate denialism.[2] In responding to Kathryn Hayhoe's and Thomas Ackerman's op-ed[3] arguing for congruence between evangelical beliefs and action in response to climate science, Beisner disputes their conclusions by converging oil and the Christian narrative in the twenty-first century as McLaurin and Eaton had in the nineteenth: "Stop and think for a moment: Innocent creatures die, are buried, are brought up out of the ground, and bring life to others. Haven't you heard that story before? Of course you have. It is the basic summary of the gospel." For Beisner, oil "literally [gives] life—long and healthy life—to billions of human beings . . . beautifully picturing the death, burial, and resurrection of our Lord and Savior Jesus Christ."[4] Beisner expands on this oil redemption narrative, citing 1 Corinthians to demonstrate how, like redeemed human bodies, oil bridges the material and spiritual. He writes, "At death the human body 'is sown a natural body; it is raised a spiritual body.' If there is a natural body, there is also a spiritual body. Thus it is written, 'The first man Adam became a living being'; the last Adam became a life-giving spirit (1 Cor. 15.3-4, 44-45)."[5] In Beisner's petro-theology, organic matter is buried as a seed, only to rise to its fulfilled spiritual form as "life giving" energy. This redemption narrative, he argues, is a much more Christian way to think about the carbon cycle than permanent carbon sequestration where death remains in the grave.

Beisner's interpretation is not unprecedented. Indeed, one of the most common early Christian metaphors of resurrection, articulated by Paul (whom Beisner cites), as well as Gregory of Nyssa and others, was the seed, buried in the ground like the body, only to rise to new life in a resurrected body.[6] That this theology directly impacted the ways Western Christians thought about the material world, its meanings and purposes, is evidenced in the fact that the term "resource" has its etymological roots in resurrection.[7] Through Christian theologies of redemption, then, minerals become resources, materials buried in death, only to rise to their true actualized form when they are most useful and valuable to humans and thus ready to be plucked from the earth. After Aristotle and at least through the Reformation, divine reason or providence was seen as guiding the development of minerals in the ground. Recall, for example, from Chapter 3, that for Mathesius and other Reformation-era mineralogists minerals were seeds planted by God, growing to full fruition when they were ready to be picked from their beds.[8]

Not only does Beisner's petro-theology draw on ancient resurrection theologies, but his petro-gospel is seemingly confirmed by the sense that oil manifests empirically verifiable results—it seems to perform what it signifies. It not only symbolizes new, transformed life, but in Beisner's theology, it can also actually bring it about, "giving life—long and healthy life—to billions of human beings."[9] Clearly, though, oil performs the life and redemption Beisner refers to only from a particularly limited perspective. As Dipesh Chakrabarty emphasizes, "the mansion of modern freedoms stands on an ever-expanding base of fossil fuel use"[10] and as the #NoDAPL, Idle No More, and NDN Collective protests clearly demonstrate, when it comes to fossil fuels, the life and freedoms they grant for some are intimately linked to the death and toxic bondage of others.[11]

On account of this resurrection drive toward new life, there has been an inability in Christian thought, affect, and practice to let something lie fallow, to embrace loss as loss and not a momentary setback invested for a later greater gain. Just as carbon sequestration registers for Beisner as anti-Gospel because it refuses to rise to new life again, so too others have concluded that this ultimate triumph of life over death, gain over loss, was an essential aspect of Christianity that made capitalism appear as a particularly Christian economy where one's sacrificial investments were never wasted, never left for dead, but would always return triumphant, redeemed with interest.

Neither Christianity nor capitalism can abide loss as a final answer—redemption of investment or capitalization on loss is too fully engrained. This shared intolerance is not coincidental, but, as economically oriented theologians have recognized, it is the result of a mutual influence and interdependence, an extended resonance and at times explicit exchange between Christianity and capitalism.[12] According to philosopher Mark C. Taylor, both Derrida and Bataille identify in Hegelianism "a transparent translation of the foundational principles of a capitalistic market economy" alongside an inability to account for loss ascribed to a latent Christian influence.[13] In *The Phenomenology of the Spirit*, Hegel claimed to preserve loss and negation within his dialectic, but as Derrida and Bataille emphasized, the one thing Hegel's symbolic economy still could not abide was unredeemed loss.[14] In Hegel's symbolic economy, negation is swallowed up, subsumed, given new meaning and purpose as it is synthesized with affirmation. Derrida notes that for Hegel, "there must be meaning . . . nothing must be definitely lost in death."[15] A symbolic economy with a theological mandate or affective compulsion to make meaning, not let anything go to waste, and turn liabilities into assets translates into an idealized capitalist economy where every investment is capitalized, every loss redeemed. As I have argued elsewhere, from this perspective, growth-based "capitalism emerges as the ultimate expression of a Christian economy because it functions by a principle of resurrection: ideally every investment dies only to return—redeemed, resurrected as a capital gain."[16]

Despite a preliminary dependence on loss or negation, as Derrida and Bataille have emphasized, in the end the loss proves to be a good investment. Beyond the irrational trauma of the death of God—of God against God, and divine absence—the loss is not total, the despair not final. In the end, the shock of loss and the irrationality of the death of God merely serves to amplify the power and triumph of reasserted life—and life now that is impervious to any of its earlier vulnerabilities since it not only overcomes negation, but subsumes it. While such alliances between resurrection and capitalist growth can be rationalized, they gain their force of impact on an affective level. Perhaps on an affective level this is what appealed to Hegel so that in spite of his criticism of some of the social effects of capitalism, he still amplifies its triumphal gesture and is compelled to "[secure] a return on every investment."[17]

Life's continual and inevitable triumph over death assumes a certain temporality, an onward march of time triumphant toward a better future guided by the hand of God. These temporalities are often more felt and embodied than thought. Many have identified the progressive temporality of capitalism, modern science, and technology as a secularized Christian salvation history.[18] Such progression was also explicitly reinforced by modern energy science.[19]

Critical analysis of the progressive linear timeline has been a regular feature of critical engagements with various iterations of capitalism. Queer and affect theories, political theology, and theological critiques of capitalism resonate around a diagnosis of the problematic temporalities of capitalism.[20] Queer theorists in particular have analyzed the ways that capitalist temporalities reinforce heteronormativity, while political and radical theologians have emphasized the ways the time of capitalism, while seeming to rely on change, is only capable of reinforcing the same disguised as radical change.[21] This, as we will see, is true of extractive capitalism in that "alternative energies" all too often promise radical change, but merely result in more of the same energy growth.

While alternative energies often do not carry through on a promise of something radically new but merely result in the same energy additions, the temporality of extractive capitalism is also much more disruptive than most analyses account for. Where capitalism is critiqued for its faith in, and reinforcement of, a linear, progressive, law-like temporality, a lens of *extractive capitalism* reveals that its temporality is also fundamentally dependent on the disruptions of loss and negation. With extractive capitalism, as with oil, the march of ordinary time is premised on an interruption—the new, exception to the ordinary.

As we look more closely once more at the intersection of energy and capitalism, we will see that energy growth has not been characterized by a smooth linear accumulation.[22] Since the Second World War, US energy consumption has been a key part of economic increase and maintaining this continued growth has required trauma—and the ability to capitalize on it.[23] Extractive, energy-intensive capitalism depends less on progressive gradual increases of accumulation and more on a crisis-driven rupture of the smooth flow of time. Resilience, the ability to capitalize on trauma, thus emerges as a new iteration of triumphant victory over death and destruction.

In this sense, extractive capitalism tracks even more closely to resurrection affects and temporalities than has typically been identified. Where capitalist temporalities might be chrononormatively linear and progressive, extractive capitalist temporalities build progress only through the disruption—death, crisis, loss—of linear time. Life here is life only in that it defies death by growing out of it. This is the case from creation accounts of life emerging *ex nihilo*—out of nothing—to redemption where triumphant resurrection emerges only out of the nihil of death and divine absence. This is the dialectic at the heart of triumphal resurrection narratives: life not only overcomes its antagonist—it subsumes it, metabolizes it, synthesizing death into new strength and newly fortified life. In this way, the triumphal life drive also centers on, turns on, depends on death—it must be metabolized, synthesized in order to render life transformed, newer, stronger, more invulnerable. Life emerges as indestructible where it is no longer threatened by death because it has subsumed it.

A key locus of intervention for a critical petro-theology therefore emerges at the heart of the Christian story. Undergirding the anthropological emphasis of Chapter 1, the doctrine of God focus of Chapter 2, the role of grace emphasized in Chapter 3, and the life and death dynamic highlighted in Chapter 4 is a secularized Christian narrative of crucifixion, death, and triumphal new, fulfilled life. To resist the affects and temporalities of extractive capitalism, then, alternatives to both the linear, orderly, expected progressive temporality of growth *and* its exceptional disruptions are needed. Exploring truly alternative energies will require a closer analysis of the imbrications of life and death, trauma, and crisis as they have been predominantly interpreted and narrated in Western Christianity through the lens of resurrection and redemption. As affect theorists have emphasized, temporalities are imbued with affect and different affects assume different temporalities.

In the conclusion I will make a case for the significance of Holy Saturday from within this accumulative life/death dialectic. The liturgical day commemorating the time/space between Christ's death and his Easter resurrection, Holy Saturday has traditionally been celebrated as a vigil, a time for keeping watch. This time/space offers an alternative to typical life/death dialectics and encourages affects and practices of vigilant witness to experiences where life is not triumphant, where death continues to interrupt its progress. In creating some space or play within the life/death dialectic, Holy Saturday presents an opening in Christian-infused temporalities to recognize alternative embodied energies that have persisted on the underside of extractive capitalism. These are not new alternatives that will break into the normative temporalities of extractive capitalism. They do not need to be uncovered, mined, or invented. The time/space of Holy Saturday points to alternative embodied energies that have remained, resisting extractive capitalism merely by their persistence.

Resilience: The Time of Extractive Capitalism

Energy and international policy decisions in the United States have frequently been swayed by reference to the preservation of an American "way of life." Encompassed are practices of exuberant consumption, high production, and intensive extraction. Yet, this "way of life" has not emerged as a natural or inevitable result of economic practices and population increase, nor has it been driven solely by the triumphs of technological innovations. Reverberating in this way of life is a certain learned response to the trauma of energy limits. Rather than being identified as experiences of shame and key moments to recalibrate consumption by exploring alternative ways of life, these energy crises have been triumphantly and resiliently overcome. Rather than a smooth accumulation of energy growth, twentieth- and twenty-first-century extractive energy capitalism has fundamentally depended on crisis, destruction, and loss, followed by triumphally resilient exponential increase. As a result, the secularized theology we find at the heart of extractive capitalism is no mere liberal progressive salvation history, but a life/death, crucifixion/resurrection dialectic where new growth depends on the resilient return of new life after negation, crisis, and destruction.

While a progress narrative does not quite account for an integral dependence on crisis functioning in the temporalities of extraction capitalism, resilience tracks more closely to the affective arch of time wherein inevitable "progress" depends on trauma, crisis, and loss. "Resilience" refers to a set of affective and cognitive resources allowing a person or group to bounce back or recover after calamity or trauma.[24] Yet, resilience is not just a synonym for adaptation or adaptability. While adaptation suggests the possibility of a new trajectory, a permanent change in response to alterations in the environment, resilience suggests a return to an original state—but with new strength, growth, and vitality. Resilience distinguishes itself from both adaptation and linear, progressive growth by emphasizing certain affects and cognitive resources that allow one to take crisis or trauma and metabolize it into strength, to come back even stronger than before. As philosopher of gender and race, Robin James, explains, "resilience is the hegemonic . . . ideology that everything is to be measured . . . by its health. And this 'health' is maintained by bouncing back from injury and crisis in a way that capitalizes on deficits so that you end up ahead of where you initially started."[25] Rather than transformation to a new state or different trajectory, resilience seeks to use a challenge, transforming it into an opportunity to return to a more "natural" state with increased vigor.

Resilience has recently been popularized in psychology and self-help genres, but philosopher Mark Neocleous has emphasized the military roots of the recent heightened emphasis on the term. He has noted a key shift toward resilience rhetoric in US Homeland Security and UK National Security documents produced after 9/11. Here resilience strategies took the place of a more traditional neoliberal emphasis on security or prevention which aimed to *avoid* catastrophe. By contrast, resilience *assumes* trauma, expects it, and has learned to capitalize on it to get ahead. In so doing, "progress" now also depends on it. In fact, Neocleous and James emphasize key connections between resilience and its assumption of and dependence on "disaster capitalism,"[26] a phenomena Naomi Klein has identified as the strategic use of national crises in various places around the world to initiate key shifts in economic policies toward less regulation. While there is certainly something distinctive about the way that resilience affects and strategies have emerged in military and neoliberal capitalist strategies since 9/11 as Neocleous and James suggest, the affective arch of resilience is also clearly building on and resonating with something much more engrained in Western culture: triumphal resurrection narratives.[27]

The affective trajectory of resilience overlaps with but remains distinct from the traditional liberal Protestant work ethic of progressive, rational, step-by-step improvement. Just as with the dynamic between grace and the Protestant work ethic outlined in Chapter 3, the resilience of resurrection depends on a break in the rationality and predictability of this narrative. It interrupts progressive growth narratives with the shock of the irrational, the paradoxical, death, loss, and destruction.

Life here is life only in that it defies death by growing out of it. This is the dialectic at the heart of triumphal resurrection narratives: life not only overcomes its antagonist, it also metabolizes it by subsuming it. Life synthesizes death into new strength, vaccinating itself against its opposition. In this way, the triumphal life drive also centers on, turns on, depends on death just as extractive capitalism now depends on crisis—death and crisis must be metabolized, synthesized in order to render life transformed, newer, stronger, more invulnerable. Life becomes indestructible when it is no longer threatened by death because it has subsumed it.

Resilience both carries particular theological weight and also, while receiving significant current—often uncritical—attention, has a history that carries certain embodied energy lessons driving energy practice and policy. The story of US energy increase can be identified as a resilience narrative. J. R. McNeill and Peter Engelke have argued that energy consumption in North America and Europe (more recently China, which in 2010 surpassed the United States in energy consumption) has followed a pattern of acceleration after 1945 rather than gradual accumulation. These authors emphasize the role of population increase and suggest that "so far humankind has influenced basic Earth systems only by accident, as an unforeseen and unintended by-product of actions undertaken for routine quests for wealth, power, and contentment."[28] Yet, there is reason to emphasize that while humans in 1945 could not have anticipated the kinds of ecological effects we see today in climate change, it is misleading to conclude that increased energy use during this time was an "unintended" by-product.[29] Rather than a smooth accumulation following population increase, significant energy spikes have followed experiences of trauma, crisis, and loss, and these increases were part of strategic plans to resiliently bounce back stronger than before. I'll highlight two key moments when white US citizens affectively learned in the midst of anxiety-provoking confrontation with limits, how to use energy to overcome their damage, to turn their liabilities into strengths, to run headlong into their anxieties about death, decay, and loss, coming out stronger and more capable of continuing the US capitalist-imperial project.

Resilience and Architectural Exuberance The first example follows the ways energy was used as a strategy to overcome key crises of the twentieth century. A history of architecture can help illuminate the ways US energy increase followed periods of trauma, with energy playing a key role in resilience strategies to overcome these challenges. After the crisis of the Great Depression and the Second World War, maintenance of the wartime state of emergency economy was a key part of the national recovery plan. This much is widely known. Not widely acknowledged but highlighted by scholar of architecture, Daniel Barber, is the role modern architecture played in these patriotic aims. Barber writes that "much of the purpose of architectural innovation in the American post-war context was towards developing means to increase energy use."[30] The key, influential example he cites is the Equitable Insurance Building in Portland, OR. This building, completed in 1947, was designed by Pietro Belluschi and was the first glass box tower ever built. It would become a pioneer of modern style, emulated time and again all over the country and then the world. This building and the many others inspired by it have also become infamous for their energy inefficiency: heating and air vents were placed on the outside walls, up against single-paned glass surrounding the entirety of the tower. Contrary to common perception that the energy inefficiency of the style of building was due primarily to a misplaced emphasis on style over substance or that energy-efficient technology hadn't caught up to the modern aesthetic, Barber explains that in designing the building in this way Belluschi "aspired to use as much energy as possible, in order to aid the national prospect of continuing to operate, quite literally, in the state of emergency that wartime production had instigated, and that was seen as essential to post-war recovery."[31]

Individual consumers did not initially drive this increase, consumption did not drive production.[32] Rather, Belluschi explicitly cites the existence of excess "cheap energy" coming from hydropower plants along the Columbia River "and the imperative to turn this abundance towards full employment after the war"[33] as key motivating factors for designing the building as he did. Barber's analysis of Belluschi's expressed desire that the building use *as much energy as possible* and his vision that the building style play a key role in maintaining a wartime state of emergency in order to help the economy and the country bounce back suggests that this key time of energy increase in US energy consumption did not follow as a natural consequence of increased population—nor was it unintended. The significant increase in energy consumption following the Second World War was a response to crisis and the affective desire to resiliently bounce back with increased vigor and vitality on the world stage. Individual consumption did not drive this expansion. An economic strategy using energy practices that resonated with a resilience affect to bounce back after crisis drove this exponential increase. In turn, imperatives to increase energy consumption with the promise of an economically redemptive end created new desires in consumers for a more energy-intensive lifestyle.

Resilience and Embodied Exuberance Even this mid-twentieth-century energy-intensification resilience strategy, though, was building on embodied, affective energy lessons learned by US Americans in the late nineteenth and early twentieth centuries. While climate concerns currently evoke a profound sense of energy emergency, the anxieties of the current crisis were foreshadowed in what might be considered the first modern energy crisis during the nineteenth century. Societies have faced shortages in fuel and energy resources since ancient times, but a profound sense of disorientation and a pervasive tenor of energy crisis pervaded late nineteenth- to early twentieth-century modern Western cultures. This is often considered the first distinctively modern energy crisis since it was directly provoked by the emergence of modern industrial society and the science of thermodynamics. Recall that while the first law of thermodynamics (1840s) had affirmed a sense that the workings of the world were being upheld by a constant, universal, seemingly benevolent and life-sustaining force, the second law, closely following in the 1850s, seemed to call this benevolent sustenance into question by emphasizing that within a closed system, energy available for human use is always diminishing. The influence of the law of entropy, or "heat death," did not remain confined to the realm of science but had widespread social influence. Such revelations led to increased anxieties about energy limits, heat death, and entropy—on all levels from the cosmic, to the national, to the bodily. Cara Daggett suggests that the intensity of this energy-induced anxiety and disorientation is comparable only to "the later energy crises of nuclear holocaust or climate change."[34]

The cosmic and scientific became intimate where signs of entropy seemed to emerge in US national resources and white male bodies. Toward the end of the nineteenth century there was an emerging recognition that what had once seemed to be a land of endless resources was showing signs of diminishment and limits. This time period marks the beginnings of the conservation movement along with increases in immigration, Black emancipation, and calls for expanded civil rights for women. As historian Carolyn de la Peña explains, it was these cultural shifts "that gave rise to fears of decreasing 'potency' and 'power' in white males."[35] The historian therefore emphasizes that the late-nineteenth-century energy crisis and its energy-intensive responses emerged as a reaction to a perceived threat to white masculine superiority and privilege.

The perceived challenge to white masculine privilege and superiority had a marked impact on anxieties about white male health and vitality. Historians mark this period as the "discovery" of fatigue. While the weariness of human muscle and wearing down of mortal bones, joints, and spirits was as ancient as high childbirth death rates or an enslaved Potosí miner's six to eight-year life-work expectancy, a wave of exhaustion among educated men in "developed" and "civilized" societies toward the end of the nineteenth century sparked the creation of "fatigue" as a new diagnostic criteria. De la Peña, for example, notes that "physical depletion among middle-class, white males reached epidemic proportions by 1900."[36] Concerns about white male fatigue were focused mainly on the bodily and mental strains of industrialization and modern life.

New York physician George Miller Beard first diagnosed a bodily energy malady in the 1860s and called it "neurasthenia." The disorder was explicitly conceptualized in relation to the second law of thermodynamics. In fact, according to de la Peña, neurasthenia was so commonly known that it was mainly through awareness of this disorder that most US residents came to be introduced to the second law of thermodynamics. Consequently, the disorder was generally seen as a particular bodily "physical manifestation of global energy depletion."[37]

Once again, in this context energy was acting to delineate genres of humanity.[38] As Todd Vogel explains in *Rewriting White*, "Only the pure and 'advanced' Anglo-Saxon was supposed to feel the pain of nervous disorders. Anglo-Saxons' heightened states, according to the best medical minds of the time, freed them from the quotidian demands of finding food. This new leisure time, in turn, allowed their minds to turn in on themselves, become overly contemplative, and render the body ill."[39] While neurasthenia was a disorder of the individual in society, the consequences of the disorder, if left untreated, were given national and even global significance. Where the disease was framed in terms of entropy, as de la Peña explains, "there appeared two options available: to find additional energy or to suffer the 'heat death' of humanity."[40] On a national level, such weakness in white males would lead to a loss of their leadership and influence in America—a concern influential leaders like Teddy Roosevelt (a neurasthenic himself who found a cure in Muscular Christianity) framed as "racial suicide."[41] The nineteenth-century energy crisis was simultaneously social and environmental, bodily and cosmic.

Many theorists and physicians like Beard saw neurasthenia as an inherently sexual disorder. In response to heightened anxieties about the insufficiency of white male energies to compete with machines and meet the demands of industrialized, mechanized modern life, nineteenth- and twentieth-century Americans sought ways of subsuming mechanistic energy within their bodies to overcome the crushing energy demands of a mechanized, industrialized society. De la Peña outlines a variety of strategies from weight lifting and exercise machines to electric belts and ingestible radium cures. While other approaches like that of Muscular Christianity focused on exercise and weight lifting to treat neurasthenia, Beard's most common prescription was electric treatments. The theory supporting the effectiveness of this treatment relied on an understanding, as nineteenth-century expert on sexuality and physiology Frederick Hollick explains, that "nervous substance and seminal fluid . . . [were] essentially the same thing."[42] In relating seminal fluid with electricity, preachers and physicians effectively imbued seminal fluid with a higher significance than mere procreation: "ejaculatory fluid became life force."[43] Concurrently, electricity was raised to a higher plane of significance. As one 1906 advertisement headline in the *Los Angeles Herald* proclaims, "The Human Body is an Electric Battery: Startling new discoveries prove beyond a doubt that 'Electricity is Life.'"[44] That bodies could be infused with electrifying energy, that electrical currents could give life, and that bodies could overcome energy limits through it, were strategies that depended on a deep culturally assumed energy theology outlined in Chapter 1 where divinity, life, high energy, and virility were intimately associated and exchangeable. In this context it became possible, as de la Peña emphasizes, "to believe that only by fully exploiting electricity . . . could life evolve to its fullest potential."[45]

Though not yet explicitly identified as resilience, the logic and its affects were clearly functioning at the time. David Butler, developer of a popular theory and method of weight training in the 1850s, promoted his method by explaining, as de la Peña summarizes, that "Not only could the Health Lift add energy to the body enervated by the pace of modern urban life, it could use the very mechanism that threatened men's obsolescence to ensure their success."[46] US Americans sought to not just overcome energy limits, but to resiliently run headlong into them—employing the very thing that threatened them in order to ultimately overcome the threat, bouncing back stronger, more vital, more energetic than ever.

In the hundred years between 1850 and 1950, in which de la Peña analyzes these strategies for overcoming energy crises, US Americans became the world's highest energy consumers.[47] During this period, a white male energy crisis was interpreted as a symptom of cosmic and global entropy, and an indicator of a national societal entropy crisis. In response to the anxieties evoked by these options, US Americans experimented with a variety of remarkable energy-enhancement strategies. Through these strategies, Americans learned coping strategies to gain a sense of overcoming, making themselves resilient in the face of such limits. Energy patterns, habits, and desires were learned by human bodies—and these bodies taught minds certain lessons about energy that continue to inform twenty-first-century US residents. These energies became fully incorporated into a taste for energy in daily life—habits and routines that became a cultural heritage, a "way of life" worth defending, worth preserving, and (especially once it comes to twentieth-century oil interests in the Middle East) worth fighting for.

Alternative *Energies?*

As early as the second law of thermodynamics, the pursuit of "alternative energies" has been driven by a logic of resilience, of an answer to a crisis and a need to come back stronger than before. In a popular science magazine, William Thomson

(Lord Kelvin) explained the second law of thermodynamics and entropy to his nineteenth-century lay audience. Seemingly anticipating an anxious response, he closed the article with a resilient conclusion: the current energy crisis will not condemn us, but merely press the urgency of discovering alternative energy sources which will strengthen us.[48] While alternatives have been pursued, where they remain driven by a resilient affective response, new "alternatives" merely result in more of the same—energy additions that continue to delineate genres of humanity.

Many and various solutions to the twenty-first-century energy crisis have been proposed. Some are relatively low tech, already achievable and adaptable for cities,[49] but those that gain the most attention and political traction—like those characterized by ecomodern masculinity[50]—depend primarily on technological solutions for producing new and different energy sources: wind, sun, nuclear, tidal energy production or other geoengineering, carbon capture techniques. A key aim of ecomodern solutions is to maintain or allow for continued growth in energy consumption while decoupling high-energy consumption from environmental destruction.[51]

Given the urgency and high stakes of climate change, many will find it reasonable to push for decarbonization by whatever means possible. Yet, Indigenous scholar Kyle Powys Whyte problematizes ways the call to urgency overlooks the fact that new renewable energies can merely recreate patterns of colonialism, domination, and marginalization.[52] All too often, alternative energy techno-solutions continue to carry the same energy values, assumptions, and desires that led to this moment of energy crisis and continue to function in ways that consolidate power, disenfranchise local—often Indigenous—populations, and create or perpetuate social and economic inequalities.

An increasing number of studies by energy humanities scholars emphasize this problem. Anthropologist Gökçe Günel, for example, closely followed the creation of an entirely new experimental city in Abu Dhabi, built from the ground up to dramatically reduce carbon emissions. In *Spaceship in the Desert,* though, Günel demonstrated how the city structures, organizations, and power dynamics remained fundamentally unchanged from a typical fossil-fueled modern city. The main difference was a change in energy inputs.[53] Cymene Howe and Dominic Boyer similarly followed the creation of several wind parks in Mexico, finding that often these wind parks continued extractivist and exploitative patterns that perpetuated colonial patterns and neoliberal economic practices.[54] Karen Rignal found much the same in analyzing a move to create a solar industry in Morocco. Rignal emphasized that renewable energy is often "based on centralized generation models that plug into existing infrastructure" that in the end serves "to perpetuate the inequalities and environmental damage associated with incumbent energy regimes."[55] The Mayapple Energy Transition Collective has summarized such concerns with a warning that "solar and wind power are sometimes assumed to have traits more conducive to a democratic and egalitarian organization of power. . . . However, renewable energy systems do not guarantee democracy and equality, as they can be easily harnessed by authoritarian and exploitative regimes."[56]

While critically analyzing alternative energy solutions, many energy humanities scholars emphasize a remaining commitment to the importance of exploring and developing renewable energy sources. Others emphasize that solutions need to focus less on exchanging energy inputs and more on changing energy systems.[57] Given the ways a resilience affect has functioned in exponential US energy increase, I think it is also crucial to emphasize that whatever the input or system, if the underlying or driving affects, desires, and habits are not addressed, existing patterns will remain and what seem to be "alternatives" will merely result in more of the same. As Sheena Wilson emphasizes, the danger of purely technoscientific solutions is that they reinforce "a fantasy that promises those of us in the West that we will be able to conveniently replace one form of energy for another and continue to live as we always have . . . . The flawed fantasy . . . is one of radical sameness—business as usual disguised as radical innovation."[58] All too often, "alternative" energies emerge merely as new inputs for established patterns of energy inequality, domination, extraction, consolidation of power, and exuberance.

Recent research demonstrates just how energy "alternatives" have functioned in precisely this way. In the Introduction, I opened this exploration of critical petro-theology by outlining a current climate conundrum: the confounding reality faced today that at least since the IPCC began its research, the more that is known about climate change and its anthropogenic causes, the more energy is consumed. Over the course of the text, I've highlighted several attempts to explain or make sense of this phenomenon: from savior tech turned tragic narratives to market-driven explanations. Along the lines of market explanations, and the fossil economy fusion Andreas Malm has described in particular, Richard York and Shannon Bell (of the Mayapple Energy Transition Collective) have identified a "displacement paradox" in the history of energy production whereby alternative fuel sources actually end up *increasing* overall energy consumption.[59] They demonstrate a pattern whereby rather than acting as true *replacements*, new energy alternatives historically have acted as energy *additions*, merely adding to a cumulative increase in energy consumption. Consequently, they argue that the language of "energy transition," commonly used among energy researchers like Vaclav Smil, the IPCC, politicians, and climate activists, is deceptive in that it does not account for the fact that in the past 200 years, "no established energy source has undergone a sustained decline with the addition of a new energy source. Rather, consumption of all energy sources has typically grown."[60] While "alternative energies" have promised transitions and radical change, in the end their cumulative effect—at least for the past 200 years—has merely been more of the same.

York and Bell point to market factors—an economic dependence on growth—informing the pursuit of alternatives that end up functioning merely as alternatives. Given the just mentioned analysis of resilience functioning in intensive energy culture, I would add that a trajectory of continual growth—economic and energy—has relied on affective, theologically informed, gut-level responses to the experience of crisis, trauma, or limitation.

York and Bell's conclusions challenge commonly proposed solutions to the climate crisis that aim to replace fossil fuels merely by expanding the use of other energy sources. Such approaches risk merely expanding the available options for energy consumption while also failing to address the ways that energy systems are tied to social and political structures that have rendered certain modes, rhythms, and patterns of being human exceptional to the interdependence of material existence. I suggest that unless we re-think/feel the underlying assumptions about energy that fuel desires, patterns, habits, and expectations about the good life and its fulfillments—those underlying theologies of energy, the ways they energize divinity, Man, and energy consumption—then technoscientific alternative energies informed by them risk merely resulting in energy additions rather than a true energy transition. Since new technologies can be infused with old patterns of white masculine petro-capitalism, technology alone will not solve the current climate crisis. We also need alternative embodied, affective, habitual energies that can, in turn, inform the kinds of technologies, sciences, and energy systems pursued.

Through the lens of critical petro-theology employed throughout this text, I have highlighted the dynamics of modern *extraction* as infused with a sovereign, exceptional, omnipotent, external input divinity that can intervene in orders of nature with force.[61] Extractive *energy*, we should now emphasize, also functions according to the ideal of the sovereign exception: it both sets the law of the ordinary, while retaining the power of interruption. We see this in the Scottish energy scientists' conceptions of energy as the irruptive, free, unreciprocal gift; in nineteenth-century US oil narratives where oil emerged as exception to the law-like order of Cartesian-Newtonian physics; with Eaton and Stewart who emphasized oil as divine gift imbued with omnipotent characteristics like unlimited supply and power; and finally, in the previous analysis of the resilience of energy exuberance, where energy consumption sets the law of the ordinary while new "alternatives" emerge as a rupture of the ordinary, as exceptions, that eventually set a new standard, a new ordinary of increased energy consumption. In an energy-intensive culture, energy provides both the foundation of the ordinary and its exception. When bent to serve an overarching progressive productivist narrative, this exceptionality turns into resilience. Given the ways energy sciences and technologies—especially new "alternatives"—have emerged as exception to the ordinary or mundane that yet sets the ordinary in motion, there is need to think carefully and critically about the implications of this exceptionality for narratives of change, the introduction of newness, and modes of resisting the established order of extractive capitalism.

The sovereign exceptionality of Man and his Energy have become mutually dependent and mutually reinforcing. In analyzing petro-theologies as I have done throughout this text, it becomes clear that true alternatives become possible only where they are grounded in a recognition of the ways overrepresented Man (Wynter) has coincided with overrepresented Energy. As Michael Marder asserts, "Today's extreme and highly destructive energy dream presents itself as the sole possible reality (better, as the possibility of producing the one necessary and sufficient reality)" that excludes other alternatives as unrealistic, utopian, unproductive.[62] Far from being less metaphysical than Aristotle's unmoved mover or Hegel's Spirit, Marder asserts that energy functions today as more stringently metaphysical than these earlier iterations. "Hiding under the sheepskin of pragmatic concerns, the latest formalization of energy is a wolf, *more intensely metaphysical* than its forerunners, given the effectiveness with which it devours time, difference, and possibilities that disagree with its flat vision of the world."[63]

Yet, clearly the dominant modern Western form of energy is merely one manifestation. Other forms emphasize flux and flow[64] rather than storage and capture. Other forms emphasize surface over depth.[65] Alternatives emerge as contemplation over action, powerlessness over power, and the fullness of the present over a striving for future actualization.[66] Many of us know this experientially—the way one can be energized through contemplation, prayer, or breath awareness, how energy can surge and diminish through a crowd in protest or celebration, how one's capacity for creative work can be either excited or hampered by a community or context, or how attending to the flux and flow of the change of seasons carries different energies. As Cara Dagget has emphasized, energy need not just be work-driven and progressive-oriented. Julia Steinberger's research, outlined in Chapter 1, points to this empirically as well. There are ways of living, modes of being where humans can experience meaningful and sustained lives with even low to moderate energy consumption—and there are ways that high-energy culture can be profoundly detrimental to human mental, physical, and social health.[67]

Yet, sovereign energy presents itself as the only option, uncontestable, unquestionable, of ultimate value and immeasurable worth. Even where the language of oil and energy as divine is no longer employed, modern energy still affectively functions in the manner of a monotheistic jealous deity. To contest it, then, is to identify current energy domination for what it is and explore alternative embodied technologies, technologies of the self and systems, through art, poetry, theopoesis, ritual, liturgy, attunement[68], protest, and community- and coalition-building—to think, feel, practice energy differently.

Holy Saturday Time/Space

I remain uncertain that Christianity, as it has been predominantly received in the white West, can offer any "solution" that won't merely continue patterns that pave the way for the expansion of Man along with his energy. That space has been conceded by the exceptionality of whiteness in claiming possession and property, that time too successfully put to work in extractive capitalism. But if there was a time/space that might create some room from within the orders of resilient driven extractive capitalism for alternative energy imaginaries, it might be something like Holy Saturday for the ways it resists the triumphal drive of resilient life by holding life/death in tension while pressing attention toward alternative energies embodied in the lives of those who have not served extractive capitalism well, who have been excluded or deemed unfulfilled by its doctrine of Man.

Given the ways resilience has functioned within extractive capitalism, pursuing true alternative energies that will not result in merely more of the same additions calls for closer attention to experiences of limitation and finitude. It calls for exploring affective responses that do not aim to subsume a limit and transform it into transcendence. Triumphal Christian resurrection has excelled at transcending limits, metabolizing the limit of death into newly vivified and fortified life, and metamorphosing trauma into triumph. Common conceptions of Christian resurrection emerge as a key stumbling block for exploring alternative energies in an energy culture profoundly influenced by the Christian tradition. For Western modern Christianity it seems contrary to the core of the faith—indeed, to life itself—to leave an investment unredeemed, let the potentiality of a seed go unactualized, let petro remain in the grave, or accept the vulnerability of shame or loss without triumphing over it. Beisner, recall, has emphasized as much, arguing that carbon sequestration is simply un-Christian in that it refuses to raise up carbon to new life again.

While the ending of John's Gospel seems to confirm the centrality of abundant life to the Gospel message and its post-resurrection culmination—"But these are written so that you may come to believe that Jesus is the Messiah, the Son of God, and that through believing you may have life in his name" (John 20:31)—there are other narratives, corresponding timelines, energies, and embodiments. Michael Marder's important reinterpretation of ancient *energeia* as excluding the drive of *potentia*-obsessed modern energy and Kathryn Tanner's insightful interventions in finance capitalism could both, for example, be seen as offering alternative perspectives on John's call to the fullness of life.[69] Tanner, like Marder, resists the stretch of modern *potentia* by drawing attention to the fullness of the present. In articulating the ways Christianity could be articulated as a direct counter to the temporalities of finance capitalism, Tanner emphasizes that finance capitalism is intensely focused on the present such that past and future possibilities are cut short. Christianity, too, she emphasizes, retains an intense focus on the present. "By virtue of such an overlap in temporal sensibility," Tanner argues, "a Christian approach to the present has the capacity to infiltrate the way finance-dominated capitalism encourages one to relate to it, and in so doing disrupt it."[70] The present focus of finance capitalism is forced by scarcity and the necessity to grasp an opportunity before it slips away. For the Christian, by contrast, the present comes into heightened focus not because its opportunities will be lost but because of the "overwhelming attractiveness of the offer" God makes to provide precisely what is needed in every moment.[71] Each and every moment divine grace is offered in full by God who is indivisible and thus never present only in part. Where every moment is filled with full divine presence, all of time is within God—past, present, and future—so that when God is present in each moment, all of time "becomes thereby ours as well in the present."[72] In this sense, the focus of finance capitalism, drawn to the present by the constant flux of fortune and passing opportunity, is directly countered by divine presence available in full, in every moment, without change.

For both Marder and Tanner, the fullness of the present resists the drive toward unlimited potentiality. Just as Tanner emphasizes the ways this grace-full orientation in the present forms a particular subjectivity that can resist the subject formation of finance capitalism, Marder emphasizes corresponding contemplative practices—like Buddhist meditation or Eastern Orthodox Hesychasm—that draw attention to the fullness of the present.[73] While Tanner does not explicitly address energy, a correspondence between her work and Marder's suggests important implications not just for finance, but also for extractive energy capitalism. From this perspective, both Tanner and Marder can be seen to emphasize the fullness of life lived in the present as an alternative energy, resisting modern energy and its capitalist spirits. Both offer remarkably compelling theologically informed alternatives to the temporalities of modern energy and finance capitalism.

Yet, a sole focus on the eternal glimmer of the present does not adequately address a context like today's extractive energy culture where entrenched patterns of injustice set the rhythms of the everyday. As I've demonstrated, in extractive capitalism time is not only stretched forward by the enticements of unlimited *potentia*, its accumulative accelerations are built on resilient responses to the continual crisis oriented interruptions of the smooth flow of progressive time. In extractive capitalism entrenched and interruptive patterns of injustice set the rhythms of the everyday. I worry, then, that a sole focus on the fullness of the present can obscure attention to the crucifixions of the past and experiences of divine abandonment that still interrupt every present moment in extractive capitalism. Such experiences could only register as exceptions to the fullness of divine presence available in each moment. I suggest there might also be something theological that draws closer attention to these interruptions, incompleteness, and uncertainties of the present. From this perspective, the lure of the sacred draws attention to those who wait in the midst of unfulfillment, abandonment, and crisis.

Holy Saturday provides this space/time, especially in its iterations that draw from feminist, womanist, postcolonial, and liberation theologians who have critiqued triumphal Christian resurrection narratives and sacrificial atonement theories.[74] Shelly Rambo and Karen Bray draw particular attention to the importance, in the contexts of these critiques and debates, of a basic rethinking of the relationship between life and death—particularly the ways life and death become profoundly unsettled through trauma.[75] Rambo argues that the typical Christian life/death dualisms and dialectics driving toward a triumphal resurrection cannot abide the disruptions of trauma. Since Freud's study of soldiers of the First World War, theorists have noted the ways that trauma disrupts a linear progression of time. A distinguishing mark of a traumatic event is that it exceeds the human's cognitive sense of the world. Since a traumatic event cannot fit within the conscious orders of the world, the survivor continually relives the event, trying unsuccessfully over and over again to make it compute. The incompatibility of the experience creates a profound disruption in the typical flow of time from past to present and future. With trauma, the present is always haunted by the past and the future cut off by an inability to imagine an alternative. Within a traditional Christian narrative arch there has been little room to attend to the sense that trauma survivors live with: where life is continually haunted by death, where the past refuses to remain in the past but keeps pushing into the present. Such experiences insist that there is something important that needs attending to in the time/space between death and life.

Rambo moves to create space for the disruptions of trauma in conversation with theologians Hans Urs von Balthasar and Adrienne von Speyr who drew particular attention to a significant gap in theological reflection on the liturgical day between Christ's death on Good Friday and resurrection on Easter Sunday. On account of the rush to affirm life and claim the triumph of resurrection, they argued, theologians have consistently overlooked Holy Saturday. In drawing attention to this gap, von Balthasar and Speyr asked, "What is it that persists between death and Resurrection?" Balthasar concludes that this time/space between life and death "is a problem of theological logic; perhaps it is *the* problem that the theologians have never attended to [. . .]."[76] On Holy Saturday, Balthasar and Speyr conclude, "the logic of life and death is shattered."[77] It resists any smooth progression from death to life and attending to this liminal time/space contests a sense of resurrection as triumph over death by subsuming it into new life. As Rambo emphasizes, "There is a witness arising from the middle that cannot simply be translated into the logic of death or life, cross or resurrection."[78] Rambo seeks to give theological significance to this middle space/time and, significantly, ties the liminal space of Holy Saturday between death and life to the disruptions of trauma.

Rambo reimagines a Christianity that attends to and does not seek to merely overcome trauma, a Christianity that makes space for these disruptive experiences of life haunted by death and death porous to life, rather than continually repressing its disruptions and thereby reproducing traumatic effects. This is what makes Rambo's work significant for Karen Bray's other-than-Christian theological engagement with the time/space of Holy Saturday. For Bray, the time of Holy Saturday is particularly significant in the context of her critical analysis of secularized neoliberal theologies of redemption. Crucially, Bray focuses in particular not just on theologics, but also on the affects of neoliberalism, redemption, and Holy Saturday disorientations. Surveying critical engagements of neoliberal capitalism, Bray notes that "few have adequately addressed how post-Fordist temporalities feel. And as such how we might learn to embody a different sense of time."[79] Bray diagnoses the affect of neoliberalism as oriented by a trap of dual temporality. Post-Fordist time feels like being stuck between the crucifixions of the past that continue to haunt long after the overt structures of enslavement, land requisition, or intensive extraction take place on the one hand, and the promises of a better, easier, more prosperous, but continually out of reach, future on the other hand. Bray articulates this, in other words, as being stuck between living "in the wake of crucifixion and the shadow of an uncertain resurrection."[80] To articulate this feeling of living in the dual temporality of neoliberalism, Bray draws on Rambo's engagement with Holy Saturday and trauma theory.

Rambo and Bray agree that Holy Saturday theologies like those articulated by Balthasar and Speyr have relied too heavily still on the promise of a redemptive Sunday. Yet, they find it important to remain with them long enough to learn how temporality, and the corresponding life/death dynamic, are being re-felt, rethought. Bray in particular importantly addresses concerns that trauma theory focuses solely on the rupture of an event and thus cannot adequately account for the slow violence or repeated traumas of systems like colonialism, slavery, or climate change.[81] Bray focuses in particular on the "cruel optimism" (Berlant) conveyed in many ableist, patriarchal, heterosexist, anti-Black forms of neoliberal redemption on offer in twenty-first-century capitalism. These traumas may be single events or, more pervasively, a series of events over generations, a slow violence that systematizes, institutionalizes, and legalizes a biopolitical lack of support for flourishing and survival. Such "unredeemed" modes of living have been marginalized, rejected, and suppressed on account of their unwillingness or inability to contribute to the progressive trajectory of capital accumulation and energy intensification. Rather than rushing to healing, wholeness, and resiliently overcoming so as to become a productive contributor to a sociopolitical economic system that favors a few and constrains the rest to lives of precarity, Bray emphasizes that her interest is not in "being saved" out of an unproductive present. Rather, her interest is in asking "how one should better remain, and so live, when unsure whether one really wants a resurrection that may not be coming."[82] In contrast to resilience, both Bray and Rambo articulate a mode of being that aims less to overcome damage and more to allow different ways of living and feeling emerge through it.

For Rambo, the middle time/space of Holy Saturday calls not for proclamation but for witness "to the truths that are in danger of being covered over and buried."[83] What Speyr describes of her mystical experiences is neither crucifixion nor redemption but an experience of endurance and persistence in the midst of loss and even divine abandonment. From her critical lens of neoliberal redemption narratives, Bray similarly emphasizes what she calls "grave attending." "Grave attending," Bray explains, witnesses "to those identities, collectivities, and possibilities assumed to be buried over and gone, the ghosts that haunt us and so gift us a sense of what we might have been and an imagination of what we might become."[84] In the space/time of such Holy Saturday grave attending, where the past continues to interrupt the completeness of the present and death infuses life, a theological divestment from resilience can begin to emerge in "caring for the gravity, the pulling down to the material world, the listening and feeling for what all its myriad emotions have to tell us and where they have to lead us."[85] In doing so, a binary between death and life, where life must seek to overcome and engulf death, loses its hold.

Reflecting on exchanges with church and neighborhood leaders who lived through Hurricane Katrina in the ninth ward, Rambo heard a witness not to the triumph of life, but to what remains: "Death persists. Life is not victorious. There is no life after the storm but only life reconceived through the storm."[86] Rambo points to biblical examples of Mary Magdalene and John's beloved disciple who testified to something that cannot be simply equated with classic interpretations of resurrection life. She explains, "Mary and the beloved disciple testify to a death event in and through which a different conception of life emerges—a picture not of victorious new life but of persistent witness to love's survival."[87] Holy Saturday time/space is not a time of reflection before moving on to happier times, it is not a moment of waiting for the arrival of a muscular Christian savior. For those suffering from climate change disasters like hurricanes, fire, and drought, and those contemplating strategies for climate mitigation, Holy Saturday vigilance is not despair, acceptance of fate, and certainly not the ratification of extractive capitalism's status quo. From the time/space of Holy Saturday vigilance, this is "*the* place and *the* time from which we can find alternative ways of living and structures of feeling that better enflesh a democratic temporality."[88] Rather than continually investing in a progress-promised future, persisting with Holy Saturday opens a space/time for attending to and investing in alternative embodied, affective energies.

In Holy Saturday the present may offer, as ever, intimations of the fullness of divine presence, but also, as ever, ruptures of abandonment, absence, and lack. Rather than turning away from the interruptions of the fullness of the present, Holy Saturday divestments "welcome hauntings of those subjectivities [neoliberalism] has tried to flee." Bray adds, "We welcome such a haunting, not so that we might vanquish our ghosts, but so that we might recover ways of relating to past, present, and future selves and others."[89] Robin James, too, suggests that in resisting resilience she is not suggesting "an opposition to or rejection of life" but calling for "investment in 'unviable practices,' practices that may help you survive but won't help you win."[90] As such, divestment, rightly understood is not just a removal of support from unsustainable investments, but also the important reinvestment in alternatives that have persisted.

Attention to the affects and temporalities of Holy Saturday addresses the gut-level response to loss which seeks to triumph over it in order to not be crushed by it—a response that continually retains the same trajectory of energy increase even through the pursuit of an alternative. It also opens space for those living in intensive-energy, resilience-driven, predominantly Christian culture to recognize the ways that predominant climate "solutions" and public policy plans to "build back better" move anxiously to return to "normal" and restore a sanctified "way of life." They thus miss the crucial moment of reflecting on what it might look like to choose an alternative path, to "reconceive life through the storm" rather than leaping to life "after the storm."

Drives to explore resilient alternative energies also obscure the alternative energies that have persisted in the bodies, lives, habits, and relations of those who would not serve the aims of extractive capitalism. Leanne Simpson, for example, emphasizes that what resistance to settler colonialism and its capitalist iterations has looked like for her and her Nishnaabeg ancestors is remaining, persisting in the face of unrelenting attempts at erasure, in doing as "we have always done."[91] Macarena Gómez-Barris similarly emphasizes modes of resistance that have emerged through those who remain—persisting in their witness to alternative perspectives and ways of life—within Latin American extractive zones.[92]

In emphasizing Holy Saturday, my aim is not to Christianize alternatives by articulating them through a frame that would be recognizably Christian. Rather, in addressing an energy-intensive culture that continues to be enchanted by the resilience of Christian resurrection, I suggest the trope of Holy Saturday might hold open time/space to attend to the persistence of life in death and death in life. I think it is crucial for those who have predominantly benefited from energy-intensive lifestyles to learn what incomplete and interrupted presences might convey about living differently in a world of climate crisis. I suspect such imaginaries could provoke greater solidarity with movements that have long resisted, long posed alternative energies that do not fit within the temporalities and affects of extractive capitalism. Holy Saturday affects demonstrate how to hold in tension, how to persist within and not consume difference into renewed strength. Rather than "mining" resources for alternative living in the Anthropocene among those who have persisted as the unredeemed of extractive capitalism, the call here is to give witness to alternative energies that have persisted and show up more fully in solidarity.

Energy Re-placements

The story of energy-resilient time is also the story of extractive space. As Jason Allen-Paisant so artfully and poignantly demonstrates in his poetics of nature walking—out of place as a Black man in a public park near his current home in Leeds—the temporalities that infuse Euro-American nature aesthetics and outdoor practices, delineated through the lens of "free time" and opportunity for leisure, are intimately tied to a deeply ingrained sense of a presumptive right to and possession of space and place.[93]

Relatedly, as emphasized in Chapter Two, Willie James Jennings has demonstrated that the story of space in the West remains intimately entwined with the story of race. Jennings points to a devouring view of space tied to a "destructive form of joining" that had become intimately entwined with Christianity.[94] In joining the Gentile to the story of the Hebrew people, Christians have predominantly forgotten that they were latecomers, mercifully grafted, according to Paul, onto the story of God's people and promises (Romans 11:17-18). Instead of God made *Jewish* flesh, the story of Christ became one of supersession, erasing, engulfing, consuming, metabolizing God's promises to the Jewish people for the "higher purpose" of a more disembodied universal Christian story. As Jennings emphasizes, this destructive form of joining profoundly limited the Christian imaginaries of intimacy and relationship with difference and space.

This destructive form of joining became the story of colonization and enslavement. It also became the history of energy-intensive culture: nineteenth century US American Harmonialism narrated the role of electricity and energy technologies as consuming nature and Indigenous lives with it, transforming them to a higher plane of existence;[95] Belluschi's new modern architecture turned consumption of hydropower into the higher power of nation-building; nineteenth- and twentieth-century American bodies absorbed mechanistic energy into their bodies, metabolizing it into new vitality and secured life. These are all patterns of what Jennings has identified as a destructive form of joining rooted in Christian supersession of Jewish history and promise.

This destructive form of joining functions in the relation between life and death as well. In addition to the capitalist dynamics of refusing to let an opportunity pass to capitalize on meaning, Derrida similarly identified the consuming dialectic of life and death in Hegel's *Logic*. In Hegel's thought death became engulfed by life so that "life no longer has any opposition" because death itself melts into something "unthinkable."[96] Such is the result of resilience as well. By metabolizing death or crisis into new strength, it is folded into a new triumphal life fully vaccinated against earlier vulnerability.

This is the broad appeal of resilience, even beside its empirical successes. It tracks in ways tantalizingly close to the affective and theological arch of Christian resurrection and redemption. Indeed, if Jennings is correct, and I believe he is, that the Christian imagination has become severely distorted and limited by its supersessionist form of joining, resilience follows precisely the affective arch of this form of redemption. In resilience, death is swallowed by life, metabolized into new strength to "build back better."[97]

But as Jennings and Kelly Brown Douglas have emphasized in their analyses of white supremacist Christianity, this articulation of the redemption story is also profoundly docetic.[98] Just as triumphal redemption narratives found ways to surpass the reality and fullness of death, for resilience redemption death is not *truly* death but merely a springboard to new life. This profoundly distorts the Christian message about life and death by rendering death merely an illusion. Christian hope is not founded on escape from death. Indeed, the best a Christian can hope for is to be joined with Christ "in a death like his" (Romans 6:5).

The docetic death denial of resilience temporalities has allowed energy to seemingly transcend the limitations of materiality and finitude. Energy has been wrapped into the logics and affects of displacement and disembodiment. It has been allowed to float free from its emplacement, surging magically from "nowhere" to the touch of a button, the flip of a switch, the turn of a key. Modern Western aesthetics of place, city, home, and nation-building have consistently obscured and camouflaged extraction and utility sites. Treated as exceptional inputs, sleights of hand in architecture and city planning create the illusion of self-sustaining magic, energy from nowhere. Re-emplacing and rematerialzing energy could take the form of heightened visibility of its functions, integrating rather than camouflaging mechanization, utility, and extraction into the aesthetics of buildings, cities, and landscapes. When localized, this would not only bring heightened accountability, but also help disenchant and rematerialize the "magic" of light, heat, sound, and entertainment "out of nothing" at the touch of a button.

The materializations of energy and intimate congruence of bodies with energy is also what the view of climate change as primarily an "emissions" problem obscures. An "emissions"-driven climate diagnosis depends on the logics as well as the practices of extractivism. "Emissions" climate change repeats the logic of its production by extracting meaning from the intra-human, the intra-bodied, the intra-creature in order to arrive at the global, the out-of-body, transcendent view, as Usher emphasizes, of emissions from nowhere. It misses and profoundly obscures the ways that energy policy and practice are intimately tied to views of what it means to be human, what divinity means, and how the sacred intersects, dwells in, acts through, or becomes manifest in the material world. In this sense, climate change is not just caused by extractivist practices. It has also been conceptually constructed, diagnosed, and described from within the framework of extractivism.

My point in critiquing predominant energy alternatives is not to take a defeatist or purist position with regard to technology and conclude that windmills or solar panels are "wrong." My point, rather, is to emphasize as I have throughout this text that there is an intimate congruence of energy with bodies, habits, affects, and theologies. I want to highlight the ways that the energy/climate crisis, though massively trans-human, trans-species, trans-national, and trans-corporational, is also profoundly intimate, coursing through and between historical and present bodies. Ecomodernist perspectives emphasize the importance of intensifying modern technology in order to decouple energy from environmental destruction. What this assumes, though, is that energy is a neutral that can be plugged into any system or culture to allow for its daily functions. To contest this sense of the neutrality or universality of energy I have emphasized the particularities of Western extractive, resilient energy and its systems and technologies that make more possible certain ways of life, certain ways of living, certain embodiments, while occluding others—and that this genre-fication of ways of being human has been a function of Western energy concepts from ancient *energeia*, to *vis viva*, to modern energy. Consequently, extending this form of energy also entails extending Man, merely continuing historical modes of colonization.

A critical petro-theology, then, does not turn away from the mechanical to focus on the "natural" or embodied, but attends more closely to the nature/culture embodiments machines create and the kinds of machines different embodiments—modes of living, values of life/death, and energies—pursue. Nor does it emphasize the personal or individual over the systemic. Emphasizing embodied energies or affects should not be taken to suggest that the climate crisis will be solved with individual, personal choices, and responsibility.[99] Rather, this approach can help examine the kinds of affect that sustain an energy-intensive culture, the kinds of "lessons our bodies teach our minds,"[100] and how they emerge at the nexus of systemic, institutional forces and flesh and blood bodies.

Modern Western energy has played an oversized role in the overrepresentation of Man in that it has tied the stakes of complying with this mode of humanism to the basic continuation of life. Current energy practices and policies favor certain bodies over others, make room for some bodies and not others, render some lives livable and others precarious. Given that energy concepts from ancient *energeia* to modern energy have so consistently functioned to delineate genres of humanity, what if in pursuing energy alternatives we expected them to take place in bodies as much as in machines?[101] If energy culture has shaped bodies, then can't different embodiments—habits, daily rhythms, orientations, and fluctuations—also contest the current monolithic energy regime? "Unproductive," fluctuating, flowing, passive, inert, incapacitated bodies have often been at odds with the aims of extractive capitalism. Ill-suited for the activation of capital or energy accumulation, such bodies manifest diverse rhythms and habits of daily life.[102] What if social movements to make room for various and more diverse embodiments were also recognized as posing alternatives to the monolithic white masculine-petro-resilient energy regime? What if we took seriously that different energies create space for, open time for, different ways of being human? What if climate movements not only created space to mourn the losses of global warming, but also created spaces to recognize the persistence of alternative energies in bodies, lives, and relations that have not well served the aims of extractive capitalism?[103] These alternative energies need not be discovered or invented. They are not novel or state-of-the-art. They do not provide a sovereign exception nor do they uphold the status quo. Such alternative energies have remained. They have persisted through histories of colonization, enslavement, misogyny, homophobia, and extractive globalization. These alternative energies need witness, attention, and the time/space of something like the life/death disruptions of Holy Saturday to remain.

Notes

1 Szeman et al., *After Oil*, 47.
2 On the Cornwall Alliance's role in promoting climate denialism, see Alumkal, *Paranoid Science*.
3 Kathryn Hayhoe and Thomas Ackerman, "Climate Change: Evangelical Scientists Say Limbaugh Wrong, Faith and Science Complement One Another," *The Christian Post*, August 21, 2013. Available online: https://www.christianpost.com/news/climate-change-evangelical-scientists-say-limbaugh-wrong-faith-and-science-compliment-one-another.html (accessed January 6, 2022).
4 E. Calvin Beisner, "Fossil Fuels, Enemy or Friend? Divine Design in the Carbon Cycle," *The Christian Post*, October 28, 2013. Available online: https://www.christianpost.com/news/fossil-fuels-enemy-or-friend-divine-design-in-the-carbon-cycle.html (accessed June 2021).
5 Ibid.
6 See Nyssa's conversation with sister Macrina in *On the Soul and Resurrection*.
7 Tina Asmussen, "The Cosmologies of the Early Modern Mining Landscape," in *Landscape and Earth in Early Modernity: Picturing Unruly Nature*, ed. Christine Göttler and Mia Mochizuki (Amsterdam, Netherlands: Amsterdam University Press, forthcoming).
8 The metaphor of oil as seed is still employed in the twenty-first century. See, for example, Penélope Plaza, "Rare Seeds: How Venezuelan Artists are Breaking the Spell of Oil," *Energy Humanities*, October 26, 2021. Available online: https://www.energyhumanities.ca/news/rare-seeds-how-venezuelan-artists-are-breaking-the-spell-of-oil (accessed October 28, 2021).
9 Ibid.
10 Chakrabarty, "The Climate of History," 208.
11 Nick Estes and Jaskiran Dhillon (eds), *Standing with Standing Rock: Voices from the #NODAPL Movement* (Minneapolis: University of Minnesota Press, 2019).
12 See, especially, Singh, *Divine Currency*.
13 Mark C. Taylor, "Capitalizing (on) Gifting," in *The Enigma of Gift and Sacrifice*, ed. Edith Wyschogrod, Jean-Joseph Goux, and Eric Boynton (New York: Fordham University Press, 2002), 50–74 (53).

14 Georges Bataille, *The Accursed Share: An Essay on General Economy, Vol. 1: Consumption*, trans. Robert Hurley (New York: Zone Books, 1991) and Jacques Derrida, "From Restricted to General Economy: A Hegelianism without Reserve," in *Writing and Difference*, trans. Alan Bass (Chicago: University of Chicago Press, 1978), 251–77. Much of Derrida's thought can be interpreted as an attempt to make room in symbolic economies of exchange for unredeemed loss or the wholly otherness of difference. In contrast to Christianity, aspects of Jewish thought can be interpreted as retaining a sense of unfulfillment: prescriptions to let land lie fallow, to leave a seat open for Elijah, or to continually keep an eye out for the messiah who (in Derrida's interpretation) will never return.
15 Derrida, "From Restricted to General Economy," 256–7.
16 Terra Schwerin Rowe, "Response to Annika and Joerg Rieger," in *The T&T Clark Handbook on Christianity and Climate Change*, ed. Ernst Conradie and Hilda Koster, 65–9 (67); see also Schwerin Rowe, *Toward a Better Worldliness*, 58.
17 Taylor, "Capitalizing (on) Gifting," 55. See Andrew Buchwalter (ed.), *Hegel and Capitalism* (Albany: State University of New York Press, 2015) on Hegel's concerns about capitalism.
18 Donna Haraway, *Simians, Cyborgs, and Women: The Reinvention of Nature* (New York: Routledge, 1991); Bauman, "Queer Values for a Queer Climate," 103–24.
19 William Thomson and his fellow evangelical interlocutors infused energy with a sense of progressive time, an irreversibility that would only march on with its steam engines and ships toward an imperial, triumphal future. See Smith, *The Science of Energy*.
20 Bray in particular makes this argument in "The Madness of Holy Saturday: Bipolar Temporality and the Queerdom of Heaven on Earth," in *Sexual Disorientations: Queer Temporalities, Affects, Theologies*, ed. Kent L. Brintnall, Joseph A. Marchal, and Stephen D. Moore (New York: Fordham University Press, 2018), 195–217. See also, Tanner, *Christianity and the New Spirit of Capitalism*; Bauman, "Queer Values for a Queer Climate"; Elizabeth Freeman, *Time Binds: Queer Temporalities, Queer Histories* (Durham: Duke University Press, 2010).
21 See Crockett, *Radical Political Theology*.
22 J. R. McNeill and Peter Engelke, *The Great Acceleration: An Environmental History of the Anthropocene Since 1945* (Cambridge: The Belknap Press of Harvard University Press, 2014).
23 K. Swart, "Trends in the Energy Market After World War II," *Journal of Power Sources* 37 (1992): 3–12.
24 See Mark Neocleous, "Resisting Resilience," *Radical Philosophy* 178 (2013): 2–7, and James, *Resilience and Melancholy*.
25 James, *Resilience and Melancholy*, 4.
26 Naomi Klein, *The Shock Doctrine: The Rise of Disaster Capitalism* (New York: Picador, 2008). This link is also cited in Bray, *Grave Attending*, 50.
27 An insight I owe to the work of Bray and de la Peña.
28 McNeill and Engelke, *The Great Acceleration*, 209.
29 Christophe Bonneuil and Jean-Baptiste Fressoz, *The Shock of the Anthropocene: The Earth, History and Us*, trans. David Fernbach (New York: Verso, 2017).
30 Daniel Barber, email exchange following his presentation at Rice Energy Symposium, "Emergency Exit" at Rice Cultures of Energy Symposium 8, April 12, 2019 (May 1, 2019).

31 Barber, email exchange. See also Barber's book since this exchange, *Modern Architecture and Climate: Design Before Air Conditioning* (Princeton: Princeton University Press, 2020).
32 See Joerg Rieger on consumption driving production rather than the reverse, in *No Rising Tide: Theology, Economics, and the Future* (Minneapolis: Fortress Press, 2009).
33 Barber, email exchange.
34 Daggett, *Birth of Energy*, 60.
35 de la Peña, *The Body Electric*, 12.
36 Ibid., 27.
37 Ibid.
38 See Chapter 1.
39 Todd Vogel, *Rewriting White: Race, Class, and Cultural Capital in Nineteenth-Century America* (New Brunswick: Rutgers University Press, 2004), 108.
40 de la Peña, *The Body Electric*, 28.
41 Ibid., 28–9.
42 Ibid., 145, citing Hollick, "Popular Treatise on Venereal Disease."
43 Ibid.
44 *Los Angeles Herald: Sunday Morning*, December 19, 1906.
45 de la Peña, *The Body Electric*, 169.
46 Ibid., 49.
47 Ibid., 1.
48 Ibid., 29.
49 David Miller, *Solved: How the World's Great Cities are Fixing the Climate Crisis* (Toronto: University of Toronto Press, 2020).
50 Martin Hultman, "The Making of an Environmental Hero: A History of Ecomodern Masculinity, Fuel Cells and Arnold Schwarzenegger," *Environmental Humanities* 2 (2013): 79–99.
51 See Caine et al., *Our High-Energy Planet*. This aim of decoupling high-energy consumption from environmental destruction through technological innovation is characteristic of ecomodernism.
52 Kyle Powys Whyte, "Too Late for Indigenous Climate Justice: Ecological and Relational Tipping Points," *WIRES Climate Change*, 2019. Available online: https://onlinelibrary.wiley.com/doi/abs/10.1002/wcc.603 (accessed January 2020).
53 Gökçe Günel, *Spaceship in the Desert: Energy, Climate Change, and Urban Design in Abu Dhabi* (Durham: Duke University Press, 2019).
54 Cymene Howe, *Ecologics: Wind and Power in the Anthropocene* (Durham: Duke University Press, 2019); Dominic Boyer, *Energopolitics: Wind and Power in the Anthropocene* (Durham: Duke University Press, 2019).
55 Karen Eugenie Rignall, "Solar Power, State Power, and the Politics of Energy Transition in Pre-Saharan Morocco," *Environment and Planning A: Economy and Space* 48: 540–57 (542).
56 Bell, Daggett, and Labuski, "Toward Feminist Energy Systems," 4.
57 In their call for an energy philosophy, Geerts et al. emphasize that different systems, like a national energy grid versus a local grid or an off-the-grid solar energy system, not only provide different ways to address a technological energy crisis but can also have the added benefit of challenging implicit assumptions, attitudes, and values. They emphasize that different systems might "induce different practices, different attitudes toward energy consumption." The authors therefore call for a shift from a general goal based on the *amount* of energy produced toward more closely attending

to the *quality* of energy—the way that these energy systems can create better or worse communities, a higher or lesser amount of attunement to natural patterns and seasons, and so on ("Towards a Philosophy of Energy," *Scientiæ Studia* 12 (2014): 105-27 (119)).

58 Wilson, "Energy Imaginaries," 380.
59 York, "Do Alternative Energy Sources Displace Fossil Fuels?" and York and Shannon Bell, "Energy Transitions or Additions? Why a Transition from Fossil Fuels Requires More than the Growth of Renewable Energy," *Energy Research and Social Science* 51 (2019): 40-3.
60 York and Bell, "Energy Transitions or Additions?" 41.
61 Chapter 2.
62 Marder, *Energy Dreams*, 27.
63 Ibid., 28.
64 See Geerts et al., "Toward a Philosophy of Energy," 121+.
65 See Marder on the surface-level, nonviolence of plant energies, *Energy Dreams*, x.
66 Ibid., 8+.
67 Steinberger and Roberts, "From Constraint to Sufficiency," 425.
68 Whitney Bauman, "CPR for Planet Earth," *Counterpoint*, February 25, 2020. Available online: https://www.counterpointknowledge.org/cpr-for-planet-earth/ Date (accessed, June 20, 2021).
69 See Chapter 1 on Marder.
70 Tanner, *Christianity and the New Spirit*, 124.
71 Ibid., 126.
72 Ibid., 130.
73 Marder, *Energy Dreams*, 44.
74 Womanists like Delores Williams have condemned the ways sacrificial atonement has served to valorize or justify the surrogacy of enslaved and minoritized women (Delores Williams, *Sisters in the Wilderness* (Maryknoll: Orbis, 1993)). See Marit Trelstad (ed.), *Cross Examinations: Readings on the Meaning of the Cross Today* (Minneapolis: Fortress, 2006) for a good survey of voices and overview of key issues. Latin American ecofeminist Ivone Gebara has diagnosed a death denial in Christianity while, relatedly and not contradictorily, ecofeminist Val Plumwood has diagnosed Western Christianity and philosophy with both death preoccupation and death denial (Ivone Gebara, *Longing for Running Water: Ecofeminism and Liberation* (Minneapolis: Fortress Press, 1999) and Plumwood, *Feminism and the Mastery of Nature*). Various theologies of the cross such as that articulated by Douglas John Hall have condemned the triumphal narratives of Christianity for the ways they have conspired with imperialism (Douglas John Hall, *The Cross in Our Context: Jesus and the Suffering World* (Minneapolis: Fortress Press, 2003)), while radical theologies like those of Clayton Crockett and death of God a/theologies like that of John Caputo contest sovereignty and thus embrace divine powerlessness (Crockett, *Radical Political Theology*; John D. Caputo, *The Weakness of God: A Theology of the Event* (Bloomington: Indiana University Press, 2006)).
75 Shelly Rambo, *Spirit and Trauma: A Theology of Remaining* (Louisville: Westminster John Knox Press, 2010).
76 von Balthasar, quoted in Rambo, *Spirit and Trauma*, 61.
77 Ibid., 42.
78 Ibid., 144.
79 Bray, "The Madness of Holy Saturday," 196.

80 Ibid., 203.
81 See Lauren Berlant's critique of trauma theory as imbued with a logic of exceptionalism—trauma as an exceptional event—in *Cruel Optimism* (Durham: Duke University Press, 2011).
82 Bray, "Madness of Holy Saturday," 211.
83 Rambo, *Spirit and Trauma*, 48.
84 Bray, *Grave Attending*, 27.
85 Ibid.
86 Rambo, *Spirit and Trauma*, 109.
87 Ibid., 110.
88 Bray, *Grave Attending*, 48.
89 Ibid., 101.
90 James, *Resilience and Melancholy*, 62.
91 Simpson, *As We Have Always Done*.
92 Gómez-Barris, Macarena, *The Extractive Zone: Social Ecologies and Decolonial Perspectives* (Durham: Duke University Press, 2017).
93 See, for example, Jason Allen-Paisant, "Those Who Can Afford Time," in *Thinking with Trees* (Manchester: Carcanet, 2021), 42–3.
94 Jennings, *Christian Imagination*, 292.
95 See Chapter 4.
96 Jacques Derrida, *Life Death*, trans. Pascale-Anne Brault and Michael Naas (Chicago: University of Chicago Press, 2020), 4. I am in debt to Beatrice Marovich, in conversation over her forthcoming work on life and death, for alerting me to this passage. See *Sister Death* (New York: Columbia University Press, 2022) for more on the dynamics of life and death in Western religion and philosophy.
97 Available online: https://www.whitehouse.gov/build-back-better/ (accessed January 30, 2022).
98 See Kelly Brown Douglas, especially "Part I: What is it about Christianity?" on Docetism, what she refers to as the "Platonized Tradition," 12–65 (*What's Faith Got to Do with It? Black Bodies/Christian Souls* (Maryknoll: Orbis, 2005)). See also Jennings, *The Christian Imagination*. Docetism was identified as a heresy early in the history of Christianity. Docetism is identified by a denial of Christ's full humanity and/or death. In these accounts Christ merely seemed human, his death merely seemed a cessation of life, and his sufferings merely masked his dispassionate divine core.
99 Recall from the intro that affect theorists explicitly resist the common idea of focusing on individual, personal feeling and so retain the importance of embodied experience while analyzing systems and institutional power dynamics those bodies are imbricated in.
100 de la Peña, *The Body Electric*, xi.
101 Some energy humanities scholars provide promising approaches. David Nye, for example, sets out to examine the complex interplay of systems and infrastructure with the "distinctive domestic patterns, work routines, urban structures, and agricultural methods" which impart "particular rhythms and contours to the everyday" lives of ordinary women and men "working, creating businesses, home-making, living in communities, seeking pleasures, and purchasing goods" (Nye, *Consuming Power,* 8 and 1 respectively). Even more than cultural habits, patterns, and social expectations of Nye's analysis, though, Karen Sayer and Carolyn de la Peña have emphasized that there is a more intimate story to tell about energy,

bodies, and culture. De la Peña's approach, emphasizing bodies in relation to machines, has been outlined earlier. For her part, Sayer emphasizes an embodied approach to energy and warns that "we will not be able to understand and therefore address climate change until we recognize the intimate relationships that have always existed between people when they purchase, consume, and labour to create energy" (Karen Sayer, "Illuminating Women: The Case of Candles in the English Home, 1815–1900," *Rachel Carson Center Perspectives* (2020): 31–5 (31)).
102 Jasbir Puar, *The Right to Maim: Debility, Capacity, Disability* (Durham: Duke University Press, 2017). Puar writes that "the body as an ability-machine takes its place among other forms of for-profit capital" (14).
103 Climate movements like Extinction Rebellion have been admirably focusing on the importance of ritualized mourning as integral to a protest movement (Available online: https://extinctionrebellion.uk/event/extinction-rebellion-feeling-nature-grief-tending-workshop/, accessed January 30, 2022). Unfortunately, Extinction Rebellion in particular still does not adequately recognize the ways social justice issues like racism and colonialism are integral to the environmental crisis.

BIBLIOGRAPHY

Acosta, Alberto, "Extractivism and Neoextractivism: Two Sides of the Same Curse," in *Beyond Development: Alternate Visions from Latin America*, edited by M. Lang and D. Mokrani, pp. 61–86, Amsterdam, Netherlands: Transnational Institute and Rosa Luxemburg Foundation, 2013.

Agricola, Georgius, *De Re Metallica*, translated by Herbert Hoover and Lou Henry Hoover, New York: Dover, 1950.

Alaimo, Stacy, "Cyborg and Ecofeminist Interventions: Challenges for an Environmental Feminism," *Feminist Studies* 20, no. 1 (1994): 133–52.

Alaimo, Stacy and Susan Heckman (eds), *Material Feminisms*, Bloomington: Indiana University Press, 2008.

Alain, Hubert, "Control: The Extractive Ecology of Corn Monoculture," *Cultural Studies* 31, no. 2–3 (2017): 232–52.

Allen, Diogenes and Eric O. Springsted, *Philosophy for Understanding Theology*, 2nd ed., Louisville: Westminster John Knox Press, 2007.

Allen-Paisant, Jason, *Thinking with Trees*, Manchester: Carcanet, 2021.

Alumkal, Antony, *Paranoid Science: The Christian Right's War on Reality*, New York: New York University Press, 2017.

Applebaum, Herbert, "The Concept of Work in Western Thought," in *Meanings of Work: Considerations for the Twenty-First Century*, edited by Frederick C. Gamst, pp. 46–78, Albany: State University of New York Press, 1995.

Aristotle, *Generation of Animals*, translated by Jeffrey Henderson, Loeb Classical Library, 366, Cambridge, MA: Harvard University Press, 1942.

Aristotle, *Metaphysics*, translated by Joe Sachs, Santa Fe: Green Lion Press, 2002.

Aristotle, *Nicomachean Ethics*, translated by Joe Sachs, Newbury: Focus, 2002.

Aristotle, *Protrepticus: A Reconstruction*, translated by Anton-Hermann Croust, Notre Dame: University of Notre Dame Press, 1964.

Asmussen, Tina, "The Cosmologies of the Early Modern Mining Landscape," in *Landscape and Earth in Early Modernity: Picturing Unruly Nature*, edited by Christine Göttler and Mia Mochizuki, Amsterdam, Netherlands: Amsterdam University Press, 2022.

Asmussen, Tina, "Spirited Metals and the Oeconomy of Resources in Early Modern European Mining," *Earth Sciences History* 39, no. 2 (2020): 371–88.

Asmussen, Tina and Pamela Long, "Introduction: The Cultural and Material Worlds of Mining in Early Modern Europe," *Renaissance Studies* 34, no. 1 (2019): 8–30.

Bacon, Francis, *Novum Organum*, edited by Joseph Devey, New York: P. F. Collier & Son, 1902.

Barad, Karen, *Meeting the Universe Halfway: Quantum Physics and the Entanglement of Matter and Meaning*, Durham: Duke University Press, 2007.

Barad, Karen, "Nature's Queer Performativity," *Qui Parle* 19, no. 2 (2011): 121–58.

Barba, Albaro Alonso, *The Art of Metals*, translated by R. H. Edward, London: S. Mearne, 1669.
Barber, Daniel, *Modern Architecture and Climate: Design Before Air Conditioning*, Princeton: Princeton University Press, 2020.
Barbour, Ian G., *Religion and Science: Historical and Contemporary Issues*, San Francisco: Harper Collins, 1997.
Barton, Isabel Fay, "Georgius Agricola's De Re Metallica in Early Modern Scholarship," *Earth Sciences History* 35, no. 2 (2016): 265–82.
Bataille, Georges, *The Accursed Share: An Essay on General Economy, Vol. 1: Consumption*, translated by Robert Hurley, New York: Zone Books, 1991.
Bauman, Whitney, "CPR for Planet Earth," *Counterpoint*, February 25, 2020, https://www.counterpointknowledge.org/cpr-for-planet-earth/ (accessed June 20, 2021).
Bauman, Whitney, "Queer Values for a Queer Climate: Developing a Versatile Planetary Ethic," in *Meaningful Flesh: Reflections on Religion and Nature for a Queer Planet*, edited by Whitney Bauman, pp. 103–24, Santa Barbara: Punctum Books, 2018.
Beisner, E. Calvin, "Fossil Fuels, Enemy or Friend? Divine Design in the Carbon Cycle," *The Christian Post*, October 28, 2013, https://www.christianpost.com/news/fossil-fuels-enemy-or-friend-divine-design-in-the-carbon-cycle.html (accessed June 21).
Bell, Shannon Elizabeth, Cara Elizabeth Daggett, and Christine Elizabeth Labuski, "Toward Feminist Energy Systems: Why Adding Women and Solar Panels Is Not Enough," *Energy Research & Social Science* 68 (2020): 1–13.
Bellamy, Brent Ryan and Jeff Diamanti, *Materialism and the Critique of Energy*, Chicago: MCM, 2018.
Bennett, Jane, *Vibrant Matter: A Political Ecology of Things*, Durham: Duke University Press, 2010.
Benz, Ernst, *The Theology of Electricity: On the Encounter and Explanation of Theology and Science in the 17th and 18th Centuries*, edited by Dennis Stillings, translated by Wolfgang Taraba, Eugene: Pickwick Publications, 1989.
Berlant, Lauren, *Cruel Optimism*, Durham: Duke University Press, 2011.
Berry, Evan, "Religion and Energy," in *Routledge Handbook on Energy Humanities*, edited by Janet Stewart and Graeme Macdonald, London: Routledge, 2022.
Berry, Evan and Robert Albro (eds), *Church, Cosmovision and The Environment: Religion and Social Conflict in Contemporary Latin America*, New York: Routledge, 2018.
Berry, Thomas, "The New Story," in *Teilhard in the Twenty-First Century: The Emerging Spirit of Earth*, edited by Arthur Fabel and Donald St. John, pp. 77–88. Maryknoll: Orbis Books, 2003.
Betcher, Sharon, *Spirit and the Politics of Disablement*, Minneapolis: Fortress, 2007.
Betancor, Orlando, *The Matter of Empire: Metaphysics and Mining in Colonial Peru*, Pittsburg, PA: University of Pittsburg Press, 2017.
Billings, J. Todd, "John Milbank's Theology of the 'Gift' and Calvin's Theology of Grace: A Critical Comparison," *Modern Theology* 21, no. 1 (2005): 87–105.
Biviano, Erin Lothes et al., "Catholic Moral Traditions and Energy Ethics for the Twenty-First Century," *Journal of Moral Theology* 5, no. 1 (2016): 1–36.
Bonneuil, Christophe and Jean-Baptiste Fressoz, *The Shock of the Anthropocene: The Earth, History and Us*, translated by David Fernbach, New York: Verso, 2017.
Bos, Abraham P., *Aristotle on God's Life-generating Power and on Pneuma as Its Vehicle*, Albany: State University of New York Press, 2019.
Bowman, Donna and Clayton Crockett (eds), *Cosmology, Ecology, and the Energy of God*, New York: Fordham University Press, 2012.
Boyer, Dominic, *Energopolitics: Wind and Power in the Anthropocene*, Durham: Duke University Press, 2019.

Boyer, Dominic and Imre Szeman (eds), *Energy Humanities: An Anthology*, Baltimore: Johns Hopkins University Press, 2017.
Braaten, Carl E. and Robert W. Jenson, *Union with Christ: The New Finnish Interpretation of Luther*, Grand Rapids: Eerdmans, 1998.
Bracken, Christopher, *The Potlatch Papers: A Colonial Case History*, Chicago: University of Chicago Press, 1997.
Bradshaw, David, *Aristotle East and West: Metaphysics and the Division of Christendom*, New York: Cambridge University Press, 2004.
Bradshaw, David, "The Concept of the Divine Energies," *Philosophy and Theology* 18, no. 1 (2006): 93–120.
Bradshaw, David, "The Divine Energies in the New Testament," *St. Vladimir's Theological Quarterly* 50, no. 3 (2006): 189–223.
Bray, Karen, *Grave Attending: A Political Theology for the Unredeemed*, New York: Fordham University Press, 2020.
Bray, Karen, "The Madness of Holy Saturday: Bipolar Temporality and the Queerdom of Heaven on Earth," in *Sexual Disorientations: Queer Temporalities, Affects, Theologies*, edited by Kent L. Brintnall, Joseph A. Marchal, and Stephen D. Moore, pp. 195–217, New York: Fordham University Press, 2018.
Bray, Karen, Heather Eaton, and Whitney Bauman (eds), *Immanent Religiosities, New Materialisms, and Planetary Thinking*, New York: Fordham University Press, 2023.
Brown Douglas, Kelly, *What's Faith Got to Do with It? Black Bodies/Christian Souls*, Maryknoll: Orbis, 2005.
Buchwalter, Andrew (ed.), *Hegel and Capitalism*, Albany: State University of New York Press, 2015.
Buell, Frederick, "A Short History of Oil Cultures: Or, the Marriage of Catastrophe and Exuberance," *Journal of American Studies* 46, no. 2 (2012): 273–93.
Buell, Lawrence, *The Environmental Imagination: Thoreau, Nature Writing, and the Formation of American Culture*, Cambridge, MA: Harvard University Press, 1995.
Burkhart, Brian, *Indigenizing Philosophy Through the Land: A Trickster Methodology for Decolonizing Environmental Ethics and Indigenous Futures*, East Lansing: Michigan State University Press, 2019.
Caine, Mark, Jason Lloyd, Max Luke, Lisa Margonelli, Todd Moss, Ted Nordhaus, Roger Pielke Jr., Mikael Román, Joyashree Roy, Daniel Sarewitz, Michale Shellenberger, Kartikeya Singh, and Alex Trembath, *Our High-Energy Planet: A Climate Pragmatism Project*, Breakthrough Institute, 2014. https://thebreakthrough.org/articles/our-high-energy-planet
Callahan, Richard Jr., Kathryn Lofton, and Chad Seales, "Allegories of Progress: Industrial Religion in the United States," *Journal of the American Academy of Religion* 78, no. 1 (2010): 1–39.
Caputo, John D., *The Weakness of God: A Theology of the Event*, Bloomington: Indiana University Press, 2006.
Carnot, Sadi, *Reflections on the Motive Power of Fire*, Mineola: Dover Publications, 1988.
Carter, J. Kameron, *Race: A Theological Account*, New York: Oxford University Press, 2008.
Caterine, Darryl, "The Haunted Grid: Nature, Electricity, and Indian Spirits in the American Metaphysical Tradition," *Journal of the American Academy of Religion* 82, no. 2 (2012): 371–97.
Chakrabarty, Dipesh, *Provincializing Europe: Postcolonial Thought and Historical Difference*, Princeton: Princeton University Press, 2000.

Chakrabarty, Dipesh, "The Climate of History: Four Theses," *Critical Inquiry* 35a, no. 2 (2009): 197–222.
Chen, Mel Y., *Animacies: Biopolitics, Racial Mattering, and Queer Affects*, Durham: Duke University Press, 2012.
Cielo, Cristina and Nancy Corrión Sarzosa, "Transformed Territories of Gendered Care Work in Ecuador's Petroleum Circuit," *Conservation and Society* 16, no. 1 (2018): 8–20.
Clayton, Phillip, *Religion and Science: The Basics*, 2nd ed., New York: Routledge, 2019.
Colebrook, Clare, "On Not Becoming Man: The Materialist Politics of Unactualized Potential," in *Material Feminisms*, edited by Stacy Alaimo and Susan Heckman, pp. 52–84, Bloomington: Indiana University Press, 2008.
Coleman, Desmond, *Alchemy and Blackness*, Dissertation, forthcoming.
Comaroff, Jean and John L. Comaroff, "Millennial Capitalism: First Thoughts on a Second Coming," *Public Culture* 12, no. 2 (2000): 291–343.
Connell, R. W., "The History of Masculinity," in *The Masculinity Studies Reader*, edited by Rachel Adams and David Savran, pp. 245–61, Malden: Blackwell, 2002.
Connolly, William, *Capitalism and Christianity: American Style*, Durham: Duke University Press, 2008.
Connolly, William, "The Evangelical-Capitalist Resonance Machine," *Political Theory* 33, no. 6 (2005): 869–86.
Conradie, Ernst, "Christianity," in *Routledge Handbook of Religion and Ecology*, edited by Willis Jenkins et al., pp. 70–8, New York: Routledge, 2017.
Conradie, Ernst and Hilda Koster (eds), *The T&T Clark Handbook on Christianity and Climate Change*, New York: T&T Clark, 2020.
Coole, Diana and Samantha Frost, *New Materialisms: Ontology, Agency, and Politics*, Durham: Duke University Press, 2010.
Coulson, Michael, *History of Mining: The Events, Technology and People Involved in the Industry that Forged the Modern World*, Hampshire: Harriman House Ltd., 2012.
Crenshaw, Kimberle, "Demarginalizing the Intersection of Race and Sex: A Black Feminist Critique of Antidiscrimination Doctrine, Feminist Theory and Antiracist Politics," *University of Chicago Legal Forum* 1, no. 1 (1989): 139–67.
Crockett, Clayton, *Radical Political Theology: Religion and Politics After Liberalism*, New York: Columbia University Press, 2011.
Crutzen, Paul and Eugene Stoermer, "The 'Anthropocene,'" *IGBP Newsletter* 41 (2000): 17–18.
Daggett, Cara New, *The Birth of Energy: Fossil Fuels, Thermodynamics, and the Politics of Work*, Durham: Duke University Press, 2019.
Daggett, Cara New, "Petro-Masculinity: Fossil Fuels and Authoritarian Desire," *Millennium* 47, no. 1 (2018): 25–44.
Daly, Herman E., John B. Cobb, and Clifford W. Cobb, *For the Common Good: Redirecting the Economy Toward Community, the Environment, and a Sustainable Future*, Boston: Beacon Press, 1994.
De Graaf, John, Vivia Boe, and Scott Simon, *Affluenza*, Oley: Bullfrog Films, 1997.
de la Peña, Carolyn Thomas, *The Body Electric: How Strange Machines Built the Modern American*, New York: New York University Press, 2003.
Derrida, Jacques, "From Restricted to General Economy: A Hegelianism without Reserve," in *Writing and Difference*, translated by Alan Bass, pp. 251–77, Chicago: University of Chicago Press, 1978.
Derrida, Jacques, *Given Time: Counterfeit Money*, translated by Peggy Kamuf, Chicago: University of Chicago, 1992.

Derrida, Jacques, *Life Death*, translated by Pascale-Anne Brault and Michael Naas, Chicago: University of Chicago Press, 2020.
Dochuk, Darren, *Anointed with Oil: How Christianity and Crude Made Modern America*, New York: Basic Books, 2019.
Dussel, Enrique D., *The Invention of the Americas: Eclipse of "the Other" and the Myth of Modernity*, New York: Continuum, 1995.
Dym, Warren Alexander, "Mineral Fumes and Mining Spirits: Popular Beliefs in the Sarepta of Johann Mathesius (1504–1565)," *Reformation & Renaissance Review* 8, no. 2 (2006): 161–85.
Eaton, S. J. M., *Petroleum: A History of the Oil Region of Venango County, Pennsylvania*, Philadelphia: J. P. Skelly, 1866.
Elshtain, Jean Bethke, *Sovereignty: God, State, and Self*, New York: Basic Books, 2008.
Engberg-Pedersen, Troels, "Gift-Giving and Friendship: Seneca and Paul in Romans 1-8 on the Logic of God's Χάρις and Its Human Response," *The Harvard Theological Review* 101, no. 1 (2008): 15–44.
Entzelt, Christoph, *De Re Metallica*, translated by Nellie E. Lutz and Lloyd M. Swan, Canton: Ohio Ferro-Alloys Corporation, 1943.
Epstein, Alex, *The Moral Case for Fossil Fuels*, New York: Portfolio/Penguin, 2014.
Estes, Nick and Jaskiran Dhillon (eds), *Standing with Standing Rock: Voices from the #NODAPL Movement*, Minneapolis: University of Minnesota Press, 2019.
Facundo, Martin, "Reimagining Extractivism: Insights from Spatial Theory," in *Contested Extractivism, Society and the State: Struggles over Mining and Land*, edited by Bettina Engles and Kristina Deitz, pp. 21–44, London: Palgrave MacMillan, 2017.
Farrington, Benjamin, *The Philosophy of Francis Bacon: An Essay on Its Development from 1603 to 1609 with New Translations of Fundamental Texts*, Liverpool: Liverpool University Press, 1964.
Ferreira da Silva, Denise, "Before Man: Sylvia Wynter's Rewriting of the Modern Episteme," in *Sylvia Wynter: On Being Human as Praxis*, edited by Katherine McKittrick, pp. 90–105, Durham: Duke University Press, 2015.
Ferngren, Gary, *Science and Religion: A Historical Introduction*, 2nd ed., Baltimore: Johns Hopkins University Press, 2017.
Freeman, Elizabeth, *Time Binds: Queer Temporalities, Queer Histories*, Durham: Duke University Press, 2010.
Freese, Barbara, *Coal: A Human History*, Cambridge: Perseus Pub., 2003.
Freudenthal, Gad, *Aristotle's Theory of Material Substance: Heat and Pneuma, Form and Soul*, New York: Oxford University Press, 1995.
Friedlingstein, P., R. M. Andrew, J. Rogelj, G. P. Peters, J. G. Canadell, R. Knutti, G. Luderer, M. R. Raupach, M. Schaeffer, D. P. van Vurren, and C. Le Quéré, "Persistent Growth of CO2 Emissions and Implications for Reaching Climate Targets," *Nature Geoscience* 7 (2014): 709–15.
Friedman, Benjamin M., *Religion and the Rise of Capitalism*, New York: Knopf, 2021.
Frigo, Giovanni, "Energy Ethics: A Literature Review," *Relations* 6, no. 2 (2018): 173–214.
Galeano, Eduardo, *The Open Veins of America: Five Centuries of the Pillage of a Continent*, translated by Cedric Belfrage, New York: Monthly Press Review, 1973.
Galen, *Galen on the Usefulness of the Parts of the Body*, translated by Margaret Tallmadge May, Ithaca: Cornell University Press, 1968.
Gebara, Ivone, *Longing for Running Water: Ecofeminism and Liberation*, Minneapolis: Fortress Press, 1999.
Geerts, Robert-Jan et al., "Towards a Philosophy of Energy," *Scientiæ Studia* 12 (2014): 105–27.

Ghosh, Amitav, "Petrofiction," *The New Republic* 2 (1992): 29–33.
Ghosh, Amitav, *The Great Derangement: Climate Change and the Unthinkable*, Chicago: University of Chicago Press, 2017.
Giddens, Paul H, *The Birth of the Oil Industry*, New York: Macmillan Co., 1938.
Gillespie, Michael Allen, *The Theological Origins of Modernity*, Chicago: University of Chicago Press, 2008.
Gilson, Etienne, *The Christian Philosophy of St. Thomas Aquinas*, translated by L. K. Shook, New York: Random House, 1956.
Gómez-Barris, Macarena, *The Extractive Zone: Social Ecologies and Decolonial Perspectives*, Durham: Duke University Press, 2017.
Grainger, Brett, *Church in the Wild: Evangelicals in Antebellum America*, Cambridge, MA: Harvard University Press, 2019.
Grau, Marion, "From Refiner's Fire to Refinery Fires: Reflections on the Combustive Element of Fire," in *Bloomsbury Handbook of Religion and Nature: The Elements*, edited by Laura Hobgood and Whitney Bauman, pp. 159–72, New York: Bloomsbury Academic, 2018.
Grau, Marion, *Of Divine Economy: Refinancing Redemption*, New York: T&T Clark, 2004.
Grau, Marion, "Petro-eschatology," in *Eschatology as Imagining the End: Faith Between Hope and Despair*, edited by Sigurd Bergmann, pp. 45–60, New York: Routledge, 2018.
Greenfield, Patrick, "Story of Cities #6: How Silver Turned Potosí into 'the First City of Capitalism,'" *The Guardian*, March 21, 2016, https://www.theguardian.com/cities/2016/mar/21/story-of-cities-6-potosi-bolivia-peru-inca-first-city-capitalism (accessed June 21, 2021).
Gregg, Melissa and Gregory J. Seigworth (eds), *The Affect Theory Reader*, Durham: Duke University Press, 2010.
Günel, Gökçe, *Spaceship in the Desert: Energy, Climate Change, and Urban Design in Abu Dhabi*, Durham: Duke University Press, 2019.
Haag, James et al. (eds), *Routledge Companion to Religion and Science*, New York: Routledge, 2012.
Halberstam, Jack, *The Queer Art of Failure*, Durham: Duke University Press, 2011.
Hall, Douglas John, *The Cross in Our Context: Jesus and the Suffering World*, Minneapolis: Fortress Press, 2003.
Hamm, Berndt, "Martin Luther's Revolutionary Theology of Pure Gift without Reciprocation," translated by Timothy J. Wengert, *Lutheran Quarterly* 29 (2015): 125–61.
Hamm, Ernst, "Mining History: People, Knowledge, Power," *Earth Sciences History* 31, no. 2 (2012): 321–6.
Haraway, Donna, *The Companion Species Manifesto: Dogs, People, and Significant Otherness*, Chicago: Prickly Paradigm Press, 2003.
Haraway, Donna, *Primate Visions: Gender, Race, and Nature in the World of Modern Science*, New York: Routledge, 1989.
Haraway, Donna, *Simians, Cyborgs, and Women: The Reinvention of Nature*, New York: Routledge, 1991.
Haraway, Donna, "Situated Knowledges: The Science Question in Feminism and the Privilege of Partial Perspective," *Feminist Studies* 14, no. 3 (1988): 575–99.
Haraway, Donna, *Staying with the Trouble: Making Kin in the Chthulucene*, Durham: Duke University Press, 2016.
Harris, Cheryl I., "Whiteness as Property," *Harvard Law Review* 106, no. 8 (1993): 1707–91.

Harrison, Peter, *The Territories of Science and Religion*, Chicago: University of Chicago Press, 2015.
Hayhoe, Kathryn and Thomas Ackerman, "Climate Change: Evangelical Scientists Say Limbaugh Wrong, Faith and Science Complement One Another," *The Christian Post*, August 21, 2013, https://www.christianpost.com/news/climate-change-evangelical-scientists-say-limbaugh-wrong-faith-and-science-compliment-one-another.html (accessed January 6, 2022).
Heidegger, Martin, "The Question Concerning Technology," in *The Question Concerning Technology and Other Essays*, translated by William Lovitt, pp. 3–35, New York: Garland Publishing, 1977.
Heimann, P. M., "Helmholtz and Kant: The Metaphysical Foundations of 'Über Die Erhaltung Der Kraft,'" *Studies in History of Philosophy and Science* 5, no. 3 (1974): 205–38.
Hessel, Dieter T. (ed.), *Energy Ethics: A Christian Response*, New York: Friendship Press, 1979.
Hobgood, Laura and Whitney Bauman (eds), *Bloomsbury Handbook of Religion and Nature: The Elements*, New York: Bloomsbury Academic, 2018.
Holm, Bo Kristian, "The Gift in Martin Luther's Theology," *Oxford Research Encyclopedia of Religion*, March 29, 2017, https://oxfordre.com/religion/view/10.1093/acrefore/9780199340378.001.0001/acrefore-9780199340378-e-356 (accessed August 25, 2021).
Holm, Poul, et al., "Humanities for the Environment—A Manifesto for Research and Action," *Humanities* 4, no. 1 (2015): 977–92.
hooks, bell, *Writing Beyond Race: Living Theory and Practice*, New York: Routledge, 2013.
Howe, Cymene, *Ecologics: Wind and Power in the Anthropocene*, Durham: Duke University Press, 2019.
Hultman, Martin, "The Making of an Environmental Hero: A History of Ecomodern Masculinity, Fuel Cells and Arnold Schwarzenegger," *Environmental Humanities* 2 (2013): 79–99.
Jackson, Zakiyyah Iman, *Becoming Human: Matter and Meaning in an Antiblack World*, New York: New York University Press, 2020.
James, Robin, *Resilience and Melancholy: Pop Music, Feminism, Neoliberalism*, Winchester: Zero Books, 2015.
Jenkins, Willis et al. (eds), *The Routledge Handbook of Religion and Ecology*, New York: Routledge, 2017.
Jenkins, Willis, Evan Berry, and Luke Kreider, "Religion and Climate Change," *Annual Review of Environment and Natural Resources* 43 (2018): 9.1–9.24.
Jennings, Willie James, *The Christian Imagination: Theology and the Origins of Race*, New Haven: Yale University Press, 2010.
Jennings, Willie James, "Binding Landscapes: Secularism, Race, and the Spatial Modern," in *Race and Secularism in America*, edited by Jonathon S. Kahn and Vincent W. Lloyd, pp. 207–38, New York: Columbia University Press, 2016.
Johnson, Bob, "Energy Slaves: Carbon Technologies, Climate Change, and the Stratified History of the Fossil Economy," *American Quarterly* 68, no. 4 (2016): 955–79.
Jones, Donna V., *The Racial Discourses of Life Philosophy: Negritude, Vitalism, and Modernity*, New York: Columbia University Press, 2012.
Josephson Storm, Jason A., *The Myth of Disenchantment Magic, Modernity, and the Birth of the Human Sciences*, Chicago: University of Chicago Press, 2017.
Joy, Morny (ed.), *Women and the Gift: Beyond the Given and All-Giving*, Indianapolis: Indiana University Press, 2013.
"Just Powers," *Just Powers* Online, 2021, https://www.justpowers.ca/about/.

Keel, Terence, *Divine Variations: How Christian Thought Became Racial Science*, Stanford: Stanford University Press, 2018.
Keller, Catherine, *Face of the Deep: A Theology of Becoming*, New York: Routledge, 2003.
Keller, Catherine, *From a Broken Web: Separation, Sexism, and Self*, Boston: Beacon, 1986.
Keller, Catherine, *Political Theology of the Earth: Our Planetary Emergency and the Struggle for a New Public*, New York: Columbia University Press, 2018.
Keller, Catherine and Stephen Moore, "Derridapocalypse," in *Derrida and Religion: Other Testaments*, edited by Yvonne Sherwood and Kevin Hart, pp. 189–208, New York: Routledge, 2005.
Kimmerer, Robin Wall, *Braiding Sweetgrass: Indigenous Wisdom, Scientific Knowledge, and the Teachings of Plants*, Minneapolis: Milkweed Editions, 2013.
Klaver, Irene, "Accidental Wildness on a Detention Pond," *Antennae, The Journal of Nature in Visual Culture* 33 (2015): 45–58.
Klein, Naomi, "Dancing the World into Being: A Conversation with Idle No More's Leanne Simpson," *YES! Magazine*. March 6, 2013, https://www.yesmagazine.org/social-justice/2013/03/06/dancing-the-world-into-being-a-conversation-with-idle-no-more-leanne-simpson (accessed August 14, 2021).
Klein, Naomi, *This Changes Everything: Capitalism Vs. the Climate*, New York: Simon & Schuster, 2014.
Klein, Naomi, *The Shock Doctrine: The Rise of Disaster Capitalism*, New York: Picador, 2007.
Kobes Du Mez, Kristin, *Jesus and John Wayne: How White Evangelicals Corrupted a Faith and Fractured a Nation*, New York: Liveright Publishing, 2021.
Koster, Hilda, "Trafficked Lands: Sexual Violence, Oil, and Structural Evil in the Dakotas," in *Planetary Solidarity: Global Women's Voices on Christian Doctrine and Climate Justice*, edited by Grace Ji-Sun Kim and Hilda P. Koster, pp. 155–78, Minneapolis: Fortress Press, 2017.
Kuhn, Thomas S., "Energy Conservation as an Example of Simultaneous Discovery," in *The Essential Tension: Selected Studies in Scientific Tradition and Change*, pp. 66–104, Chicago: University of Chicago Press, 1977.
Leibniz, Gottfried, "On the Doctrine of Malebranche: A Letter to M. Remond De Montmort, Containing Remarks on the Book of Father Tertre Against Father Malebranche," in *The Philosophical Works of Leibnitz*, edited and translated by George Martin Duncan, pp. 223–37, New Haven: Tuttle, Morehouse & Taylor, 1890.
LeMenager, Stephanie, *Living Oil: Petroleum Culture in the American Century*, New York: Oxford University Press, 2014.
Lindberg, David and Ronald Numbers (ed.), "Introduction," in *God & Nature: Historical Essays on the Encounter between Christianity and Science*, edited by David Lindberg and Ronald Numbers, pp. 1–18, Berkeley: University of California Press, 1986.
Lindsay, Robert Bruce, *Energy: Historical Development of the Concept*, Stroudsburg: Dowden, Hutchinson and Ross, 1975.
Lloyd, Vincent W. (ed.), *Race and Political Theology*, Stanford: Stanford University Press, 2012.
Lo Bello, Anthony, *Origins of Mathematical Words: A Comprehensive Dictionary of Latin, Greek, and Arabic Roots*, Baltimore: Johns Hopkins University Press, 2013.
Lugones, María, "Heterosexualism and the Colonial/Modern Gender System," *Hypatia* 22, no. 1 (2007): 186–209.
Luther, Martin, "Sermon on Two Kinds of Righteousness (1519)," in *The Annotated Luther, Vol. 2: Word and Faith*, edited by Kirsi Stjerna, translated by Else Marie Wiberg Pedersen, pp. 9–24, Minneapolis: Fortress Press, 2015.

Malm, Andreas, *Fossil Capital: The Rise of Steam Power and the Roots of Global Warming*, Brooklyn: Verso, 2016.
Manolopoulos, Mark, *If Creation is a Gift*, New York: State University of NY Press, 2009.
Marder, Michael, *Energy Dreams: Of Actuality*, New York: Columbia University Press, 2017.
Marovich, Beatrice and Alex Dubilet, "Negotiating Terrain: Gender and the Postsecular?" *Journal for Cultural and Religious Theory* 16, no. 2 (2017): 109–25.
Marovich, Beatrice, *Sister Death*, New York: Columbia University Press, 2022.
Martinez, D. M. and B. W. Ebenhack, "Understanding the Role of Energy Consumption in Human Development Through the Use of Saturation Phenomena," *Energy Policy* 36, no. 4 (2008): 1430–35.
Marvin, Carolyn, *When Old Technologies Were New: Thinking About Electric Communication in the Late Nineteenth Century*, New York: Oxford University Press, 1988.
Mauss, Marcel, *The Gift: The Form and Reason for Exchange in Archaic Societies*, translated by W. D. Hall, New York: W. W. Norton, 1990.
Mbembe, Achille, *Critique of Black Reason*, translated by Laurent Dubois, Durham: Duke University Press, 2017.
McFague, Sallie, *Blessed are the Consumers*, Minneapolis: Augsburg Fortress, 2013.
McGrath, Alister, *Christian Theology: An Introduction*, 6th ed., New York: John Wiley and Sons, 2016.
McGrath, Alister, *The Re-Enchantment of Nature: Science, Religion and the Human Sense of Wonder*, London: Hodder & Stoughton, 2003.
McGrath, Alister, *Science and Religion: A New Introduction*, 3rd ed., Hoboken: Wiley Blackwell, 2020.
McLaurin, John J., *Sketches in Crude Oil: Some Accidents and Incidents of the Petroleum Development in All Parts of the Globe*, 2nd ed., Harrisburg: Published by the Author, 1898.
McNeill, J. R. and Peter Engelke, *The Great Acceleration: An Environmental History of the Anthropocene Since 1945*, Cambridge: The Belknap Press of Harvard University Press, 2014.
McRuer, Robert, *Crip Theory: Cultural Signs of Queerness and Disability*, New York: New York University Press, 2006.
Merchant, Carolyn, *The Death of Nature: Women, Ecology, and the Scientific Revolution*, New York: HarperCollins Publishers, 1980.
Merchant, Carolyn, "Mining the Earth's Womb," in *Philosophy of Technology, The Technology Condition: An Anthology*, edited by Robert C. Sharff and Val Dusek, 2nd ed., pp. 471–81, Malden: Wiley Blackwell, 2014.
Merchant, Carolyn, "The Secrets of Nature: The Bacon Debates Revisited," *Journal of the History of Ideas* 69, no. 1 (2008): 147–62.
Mezzadra, Sandro and Brett Neilson, "On the Multiple Frontiers of Extraction: Excavating Contemporary Capitalism," *Cultural Studies* 31, no. 2–3 (2017): 185–204.
Mignolo, Walter D. and Catherine E. Walsh, *On Decoloniality: Concepts, Analytics, Praxis*, Durham: Duke University Press, 2018.
Milbank, John, *Being Reconciled: Ontology and Pardon*, New York: Routledge, 2003.
Milbank, John, "Can a Gift Be Given? Prolegomena to a Future Trinitarian Metaphysic," *Modern Theology* 11, no. 1 (1995): 119–61.
Milbank, John, Catherine Pickstock, and Graham Ward (eds), *Radical Orthodoxy: A New Theology*, New York: Routledge, 1999.

Miller, David, *Solved: How the World's Great Cities are Fixing the Climate Crisis*, Toronto: University of Toronto Press, 2020.
Mirowski, Philip, *More Heat than Light*, Cambridge: Cambridge University Press, 1989.
Mitchell, Timothy, *Carbon Democracy: Political Power in the Age of Oil*, New York: Verso, 2011.
Moltmann, Jürgen, *God in Creation: A New Theology of Creation and the Spirit of God*, Minneapolis: Fortress Press, 1993.
Moltmann, Jürgen, *Trinity and the Kingdom: The Doctrine of God*, Minneapolis: Fortress Press, 1993.
Morrison, Mark, Roderick Duncan, and Kevin Parton, "Religion Does Matter for Climate Change Attitudes and Behavior," *PLoS ONE* 10, no. 8 (2015): e0134868. doi:10.1371/journal.pone.0134868.
Morton, Timothy, "Queer Ecology," *PMLA* 125 (2010): 273–82.
Mumford, Lewis, *Technics and Civilization*, New York: Harcourt, Brace and Company, 1934.
Neocleous, Mark, "Resisting Resilience," *Radical Philosophy* 178 (2013): 2–7.
Nielsen, Karen M., "The Private Parts of Animals: Aristotle on the Teleology of Sexual Difference," *Phronesis* 53, no. 4/5 (2008): 373–405.
Nikiforuk, Andrew, *The Energy of Slaves*, Vancouver: Greystone Books, 2012.
Noble, David F., *The Religion of Technology: The Divinity of Man and the Spirit of Invention*, New York: Alfred A. Knopf, 1997.
Norris, John A., "The Providence of Mineral Generation in the Sermons of Johann Mathesius (1504–1565)," in *Geology and Religion: A History of Harmony and Hostility*, edited by M. Kölbl-Ebert, pp. 37–40, London: The Geological Society, 2009.
Northcott, Michael, *A Political Theology of Climate Change*, Grand Rapids: William B. Eerdmans Publishing Co, 2013.
Nye, David E., *Consuming Power: A Social History of American Energies*, Cambridge, MA: MIT Press, 1999.
Nyssa, Gregory of, "Address on Religious Instruction," in *Christology of the Later Fathers*, edited by Edward R. Hardy, pp. 268–326, Philadelphia: Westminster Press, 1954.
Oakley, Francis, *Omnipotence, Covenant and Order: An Excursion in the History of Ideas from Abelard to Leibniz*, Cornell: Cornell University Press, 1984.
Oakley, Francis, *Politics and Eternity: Studies in the History of Medieval and Early-Modern Political Thought*, Leiden: Brill, 1999.
Oberman, Heiko Augustinus, *Luther: Man Between God and the Devil*, New Haven: Yale University Press, 1989.
Olson, Richard, *Science and Religion (1450–1900): From Copernicus to Darwin*, Baltimore: Johns Hopkins University Press, 2004.
Oreskes, Naomi and Erik M. Conway, *Merchants of Doubt: How a Handful of Scientists Obscured the Truth on Issues from Tobacco Smoke to Global Warming*, New York: Bloomsbury Press, 2010.
Osterhammel, Jürgen, *The Transformation of the World: A Global History of the Nineteenth Century*, translated by Patrick Camiller, Princeton: Princeton University Press, 2015.
Ozment, Steven E., *The Age of Reform (1250–1550): An Intellectual and Religious History of Late Medieval and Reformation Europe*, New Haven: Yale University Press, 1980.
Park, Katharine, *Secrets of Women: Gender, Generation, and the Origins of Human Dissection*, New York: Zone Books, 2010.

Pelikan, Jaroslav, *The Christian Tradition: A History of Development of Doctrine, Book 1: The Emergence of the Catholic Tradition (100–600)*, Chicago: University of Chicago Press, 1971.
Peppard, Christiana Z., Julia Watts Belser, Erin Lothes Biviano, and James B. Martin-Schramm, "What Powers US? A Comparative Religious Ethics of Energy Sources, Power, and Privilege," *Journal of the Society of Christian Ethics* 35, no. 1 (2016): 3–25.
Perez Sheldon, Myrna and Naomi Oreskes, "The Religious Politics of Scientific Doubt," in *The Wiley Blackwell Companion to Religion and Ecology*, edited by John Hart, pp. 348–67, Hoboken: Wiley Blackwell, 2017.
Perez Sheldon, Myrna, Ahmed Ragab, and Terence Keel (eds), "Introduction," *Critical Approaches to Science and Religion*, NY: Columbia University Press, 2023.
Pietsch, B. M., "Lyman Stewart and Early Fundamentalism," *Church History* 82, no. 3 (2013): 617–46.
Plaza, Penélope, "Rare Seeds: How Venezuelan Artists are Breaking the Spell of Oil," *Energy Humanities*, October 26, 2021, https://www.energyhumanities.ca/news/rare-seeds-how-venezuelan-artists-are-breaking-the-spell-of-oil (accessed October 28, 2021).
Plumwood, Val, *Feminism and the Mastery of Nature*, London: Routledge, 1993.
Pontifical Academy of Sciences, *Mankind and Energy: Needs, Resources, Hopes*, edited by André Blanc-Lapierre, Amsterdam, Netherlands: Elsevier, 1982.
Posadas, Jeremy, "The Refusal of Work in Christian Ethics and Theology," *Journal of Religious Ethics* 45, no. 2 (2017): 330–61.
Primavesi, Anne, *Gaia's Gift: Earth, Ourselves and God after Copernicus*, New York: Routledge, 2004.
Puar, Jasbir, *The Right to Maim: Debility, Capacity, Disability*, Durham: Duke University Press, 2017.
Putney, Clifford, *Muscular Christianity: Manhood and Sports in Protestant America, 1880–1920*, Cambridge, MA: Harvard University Press, 2001.
Rambo, Shelly, *Spirit and Trauma: A Theology of Remaining*, Louisville: Westminster John Knox Press, 2010.
Rasmussen, Larry, Normand Laurendeau, and Dan Solomon, "Introduction to 'The Energy Transition: Religious and Cultural Perspectives,'" *Zygon* 46, no. 4 (2011): 872–89.
Rieger, Joerg, *No Rising Tide: Theology, Economics, and the Future*, Minneapolis: Fortress Press, 2009.
Rignall, Karen Eugenie, "Solar Power, State Power, and the Politics of Energy Transition in Pre-Saharan Morocco," *Environment and Planning A: Economy and Space* 48, no. 3: 540–57.
Rivera, Myra, *The Touch of Transcendence: A Postcolonial Theology of God*, Louisville: Westminster John Knox Press, 2007.
Robertson, Charles, "Allegory and Ambiguity in Michelangelo's 'Slaves,'" in *The Slave in European Art: From Renaissance Trophy to Abolitionist Emblem*, edited by Elizabeth McGrath and Jean Michel Massing, pp. 39–62, London: The Warburg Institute, 2012.
Rowe, Terra Schwerin, *Toward a Better Worldliness: Ecology, Economy, and the Protestant Tradition* Minneapolis: Fortress Press, 2017.
Rowe, Terra Schwerin, "Response to Annika and Joerg Rieger," in *The T&T Clark Handbook on Christianity and Climate Change*, edited by Ernst Conradie and Hilda Koster, pp. 65–9, New York: Bloomsbury, 2019.
Rowe, Terra Schwerin, "The Crux of the Matter: Theology of the Cross and the Modern Extractive Imaginary," in *The Crux of Theology: Freedom, Justice, Peace*, edited by Allen Jorgenson and Kris Kvam, Lexington Books, 2022.

Rubenstein, Mary-Jane, *Pantheologies: Gods, Worlds, Monsters*, New York: Columbia University Press, 2018.
Rubenstein, Mary-Jane, "Science," in *The Palgrave Handbook of Radical Theology*, edited by C. D. Rodkey and J. E. Miller, pp. 747–56, New York: Palgrave, 2018.
Ruether, Rosemary Radford, *New Woman, New Earth: Sexist Ideologies and Human Liberation*, New York: Seabury Press, 1975.
Ruffner, James A., "Agricola and Community," in *Religion, Science and Worldview: Essays in Honor of Richard S. Westfall*, edited by Margaret Osler and Paul Farber, pp. 297–324, New York: Cambridge University Press, 1985.
Rundell Jr, Walter, "Centennial Bibliography: Annotated Selections of the History of the Petroleum Industry in the United States," *The Business History Review* 33, no. 3 (1959): 429–47.
Sabin, Paul, "'A Dive into Nature's Great *Grab-bag*': Nature, Gender and Capitalism in the Early Pennsylvania Oil Industry," *Pennsylvania History* 66, no. 4 (1999): 472–505.
Said, Edward W., *Orientalism*, New York: Vintage Books, 1978.
Sayer, Karen, "Illuminating Women: The Case of Candles in the English Home, 1815–1900," *Rachel Carson Center Perspectives* 1, no. 1 (2020): 31–5.
Schaefer, Donovan O., *Religious Affects: Animality, Evolution, and Power*, Durham: Duke University Press, 2015.
Schmitt, Carl, *Political Theology: Four Chapters on the Concept of Sovereignty*, translated by George Schwab, Cambridge, MA: MIT Press, 1985.
Scott, David, "The Re-Enchantment of Humanism: An Interview with Sylvia Wynter," *Small Axe* 8 (2000): 119–207.
Scott, Heidi C. M., *Fuel: An Ecocritical History*, London: Bloomsbury Academic, 2020.
Serje, Margarita, "ONGs, Indios y Petróleo: El Caso U'wa a Través de los Mapas del Territorio en Disputa," *Bulletin de l'Institut Français d'études Andines* 32, no. 1 (2003), http://journals.openedition.org/bifea/6398, doi: 10.4000/bifea.6398.
Sideris, Lisa, *Consecrating Science: Wonder, Knowledge, and the Natural World*, Oakland: University of California Press, 2017.
Simpson, Leanne Betasamosake, *As We Have Always Done: Indigenous Freedom Through Radical Resistance*, Minneapolis: University of Minnesota Press, 2017.
Singh, Devin, *Divine Currency: The Theological Power of Money in the West*, Stanford: Stanford University Press, 2018.
Sittler, Joseph, "Called to Unity," *The Ecumenical Review* 14 (1962): 177–87.
Sittler, Joseph, "The Care of the Earth," in *Evocations of Grace: Writings on Ecology, Theology, and Ethics*, edited by Steven Bouma-Prediger and Peter Bakken, pp. 51–8, Grand Rapids: Eerdmans, 2000.
Smil, Vaclav, *Energy at the Crossroads, Global Perspectives and Uncertainties*, Cambridge, MA: MIT Press, 2003.
Smil, Vaclav, *Energy in World History*, Boulder: Westview Press, 1994.
Smil, Vaclav, "Science, Energy, Ethics, and Civilization," in *Visions of Discovery: New Light on Physics, Cosmology, and Consciousness*, edited by R. Y Chiao et al., pp. 709–29, Cambridge: Cambridge University Press, 2010.
Smith, Crosbie "Natural Philosophy and Thermodynamics: William Thomson and the 'Dynamical Theory of Heat,'" *The British Journal for the History of Science* 9, no. 3 (1976): 293–319.
Smith, Crosbie, *The Science of Energy: A Cultural History of Energy Physics in Victorian Britain*, Chicago: University of Chicago Press, 1998.
Smith, Crosbie and M. Norton Wise, *Energy and Empire: A Biographical Study of Lord Kelvin*, Cambridge: Cambridge University Press, 1989.

Smith, J. Z., *To Take Place: Toward Theory in Ritual*, Chicago: University of Chicago Press, 1987.
Stinson, Robert, "Ida M. Tarbell and the Ambiguities of Feminism," *The Pennsylvania Magazine of History and Biography* 101, no. 2 (1977): 217–39.
Storyhill, "I-90," Recorded 2001, Track 28 on *Reunion*, Story Hills Records.
Swart, K., "Trends in the Energy Market After World War II," *Journal of Power Sources* 37, no. 1–2 (1992): 3–12.
Szeman, Imre, *On Petrocultures: Globalization, Culture and Energy*, Morgantown: West Virginia University Press, 2019.
Szeman, Imre, "On the Politics of Extraction," *Cultural Studies* 31, no. 2–3 (2017): 440–7.
Szeman, Imre and Jeff Diamanti (eds), *Energy Culture: Art and Theory on Oil and Beyond*, Morgantown: West Virginia University Press, 2019.
Szeman, Imre and Jennifer Wenzel, "What Do We Talk about When We Talk about Extractivism?" *Textual Practice* 35, no. 3 (2021): 505–23.
Szeman, Imre, Lynn Badia, Jeff Diamanti, Michael O'Driscoll, and Mark Simpson (eds), *After Oil*, Edmonton: Petrocultures Research Group, 2016.
Steinberger, Julia K., "Energizing Human Development," http://hdr.undp.org/en/content/energising-human-development (accessed January 2020).
Steinberger, Julia K. and J. Timmons Roberts, "From Constraint to Sufficiency: The Decoupling of Energy and Carbon from Human Needs, 1975–2005," *Ecological Economics* 70 (2010): 425–33.
Steinberger, Julia K., Yannick Oswald, and Anne Owen, "Large Inequality in International and Intranational Energy Footprints Between Income Groups and Across Consumption Categories," *Nature Energy* 5 (2020): 231–9.
Tanev, Stoyan, *Energy in Orthodox Theology and Physics: From Controversy to Encounter*, Eugene: Pickwick, 2017.
Tanner, Kathryn, *Christianity and the New Spirit of Capitalism*, New Haven: Yale University Press, 2019.
Tanner, Kathryn, *Economy of Grace*, Minneapolis: Fortress Press, 2005.
Tanner, Kathryn, *God and Creation in Christian Theology*, Minneapolis: Fortress, 2005.
Tarbell, Ida B, "The Business of Being a Woman," in *More than a Muckraker*, edited by Robert Kochersberger, pp. 118–28, Knoxville: University of Tennessee Press, 2017.
Tarbell, Ida B, *History of the Standard Oil Company*, 2 vols, New York: McClure, Phillips and Company, 1904.
Taylor, Bron (ed.), *Encyclopedia of Religion and Nature*, London: Continuum, 2008.
Taylor, Charles, *Modern Social Imaginaries*, Durham: Duke University, 2003.
Taylor, Mark C., "Capitalizing (on) Gifting," in *The Enigma of Gift and Sacrifice*, edited by Edith Wyschogrod, Jean-Joseph Goux, and Eric Boynton, pp. 50–74, New York: Fordham University Press, 2002.
Trelstad, Marit (ed.), *Cross Examinations: Readings on the Meaning of the Cross Today*, Minneapolis: Fortress, 2006.
Tsing, Anna, *Friction: An Ethnography of Global Connection*, Princeton: Princeton University Press, 2005.
Tuana, Nancy, *The Less Noble Sex: Scientific, Religious, and Philosophical Conceptions of Woman's Nature*, Bloomington: Indiana University Press, 1993.
Tuveson, Ernest Lee, *Redeemer Nation: The Idea of America's Millennial Role*, Chicago: University of Chicago, 1968.
Uribe Botero, Ángela, *Petróleo Economía y Cultura el Caso U'wa*, Bogotá, Columbia: Editorial Universidad del Rosario, 2005.

Usher, Phillip John, *Exterranean: Extraction in the Humanist Anthropocene*, New York: Fordham, 2019.
US Catholic Bishops, "Reflections on the Energy Crisis," Washington: United States Catholic Conference, 1981.
Vogel, Todd, *Rewriting White: Race, Class, and Cultural Capital in Nineteenth-Century America*, New Brunswick: Rutgers University Press, 2004.
Wajcman, Judy, *TechnoFeminism*, Cambridge: Polity, 2004.
Wallace, Mark I., *When God Was a Bird: Christianity, Animism, and the Re-Enchantment of the World*, New York: Fordham University Press, 2019.
Weatherford, Jack, *Indian Givers: How the Indians of the Americas Transformed the World*, New York: Three Rivers Press, 1988.
Weber, Max, *The Protestant Ethic and the "Spirit" of Capitalism*, edited and translated by Peter Baehr and Gordon Wells, New York: Penguin Books, 2002.
Weeks, Kathi, *The Problem with Work: Feminism, Marxism, Antiwork Politics, and Postwork Imaginaries*, Durham: Duke University Press, 2011.
Weheliye, Alexander G., *Habeas Viscus: Racializing Assemblages, Biopolitics, and Black Feminist Theories of the Human*, Durham: Duke University Press, 2014.
Weinstein, Jami and Claire Colebrook (eds), *Posthumous Life: Theorizing Beyond the Posthuman*, New York: Columbia University Press, 2017.
Weszkalnys, Gisa, "Geology, Potentiality, Speculation: On the Indeterminacy of First Oil," *Cultural Anthropology* 30, no. 4 (2015): 611–39.
White, Leslie A., "Energy and the Evolution of Culture," *American Anthropologist* 45, no. 3 (1943): 335–56.
White, Lynn, "The Historical Roots of Our Ecologic Crisis," *Science* 155, no. 3767 (1967): 1203–7.
Whyte, Kyle Powys, "Too Late for Indigenous Climate Justice: Ecological and Relational Tipping Points," *WIRES Climate Change* 11, no. 1 (2020), https://onlinelibrary.wiley.com/doi/abs/10.1002/wcc.603 (accessed January 2020).
Williams, Delores, *Sisters in the Wilderness*, Maryknoll: Orbis, 1993.
Williams, Delores, "Sin, Nature and Black Women's Bodies," in *Ecofeminism and the Sacred*, edited by Carol Adams, pp. 24–9, New York: Continuum, 1994.
Wilson, Sheena, "Energy Imaginaries: Feminist and Decolonial Futures," in *Materialism and the Critique of Energy*, edited by Brent Ryan Bellamy and Jeff Diamanti, pp. 377–412, Chicago: MCM Publishing, 2018.
Wilson, Sheena, "Gender," in *Fueling Culture: 101 Words for Energy and Environment*, edited by Jennifer Wenzel and Patricia Yaeger, pp. 174–7, New York: Fordham University Press, 2017.
Wilson, Sheena, "Gendering Oil: Tracing Western Petrosexual Relations," in *Oil Culture*, edited by Ross Barrett and Daniel Worden, pp. 244–63, Minneapolis: University of Minnesota Press, 2014.
Wilson, Sheena, Imre Szeman and Adam Carlson (eds), *Petrocultures: Oil, Politics, Culture*, Chicago: McGill-Queen's University Press, 2017.
Wynter, Sylvia, "1492: A New World View," in *Race, Discourse, and the Origin of the Americas: A New World View*, edited by Vera Lawrence Hyatt and Rex Nettleford, pp. 5–57, Washington: Smithsonian Institution, 1995.
Wynter, Sylvia, "Unsettling the Coloniality of Being/Power/Truth/Freedom: Towards the Human, After Man, Its Overrepresentation—An Argument," *CR: The New Centennial Review* 3, no. 3 (2003): 257–337.

Xu, Yangyang and Veerabhadran Ramanathan, "Well Below 2C: Mitigation Strategies for Avoiding Dangers to Catastrophic Climate Change," *Proceedings of the National Academy of Sciences of the United States of America* 114, no. 39 (2017): 10315–23.

Yaeger, Patricia, "Editor's Column: Literature in the Ages of Wood, Tallow, Coal, Whale Oil, Gasoline, Atomic Power, and Other Energy Sources," *PMLA* 126, no. 2 (2011): 305–26.

York, Richard, "Do Alternative Energy Sources Displace Fossil Fuels?" *Nature Climate Change* 2 (2012): 441–4.

York, Richard and Shannon Bell, "Energy Transitions or Additions? Why a Transition from Fossil Fuels Requires More than the Growth of Renewable Energy," *Energy Research and Social Science* 51 (2019): 40–3.

Yusoff, Kathryn, *A Billion Black Anthropocenes or None*, Minneapolis: University of Minnesota Press, 2018.

Zuck, Rochelle Raineri, "The Wizard of Oil: Abraham James, the Harmonial Wells, and the Psychometric History of the Oil Industry," in *Oil Culture*, edited by Ross Barrett and Daniel Worden, pp. 19–42, Minneapolis: University of Minnesota Press, 2014.

INDEX

acceleration, accelerationism 155, 164
Acosta, Alberto 64
affect 4, 5, 8, 9, 12–17, 29, 30, 43, 46, 49, 59 n.107, 65, 93, 99, 105, 110, 135, 139, 140, 150–6, 158–63, 165, 167–70, 175 n.99
Africa/African 47, 73, 78, 80, 87 n.71, 123, 133, 137, 143 n.12
After Oil Collective 4–6, 10, 11
Agricola, Georgius 64, 74, 75, 87 n.80, 99, 100, 102–6, 111, 113
Alaimo, Stacy 124
alchemy 49, 50, 128
Allen, Paula Gunn 96, 115
Allen-Paisant, Jason 168
America
    Native American 80, 129, 130, 137, 139
    North America 66, 68, 73, 76–8, 82, 87, 96, 97, 103, 106, 140, 141, 154, 168
    South America 68, 73, 74, 78, 82, 87, 96, 97, 103, 106, 167, 174 n.74
    United States of America 1, 5, 7–9, 18, 30, 48–53, 67, 107, 125, 127, 128, 133, 135, 136, 153, 155–8, 168
American Petroleum Institute (API) 136, 145 n.78
Anglo-Saxon 45, 47, 129, 130, 137, 157
animism 50, 123, 124
anointed 137, 138
Anselm of Canterbury 70
anthropocene 2, 5, 64, 76, 168
anthropogenic 3, 30, 53, 91, 160
Aquinas, Thomas 40, 41, 67, 68, 70–2, 98
architecture 52, 155, 168, 169
Aristotle 17, 30–46, 62, 100, 101, 114, 138, 150, 161
Asia/Asian 78, 133

Asmussen, Tina 83 n.10, 84 n.33, 116 n.2, 119 n.40
atheism 31, 50, 51
Augustine of Hippo 67–70, 97, 98, 132
autonomy 5, 6, 98

Bacon, Francis 12, 25 n.90, 62, 64, 132, 133, 137
Barad, Karen 4, 63, 124, 142 n.3
Barber, Daniel 155, 156
Bataille, Georges 151
Bauman, Whitney 16, 24 n.78, 140, 141
Beard, George Miller 157
Bell, Shanon 8, 160, 161
Benedict, Benedictine monasticism 42, 92, 112
Bennett, Jane 124, 126, 142 n.3
Benz, Ernst 49
Berry, Evan 24 n.78, 26 n.96
Berry, Thomas 13
biblical 2, 8, 34, 39, 93, 100, 110, 111, 120, 121 n.95, 131, 133, 134, 144 n.49, 166
blessing 48, 103, 111, 112, 121 n.98, 133
Boyer, Dominic 4, 6, 159
Bradshaw, David 35, 39, 40
Bray, Karen 15, 164–7, 172 nn.20, 26, 27
Buddha/Buddhist 37, 47, 164
Buell, Frederick 6, 7, 21 n.38
Burkhart, Brian 114, 139

Calvin/Calvinist 51, 98, 118 n.32
Canada, Canadian 4, 22 n.60, 137
capitalism 42, 59 n.123, 95–7, 111, 112, 121 n.103, 154, 165, 166
    Christianity (or Protestantism) and capitalism 10, 14, 16, 25 n.80, 42, 92, 94, 103, 107, 112, 115, 116 n.6, 117 n.21, 121 n.108, 150, 151

Index

extractive capitalism   3, 17–19, 64, 91, 92, 94, 99, 103, 110, 113–15, 116 n.2, 119 n.37, 152, 153, 162–4, 167, 168, 170, 171
  finance capitalism   18, 93, 94, 113, 114, 163, 164
  petro (or fossil) capitalism   20 n.19, 92, 113, 142, 161
Capitalocene   5, 61
carbon   89 n.116, 140, 149, 150, 159, 163
  carbon dioxide   91
  carbon emissions   10, 30, 54, 159
  decarbonization   8, 93, 114, 115, 159
  hydrocarbons   9, 14, 24, 53
Carnot, Sadi   33, 34
cars   5, 145 n.77
Carter, J. Kameron   15, 63
Caterine, Darryl   49, 50, 129
Catholic, Roman Catholic   23 n.75, 47, 73, 100, 102, 103, 107
Caucasian   47, 129, 130
Chakrabarty, Dipesh   5, 12, 150
Chalmers, Thomas   51, 104, 105
Chen, Mel Y.   139, 140
Christ   39, 40, 48, 149
  Christ and redemption   18, 153, 163, 165, 169
  Christ figure   133–5
  Christ-like   18
Christian, Christianity   45, 70–2, 76, 93, 162, 168, 172 n.14
  Christian anti-Semitism (anti-Judaism)   63, 77
  Christian evangelicalism   145 n.58
  Christian history   39, 151
  Christian identity   63, 77, 168
  Christianity and capitalism   151, 163
  Christianity and colonialism   87 n.71, 88–9 n.109
  Christianity and dominion   13, 124
  Christianity and *energeia*   40
  Christianity and gender   3, 17
  Christianity and gift   117–18 n.28
  Christianity and masculinity   1, 136
  Christianity and oil   9, 10, 14, 19 n.2, 29, 48, 125, 130, 131, 137, 138, 140, 149, 150
  Christianity and technology   132
  Christianity and work   41, 42, 92, 94, 113
  Christian redemption   163, 164, 169, 174 n.74
  Christian temporality   102, 120 n.93, 121 n.97, 153
  Christian theology   15, 39, 40, 45, 49, 56 n.40, 57 n.68, 63, 67–9, 78, 97, 98, 107, 132, 152, 175 n.98
  medieval Christianity   112
  muscular Christianity   46, 47, 146 n.81, 157, 167
Civil War   108
Clausius, Rudolf   33, 34
climate
  climate change   2–4, 9, 10, 14, 21 n.38, 23 n.65, 24 n.78, 30, 53, 54, 91, 94, 124, 126, 155, 156, 159, 160, 167, 176 n.101
  climate conundrum   3–6, 13, 30, 91, 93, 160
  climate denialism   9, 24, 30, 171 n.2
  climate science   4, 6, 13, 149
coal   22 n.53, 31, 33, 48, 75, 91, 107, 111, 121 n.98
Colebrook, Clare   39, 125
colonial, colonialism, colonization, neocolonialism   2, 8, 12, 31, 62, 64, 65, 67, 76–8, 80, 89 n.109, 96, 97, 114, 115, 123, 137, 159, 166, 167, 176
conflict thesis   11, 13, 25 n.81
Connolly, William   16, 63, 93, 116 n.10
conquistador   80–2
consumption   3, 9, 13, 17, 21 n.38, 22 n.53, 24 n.78, 30, 31, 35, 38, 52–4, 60 n.134, 91, 92, 94, 110, 114, 124, 129, 137, 152–6, 159–62, 168, 173 n.32
contemplation, contemplative   31, 35–7, 39, 41, 42, 47, 112, 157, 162, 164, 167
Cornwall Alliance for the Stewardship of Creation   149, 171 n.2
crisis   18, 68, 152–6, 158, 160, 164, 169
  climate crisis   2, 3, 6, 9, 11, 14, 19, 36, 52, 53, 61, 91, 161, 168, 170
  energy crisis   31, 36, 37, 156–9, 173 n.57

environmental crisis 4, 13, 26 n.93, 38, 124, 176
Crockett, Clayton 24 n.78, 174 n.74
crucifixion 152, 153, 164–6
cruel optimism 166, 175 n.81

Daggett, Cara 7, 8, 10, 21 n.51, 22 n.53, 50, 92, 93, 105, 106, 113, 156
Daly, Herman 54 n.2
Darwin, Charles/Darwinist 46, 52
Davis, Andrew Jackson 49, 50, 59 n.110, 128–30
de Acosta, José 73
death 18, 19, 26 n.91, 51, 85 n.49, 105, 106, 125, 137, 139–41, 149–57, 162–71, 174 n.74, 175 nn.96, 98
decolonial/postcolonial 2, 4, 5, 11, 12, 15, 18, 30, 94, 123, 124, 139, 142, 147 n.111, 164
de la Peña, Carolyn 49, 156–8, 172 n.27, 175–6 n.101
Derrida, Jacques 36, 116 n.15, 151, 169, 172 n.14
Descartes, Rene/Cartesian 32, 33, 82, 127, 128, 135, 139, 161
de-work, postwork 93, 94, 113–15
Dhillon, Jaskiran 171 n.11
disenchantment, myth of disenchantment 11–14, 18, 19, 26 nn.91, 93, 31, 38, 48, 50, 59 n.107, 113, 124, 125, 141, 142
dispensational premillennialism 110, 120 n.93
displacement 63, 65–7, 75, 77, 78, 80–2, 169
displacement paradox 160
divinity 13, 14, 17, 23 n.68, 31, 32, 38, 39, 41, 43, 46, 48–52, 54, 61, 67, 69, 81, 82, 86 n.70, 99, 109–11, 128, 138–40, 144 n.50, 158, 161, 169
docetic, docetism 77, 169, 175 n.98
Dochuk, Darren 1, 121 n.98, 131, 133
doctrine of creation 67, 68
Doctrine of Discovery 73, 76, 87 n.71
doctrine of God 66, 68, 69, 97, 152
Douglas, Kelly Brown 63, 84, 169, 175 n.98
Drake, "Colonel" Edwin 6, 108

dunamis 33, 35–9, 55 n.8, 61, 63, 67, 70–2, 78, 79, 81, 163, 164, *see also* potentia
Dussel, Enrique 79
Dym, Warren Alexander 87 n.80, 99, 100, 102

Easter 153, 165
Eastern Orthodox Christianity 24–5 n.78, 37, 39, 40, 164
Eaton, Rev. S. J. 107–10, 113, 123, 135, 149, 161
ecomodernism 53, 170, 173 n.51
ecotheology 18, 20 n.21, 38, 123, 124, 139
Edinburgh 51, 104
electrical theology 49, 59 n.107
electricity 14, 22 n.61, 24, 25 n.81, 31, 32, 34, 41, 48–50, 58 n.102, 125, 128–30, 137, 144 n.37, 158, 168
Elshtain, Jean Bethke 69, 72, 85 n.39
embryology 41, 43, 44
emergency 109, 155, 156
emissions 2, 3, 10, 17, 19 n.12, 30, 54, 61, 91, 92, 159, 169
enchantment, re-enchantment 12–18, 31, 38, 52, 112, 113, 124–6, 128, 135, 137, 141, 142
energeia 17, 25 n.78, 30–3, 35–41, 43, 45, 48, 51, 56 n.51, 61, 93, 163, 170
energy
    energy conservation 32–4, 51–3
    energy humanities 3, 4, 6, 9–11, 14, 23 n.68, 33, 43, 64, 89 n.116, 92, 139, 159, 160, 175 n.101
    energy poverty 8, 31
    energy science 14, 24–5 n.78, 30, 32, 38, 48, 50, 51, 55 n.6, 61, 94, 99, 103–6, 128
    laws of energy 32–4, 46, 51, 55 n.16, 61, 104, 156–61
energy ethics 24 n.75
    Christian energy ethics 10, 23 n.75
entropy 34, 51, 55 n.16, 105, 156–9
environmental humanities 3–5, 30, 91, 92, 142 n.3
Eriugena, John Scottus 132
Estes, Nick 171 n.11

evangelical, evangelicalism   9, 15, 16,
    23 n.71, 24, 49–51, 59 n.107,
    93, 104–7, 112, 114, 128, 136,
    144 n.50, 145 n.58, 149, 172 n.19
evolution, evolutionary   3, 9, 23 n.71,
    25 n.81, 30, 43, 46, 52, 64, 141
exception/exceptionalism   1, 19, 39, 48,
    66, 67, 72, 73, 79, 80, 82, 84–5
    n.39, 113, 124, 137, 138, 152,
    161, 164, 169, 171, 175 n.81
   white exceptionalism   63, 68, 81, 82,
    89 n.113, 162
Extinction Rebellion   167 n.103
extractive capitalism   3, 17–19, 92, 94,
    99, 103, 110, 113, 114, 119 n.37,
    151–4, 161–4, 167, 168, 170, 171
extractive imaginary   64, 65, 81

fall (the fall into sin)   34, 51, 70, 71, 93,
    104–6, 132, 136
fatigue   157
feminism, feminist   1, 3, 6–8, 15, 16, 18,
    22 n.60, 56 n.40, 62, 92, 93, 113,
    115, 117 n.17, 124, 125, 139,
    141, 164
   decolonial, postcolonial feminism   2,
    4, 30
   ecofeminism   2, 4, 8, 62, 77, 123, 141,
    174 n.74
   intersectional feminism   2, 6, 8,
    22 n.56, 114, 164
finance capitalism, see under "capitalism"
Finnish Interpretation of Luther   118
fossil economy   75, 91, 160, see also fossil
    capitalism; petro-capitalism
freedom   5–8, 13, 22 n.60, 29, 68, 70–2,
    79, 80, 106, 113, 133, 138, 150
Freudenthal, Gad   43, 44, 138
fuel   2, 7, 11, 15, 36, 38, 45, 156, 160
   fossil fuel   3, 5–8, 10, 22 n.53, 24, 30,
    89 n.116, 91, 92, 106, 133, 137,
    138, 150, 159, 160
fulfillment   2, 3, 7, 15, 17, 30–2, 35–45,
    48, 52–4, 61, 72, 93, 102, 107,
    132, 139, 161, 164, 172
fundamentalism   19 n.2, 107, 111

Galeano, Eduardo   82 n.2
Galen of Pergamon   45, 46

Galileo   32, 43
Galvani, Luigi   48
Genesis   101, 134
geology, geological   25 n.81, 76, 134,
    144 n.49
geotheology   50, 92, 106
Ghosh, Amitav   5, 6, 9, 10, 126
Gidden, Paul   7
gift   18, 41, 48, 51, 75, 94–9, 101–6, 108–
    11, 113–15, 117 n.28, 118 nn.29,
    32, 119 n.37, 121, 134
   free gift   8, 87 n.76, 94–9, 103–7, 110,
    113–16, 118 n.32, 119 n.37, 161
Gillespie, Michael   86 n.66, 88 n.104
Glissant, Édouard   80
God, gods   2, 14, 17, 26 n.91, 39–42,
    46, 48, 49, 51, 59 n.119, 66–78,
    89 n.114, 93, 97–112, 120 n.93,
    121, 123, 132, 133, 150–2, 163,
    168, 174 n.74
gold   48, 74, 84 n.38, 101, 108, 111, 112
Gómez-Barris, Macarena   167
Good Friday   165
Gospel   48, 77, 100–3, 105, 107, 110, 111,
    113, 123, 135, 149, 150, 163
   Gospel of Work   42, 57 n.64
   prosperity gospel   14, 103
grace   13, 17, 18, 67, 87 n.76, 93, 94,
    97–9, 103–10, 112–15, 118 n.29,
    152, 154, 163
Grainger, Brett Malcom   49, 59 n.107,
    144 n.50
Grau, Marion   24 n.78, 117 n.21,
    146 n.89
Gross Domestic Product (GDP)   30, 54
Günel, Gökçe   159

Hansen, James   3
Haraway, Donna   4, 21 n.31, 141
Harmonialism   129, 130, 168
Harris, Cheryl   89 n.113
Hayhoe, Kathryn   149
heat   32–5, 41, 43–52, 58 n.83, 59 n.119,
    61, 91, 93, 100–2, 105, 106, 138,
    155–7, 169
Hebrew   41, 168
   Hebrew Bible   40, 134
Hegel, Hegelianism   79, 151, 162, 169,
    172 n.17

Heidegger, Martin 36, 61, 62
Heraclitus 43, 57 n.68
Hessel, Dieter T. 23 n.75
Hesychasm 37, 164
hetero-
  hetero-capitalist-patriarchy 2
  heteronormativity 151
  heteropatriarchy 19
  heterosexism 8, 166
  heterosexual 96
Higgins, Patillo 123, 131, 144 n.49
Holy Saturday 19, 153, 162–8, 171
Holy Spirit 97
hooks, bell 19 n.8
Howe, Cymene 6, 159
Hugh of St. Victor 132
Human Development Index (HDI) 53, 60 nn.129–30
humanities 12, 13, 23 n.68, *see also* energy, energy humanities; environmental humanities
hydrocarbons, *see* carbon

Idle No More 114, 115
imaginary 5, 38, 61, 62, 65, 75, 77, *see also* extractive imaginary
imperial, imperialist 2, 3, 12, 14, 15, 20 n.19, 104, 155, 172 n.19, 174 n.74
incarnation 49, 69, 77
indigenous 64, 65, 73, 96, 114, 115, 129, 137, 139, 142, 159, 168
instrumentalization, instrumental value 13, 87 n.71, 114, 115, 124, 130, 142
Intergovernmental Panel of Climate Change (IPCC) 3, 20 n.15, 60 n.60, 160
intersectional 2, 4, 6, 9, 16, 22 n.56, 93, 114
intrinsic value 114, 115

Jackson, Zakiyyah Iman 80, 81, 142 n.3
James, Abraham 130, 137
James, Robin 154, 167
Jennings, Willie James 63, 76–8, 81, 123, 168, 169
Jerome 69–72
Jewish, Jews, Judaism 63, 77, 78, 137, 168, 172 n.14

Johnson, Bob 6, 89 n.116
Jones, Donna V. 123, 125
Joule, James 33

Kant, Immanuel 16, 33, 95
Keel, Terence 15, 63
Keller, Catherine 14, 56 n.40, 67, 84 n.39
Kimmerer, Robin Wall 96, 147 n.110
kinesis 36
Klein, Naomi 23 n.65, 65, 91, 154
Koster, Hilda 24 n.78
Kuhn, Thomas 33

Labor, labora 33, 35, 41, 42, 47, 62, 80, 81, 84 n.38, 91–5, 99, 103, 108, 111–13, 115, 133, 135–7, 145 n.76
Latour, Bruno 12, 15, 19 n.12
Leibniz, Gottfried Wilhelm 32, 33
LeMenager, Stephanie 5, 7, 8, 22 n.60, 139, 140, 146 n.99
liberation 89 n.116, 137, 138
  liberation theology 164, 174 n.74
life 1, 5, 12, 14, 17, 18, 26, 29–31, 38, 40–3, 47–52, 54, 61, 64, 65, 71–3, 85 n.49, 93, 100, 105, 107, 109, 112–15, 125, 126, 130–2, 135, 137–41, 143 nn.3, 10, 149–54, 156–8, 161–71, 175 n.96
lifestyle 3, 6, 8, 22 n.53, 53, 135, 156, 168
light 34, 81, 82, 101, 105, 107–9, 133–6, 169
Lloyd, Vincent 15
local, localize 2, 10, 11, 19, 63, 79, 95, 100, 105, 115, 116, 130, 139, 159, 169, 173
  delocalize 19
Locke, John 38, 42
logos 43, 44, 57 n.68, 67–70, 72–5, 85 n.57, 86 n.70, 124
Lugones, María 96, 115
Luther, Martin, Lutheran 42, 97–100, 107–9, 118 nn.29, 32, 123
Lyell, Charles 47, 76

McLaurin, John J. 127, 133–5, 137, 149
magic, magicians 5, 10–15, 26 n.90, 62, 87 n.80, 128, 135, 141, 169

magnetism   31, 32, 34, 48–50, 50 n.102, 128, 130
Malm, Andreas   20 n.15, 91, 92, 160
Marder, Michael   10, 36–41, 43, 61, 67, 161–4
Marovich, Beatrice   25 n.98, 175 n.96
Martyr, Justin   40, 67
Marvin, Carolyn   49
Marx, Karl   42, 111
masculinity   1, 2, 6, 7, 16, 17, 29, 32, 45, 46, 52, 62, 71, 80, 81, 93, 98, 125, 128, 129, 132, 139, 140, 157, 161, 171
materiality   63, 67, 77–9, 81, 123, 125, 130, 131, 138, 140, 141, 143 n.3, 169
Mathesius, Johann   87 n.80, 100–8, 110, 111, 113, 123, 150
matter   4, 18, 39, 43–5, 49, 50, 53, 63, 65, 66, 76, 79–82, 123–31, 137–42, 143 nn.3, 10, 150
Mauss, Marcel   12, 95, 97, 116 n.15, 117 n.18
Maxwell, James Clerk   50, 104, 105
Mayapple Energy Transition Collective   4, 7, 8, 21 n.51, 159, 160
Mbembe, Achille   47, 62, 84 n.25, 89 nn.114, 116, 143 n.12
mechanist, mechanistic, mechanism   4, 5, 12, 16, 34, 51, 92, 110, 114, 123, 125, 127, 128, 139, 143 n.3, 157, 158, 168
meditation   164
Melanchthon, Phillip   100
menstrual fluid   44, 57 n.73
Merchant, Carolyn   62, 87 n.80, 123, 127
metal, metallic   74, 101
metallurgist   100, 101
metaphysics, metaphysical   33, 36, 49, 50, 57 n.69, 72, 87 n.71, 116, 161, 162
Mexico   159
Mezzandra, Sandro   64, 65
Middle East   6, 158
Milbank, John   117 n.28
mineral, mineralogy, mineralogical   61, 62, 64–6, 68, 73–6, 80–2, 84 n.38, 91, 99–103, 106, 107, 120 n.78, 133, 141, 150
mining   2, 64–7, 73–5, 87 nn.71, 76, 80, 88 n.86, 94, 99–103, 110, 111, 113, 116 n.2, 123, 168
Mirowski, Phillip   34, 55 nn.6–7, 104
Morton, Tim   140
Mumford, Lewis   52, 53, 59 n.123
muscular Christianity   46, 47, 136, 146 n.81, 157

national parks   5
NDN Collective   114, 150
Neocleous, Mark   154
neoliberalism   17, 64, 93, 114, 117 n.17, 154, 159, 165–7
neurasthenia   157
new materialism   18, 123–5, 138, 142 n.3, 143 n.10
Newton, Isaac   12, 26 n.90, 43, 82, 127, 128, 135, 139, 161
Niagara Bible Conference   110, 120 n.93
Nielsen, Karen M.   44
Nikiforuk, Andrew   58
Noble, David. F.   131, 132
#NoDAPL   90, 114, 116 n.3, 150, 171 n.11
nominalism, nominalist   68, 72, 74, 75, 86 n.66, 97, 118 n.32
Norris, John A.   101
Northcott, Michael   14, 24 n.78, 71, 75
nuclear   2, 156, 159
Nye, David   175 n.101
Nyssa, Gregory of   69–72, 85 n.52, 150, 171 n.6

Ockham, William of   68, 72, 74, 86 nn.66, 70, 97, 98, 112
omnipotence, omnipotent   12, 14, 18, 34, 51, 59 n.119, 67–72, 84 n.39, 97, 104, 107, 109, 112, 113, 161
ontology, ontological   45, 68, 96, 115, 116, 118 n.32, 135, 140, 141
Oreskes, Naomi   9
Origen   67
original sin   51

Palamas, Gregory   40, 41
Park, Kathrine   62

Parmenides 32, 33, 55 n.6, 116
patriarchy, patriarchal, patriarchalism 2, 8, 19, 89 n.109, 123, 166
Paul, St. 17, 30, 39–41, 45, 56 n.51, 101, 150, 168
Perez Sheldon, Myrna 9, 23 n.71, 25 n.87
perfect, perfection 1, 31, 38, 44, 45, 53, 54, 69–71, 73, 100–3, 108, 132
Perry, Rick 137
petro-
    petro-capitalism, petro-capitalocene 61, 92, 94, 113, 141, 161
    petroculture 3–5, 7–9, 13, 29, 64, 89 n.116, 137–9, 149
    Petrocultures Research Group 6, 149
    petro-eschatology 24 n.78
    petrofiction 6
    petroleum 4, 5, 7, 8, 10, 14, 15, 18, 99, 107, 109, 110, 125–7, 131, 133–9, 149, 163 (*see also* fossil fuel)
    petro-masculine 1, 2, 7, 8, 22 n.53, 140, 171
    petro-Reformers 108
    petro-theology 11, 14, 15, 17, 93, 109, 135, 138, 141, 150, 152, 160, 161, 170
Pew, J. Edgar, Pew family 131, 136
physics 24 n.78, 25 n.81, 32, 34, 104, 161
Pietsch, B. M. 110–12
place 65–7, 77–80, 167–70
plastic, plasticization 2, 8, 80–2
Plato 35, 38, 41, 68, 72, 77, 114, 136, 175 n.98
pneuma 45, 138
political theology 14, 15, 63, 67, 85 n.39, 151
pollution 2
Posadas, Jeremy 42, 93
postsecular 14, 15, 17, 38
potency 36, 37, 46, 156
potentia 33, 35–9, 45, 55 n.8, 61, 63, 67, 70–2, 78, 79, 81, 163, 164, *see also dunamis*
potestas 37, 63, 67, 70, 72
Potosí 73–5, 80, 81, 87 nn.71, 78, 99, 119 n.39, 157
production 1, 13, 14, 17, 30, 35, 38, 52–4, 59 n.123, 60 n.134, 62, 66, 73, 76, 99, 109, 113, 114, 125, 137, 145 n.75, 153, 155, 159, 160, 173 n.32
progress, progression, progressive 22 n.60, 35, 36, 40, 41, 47, 49–51, 93, 115, 121 n.97, 129, 130, 132, 151–4, 161, 162, 164–7, 172 n.19
protestant 42, 47, 49–51, 57 n.64, 92–4, 97, 98, 100, 102–5, 107, 109–12, 114, 115, 117 n.28, 118 n.29
    protestant work ethic 18, 57 n.62, 94, 103, 107, 110–12, 121 n.98, 126, 145 n.75, 154
providence 58 n.83, 75, 101–3, 108, 109, 113, 120 n.78, 133, 150

queer 15, 124, 139–41, 151, 172 n.20

race/racialization 2, 6–8, 11, 15, 17, 18, 30, 31, 38, 39, 45, 47, 48, 62, 63, 65, 67, 75–82, 95, 96, 123–5, 129, 130, 132, 137, 139–41, 154, 157, 168
Rambo, Shelly 164–6
Rankine, William 50, 104
Rasmussen, Larry 10
reciprocity, reciprocal 31, 40, 94–8, 104, 105, 109, 114–16, 117 n.17, 118 nn.28, 29, 32, 141, 161
redemption, redeem 11, 17, 18, 30, 41, 69, 104, 105, 107, 125, 130–9, 149–52, 163, 165, 166, 168, 169, 172
reformation, reformers 18, 72, 87 n.76, 92, 94, 97–103, 107–13, 118 n.32, 150
renewable 5, 10, 159, 160
resilience 152–6, 158, 160, 161, 163, 166, 167, 169
resource 15, 31, 41, 47, 48, 52, 53, 61, 64, 66, 74, 80, 99, 102, 107–11, 121 n.98, 125, 141, 150, 153, 156, 168
resurrect, resurrection 18, 19, 71, 85 n.49, 135, 138, 141, 149–54, 163–7, 169
Rieger, Joerg 173 n.32
Rignal, Karen 159
risk 94, 110, 112, 113

Rivera, Myra   147 n.111
Rockefeller, John D.   1, 6, 110, 111, 121 n.97, 145 n.75
Roosevelt, Teddy   157
Rubenstein, Mary-Jane   15, 47
Ruether, Rosemary Radford   58 n.89

Sabin, Paul   111, 121 n.99, 126–8, 143 n.24
Said, Edward   47
Saxony   18, 74, 75, 94, 99, 101, 113, 123
Schaefer, Donovan   15, 16
Schmitt, Carl   84–5 n.39
science, *see* climate, climate science; energy, energy science
Scottish   18, 50, 51, 92, 104, 106, 111, 113, 161
Scotus, Duns   72, 73, 86 nn.66, 69
secular, secularized, secularization, postsecular   12–17, 38, 42, 43, 63, 66, 85 n.39, 98, 99, 111, 113, 125, 131, 136, 151–3, 165
seed   57 n.68, 101, 103, 107, 150, 163, 171 n.8
semen   44, 57 n.73, 138
Sideris, Lisa   16, 27 n.113
Silva, Denise   80
silver   73, 99–101, 119 nn.39, 51
Simpson, Leanne Betasamosake   65, 115, 167
Sin   51, 105, 106, *see also* original sin
Sinclair, Upton   6–8
Singh, Devin   116 n.6
Sittler, Joseph   13, 26 n.93, 56 n.44
1619 Project   91
slavery, slave, enslaved   12, 48, 61, 62, 67, 73, 75, 76, 79–82, 86, 87, 88 n.88, 89 n.116, 93, 99, 133, 157, 165, 166, 168, 171, 174 n.74
slow violence   166
Smil, Vaclav   21 n.38, 53, 60 n.129, 160
Smith, Adam   42
Smith, Crosbie   34, 35, 50, 51, 55 n.7, 59 n.119, 104, 105
Smith, J. Z.   77
solar   105, 159, 170, 173 n.57
soul   39, 45, 79, 98, 101, 102, 105, 111
sovereignty   8, 19, 63, 66–9, 80, 85 n.39, 97, 174 n.74

space   3, 7, 15, 19, 65, 67, 77, 78, 123, 139, 153, 162, 164–8, 171
speculation   58 n.88, 76, 113
Spencer, Herbert   46, 47, 52, 58 n.85
Spindletop   106, 123, 131
spiritualism   49, 50, 59 n.110, 128–31
Standard Oil   1, 111, 136, 145 nn.75–6
Steinberger, Julia   54, 60 nn.128, 129, 134, 162
Stewart, Lyman   1, 18, 19 n.2, 107, 110–13, 121 n.94, 131
Stoics   35, 41, 57 nn.59, 68, 67, 103, 107
Storm, Jason   11–13, 18, 26 nn.90–1, 59 n.107, 113, 125, 128, 142, 147 n.108
supersessionism   168, 169
Szeman, Imre   4, 6, 20 n.21, 21 n.27, 83 n.22

Tait, Peter Guthrie   50, 104
Tanner, Kathryn   57 n.62, 86 n.70, 93, 94, 113, 114, 116 n.6, 117 n.21, 118 n.29, 121 n.108, 163, 164
Tarbell, Ida   1, 2, 5, 7–9, 17, 31, 47, 145 n.76
Taylor, Mark C.   151
Teapot Dome Scandal   7, 136, 145
technology   4, 5, 13, 15, 20, 24 n.78, 25 n.81, 45, 49, 50, 76, 91, 99, 128, 129, 131, 132, 137, 151, 155, 161, 170
temporality   37, 151–3, 163–9
theophany   18
theosis   40
thermodynamics   24 n.78, 25 n.81, 31–4, 43, 45, 46, 51, 52, 55 n.16, 61, 92, 104, 128, 156–9
Thomson, James   50
Thomson, William (Lord Kelvin)   34, 50, 51, 55 n.19, 59 n.119, 104, 113, 128, 158, 172 n.19
Titusville   106–8, 126
transcendence   2, 16, 19, 29, 49, 65, 69, 77, 79, 81, 85 n.49, 128, 132, 134, 136, 142, 147 n.111, 163, 169
trauma   18, 151–5, 160, 163–6, 175 n.81
trickster   18, 115, 140, 141
trinity   31, 69, 85 n.52, 98

Tsing, Anna   113
Tuana, Nancy   44, 45, 57 nn.73, 82, 58 n.88
Tuveson, Ernest Lee   145 n.59

U'wa   141–2
Union Oil   110
United Nations (UN)   3, 60 nn.129, 130, 134
United States of America   2, 5, 7, 9, 10, 12, 13, 16, 18, 19 n.2, 23 n.75, 24 n.78, 30, 42, 46–9, 53, 57 n.64, 59 n.110, 67, 107, 111, 113, 120 n.93, 121 n.98, 123, 125, 127, 130, 132–6, 142, 144 n.50, 145 n.76, 146 n.81, 152–8, 160, 161, 168
Usher, Phillip   2, 19 n.12

vein   62, 74, 88 n.86, 101
vigil   153, 167
virility   8, 49, 52, 158
vis viva   30, 32–5, 43, 170
vital   43–6, 57 n.69, 158
voluntarism   68
von Balthasar, Hans Urs   165
von Helmholtz, Hermann   33
von Speyr, Adrienne   165

waste   98, 104–6, 111, 150, 151
Weber, Max   12, 18, 42, 63, 111, 113, 126
Weeks, Kathi   93
Weheliye, Alexander   79

weight lifting [health lift]   158
Weszkalnys, Gisa   113, 125
White, Leslie   52, 53
White, Lynn   13, 124
white, whiteness   3, 6–8, 24 n.78, 38, 47, 54, 62, 63, 66, 68, 78, 79, 81, 82, 88 n.102, 113, 155–8, 161, 162, 170
white supremacy   2, 19, 157, 169
Whyte, Kyle Powys   159
wildcatter   112
Williams, Delores   88 n.109, 174 n.74
Wilson, Sheena   6–8, 22 n.60, 137, 160
wind   159, 170
Wittenberg   99, 100
womanist   4, 18, 62, 77, 123, 164, 174 n.74
work   18, 32, 34–7, 39, 41–5, 49, 51, 52, 55 n.23, 57 nn.59, 62, 64, 61, 72–5, 91–7, 99, 102, 103, 105–8, 110–16, 118 n.29, 119 n.37, 121 n.98, 126, 129, 138, 145 nn.75–6, 154, 157, 162, 175 n.101
Wynter, Silvia   30, 38, 62, 80, 135, 142 n.3, 161

York, Richard   160, 161
Yusoff, Kathryn   19 n.10, 62, 73, 76–9, 88 n.102, 123

Zuck, Rochelle Raineri   23 n.73, 59 n.110, 130, 144 n.37